中国国际减贫中心
IPRCC International Poverty Reduction Center in China

全球减贫与发展经验分享系列
The Sharing Series on Global Poverty
Reduction and Development Experience

国际减贫年度报告 2024

中国国际减贫中心　编著

中国财经出版传媒集团

经济科学出版社
Economic Science Press
·北 京·

图书在版编目（CIP）数据

国际减贫年度报告. 2024 / 中国国际减贫中心编著
. --北京：经济科学出版社，2024.7
ISBN 978-7-5218-5806-8

Ⅰ. ①国⋯　Ⅱ. ①中⋯　Ⅲ. ①贫困问题–研究报告–
世界–2024　Ⅳ. ①F113.9

中国国家版本馆CIP数据核字（2024）第074463号

责任编辑：吴　敏
责任校对：易　超
责任印制：张佳裕

国际减贫年度报告2024

GUOJI JIANPIN NIANDU BAOGAO 2024

中国国际减贫中心　编著

经济科学出版社出版、发行　新华书店经销

社址：北京市海淀区阜成路甲28号　邮编：100142

总编部电话：010-88191217　发行部电话：010-88191522

网址：www.esp.com.cn

电子邮箱：esp@esp.com.cn

天猫网店：经济科学出版社旗舰店

网址：http://jjkxcbs.tmall.com

北京季蜂印刷有限公司印装

710×1000　16开　18.25印张　370000字

2024年7月第1版　2024年7月第1次印刷

ISBN 978-7-5218-5806-8　定价：82.00元

（图书出现印装问题，本社负责调换。电话：010-88191545）

（版权所有　侵权必究　打击盗版　举报热线：010-88191661

QQ：2242791300　营销中心电话：010-88191537

电子邮箱：dbts@esp.com.cn）

《国际减贫年度报告 2024》
课 题 组

中国国际减贫中心

李　昕　徐丽萍　贺胜年

刘欢欢　姚　远　武黎明

中央财经大学

高菠阳　戴俊骋　欧变玲

王优容　张　鹏　江　涛

其他编写人员

孟　越　蒋译瑶　李真桢　赵康华　韩湘婷

郑美欣　冯月蓉　周文婧　皮福玲　陈　琪

总序

消除贫困是人类梦寐以求的理想，人类发展史就是与贫困不懈斗争的历史。中国拥有14亿人口，是世界上最大的发展中国家，基础差、底子薄，发展不平衡，长期饱受贫困问题困扰。消除贫困、改善民生、实现共同富裕是社会主义的本质要求，是中国共产党的重要使命。为兑现这一庄严政治承诺，100多年来，中国共产党团结带领中国人民，以坚定不移、顽强不屈的信念和意志与贫困进行了长期艰苦卓绝的斗争。自改革开放以来，中国实施了大规模、有计划、有组织的扶贫开发，着力解放和发展社会生产力，着力保障和改善民生，取得了前所未有的伟大成就。党的十八大以来，以习近平同志为核心的党中央把脱贫攻坚摆在治国理政的突出位置，习近平总书记亲自谋划、亲自挂帅、亲自督战，推动实施精准扶贫精准脱贫基本方略，动员全党全国全社会力量，打赢了人类历史上规模空前、力度最大、惠及人口最多的脱贫攻坚战。

脱贫攻坚战的全面胜利，离不开有为政府和有效市场的有机结合。八年间，以习近平同志为核心的党中央加强对脱贫攻坚的集中统一领导，发挥中国特色社会主义制度能够集中力量办大事的政治优势，把减贫摆在治国理政的突出位置，为脱贫攻坚提供了坚强政治和组织保证。广泛动员市场、社会力量积极参与，实施"万企帮万村"等行动，鼓励民营企业和社会组织、公民个人参与脱贫攻坚，促进资金、人才、技术等要素向贫困地区集聚。截至2020年底，现行标准下9899万农村贫困人口全部脱贫，832个贫困县全部摘帽，12.8万个贫困村全部出列，区域性整体贫困得到解决，完成了消除绝对贫困的艰巨任务，建成了世界上规模最大的教育体系、社会保障体系、医疗卫生体系，实现了快速发展与大规模减贫同步、经济转型与消除绝对贫困同步。

一直以来，中国始终是世界减贫事业的积极倡导者、有力推动者和重要贡献者。按照世界银行国际贫困标准，改革开放以来，中国减贫人口占同期全球减贫人口70%以上，占同期东亚和太平洋地区减贫人口的80%。占世界人口近五分之一的中国全面消除绝对贫困，提前10年实现联合国2030年可持续发展议程的减贫目标，不仅是中华民族发展史上具有里程碑意义的大事件，也是人类减贫史乃至人类发展史上的大事件，为全球减贫事业发展和人类发展进步作出了重大贡献。

中国立足自身国情，把握减贫规律，走出了一条中国特色减贫道路，形成了中国特色反贫困理论，创造了减贫治理的中国样本。坚持以人民为中心的发展思想，坚定不移走共同富裕道路，是扶贫减贫的根本动力。坚持把减贫摆在治国理政突出位置，从党的领袖到广大党员干部，目标一致、上下同心，加强顶层设计和战略规划，广泛动员各方力量积极参与，完善脱贫攻坚制度体系，保持政策连续性稳定性。坚持用发展的办法消除贫困，发展是解决包括贫困问题在内的中国所有问题的关键，是创造幸福生活最稳定的途径。坚持立足实际推进减贫进程，因时因势因地制宜，不断调整创新减贫的策略方略和政策工具，提高贫困治理效能，精准扶贫方略是打赢脱贫攻坚战的制胜法宝，开发式扶贫方针是中国特色减贫道路的鲜明特征。坚持发挥贫困群众主体作用，调动广大贫困群众积极性、主动性、创造性，激发脱贫内生动力，使贫困群众不仅成为减贫的受益者，也成为发展的贡献者。

脱贫攻坚战取得全面胜利后，中国政府设立了5年过渡期，着力巩固拓展脱贫攻坚成果，全面推进乡村振兴。按照党的二十大部署，在以中国式现代化全面推进中华民族伟大复兴的新征程上，中国正全面推进乡村振兴，建设宜居宜业和美乡村，向着实现人的全面发展和全体人民共同富裕的更高目标不断迈进。中国巩固拓展脱贫成果和乡村振兴的探索和实践，将继续为人类减贫和乡村发展提供新的中国经验和智慧，为推动构建没有贫困的人类命运共同体贡献中国力量。

面对国际形势新动向新特征，习近平总书记提出"一带一路"倡议、全球发展倡议等全球共同行动，将减贫作为重点合作领域，致力于推动构建没有贫困、共同发展的人类命运共同体。加强国际减贫与乡村发展经验分享，助力全球减贫与发展进程，业已成为全球广泛共识。为此，自2019年起，中国国际减贫中心与比尔及梅琳达·盖茨基金会联合实施国际合作项目，始终坚持站在未来的角度、政策的高度精心谋划项目选题，引领国内外减贫与乡村发展前沿热点和研究走向。始终坚持将中国减贫与乡村发展经验与国际接轨，通过国际话语体系阐释中国减贫与乡村振兴道路，推动中国减贫与乡村发展经验的国际化传播，至今已实施了30余个研究项目，形成了一批形式多样、影响广泛的研究成果，部分成果已在相关国际交流活动中发布。

　　为落实全球发展倡议，进一步促进全球减贫与乡村发展交流合作，中国国际减贫中心精心梳理研究成果，推出四个系列丛书，包括"全球减贫与发展经验分享系列""中国减贫与发展经验国际分享系列""国际乡村发展经验分享系列"和"中国乡村振兴经验分享系列"。

　　"全球减贫与发展经验分享系列"旨在跟踪全球减贫进展，分析全球减贫与发展趋势，总结分享各国减贫经验，为推动联合国2030可持续发展议程、参与全球贫困治理提供知识产品。该系列主要包括"国际减贫年度报告""国际减贫理论与前沿问题"等全球性减贫知识产品，以及覆盖非洲、东盟、南亚、拉丁美洲及加勒比地区等区域性减贫知识产品。

　　"中国减贫与发展经验国际分享系列"旨在讲好中国减贫故事，向国际社会分享中国减贫经验，为广大发展中国家实现减贫与发展提供切实可行的经验。该系列聚焦中国精准扶贫、脱贫攻坚和巩固拓展脱贫攻坚成果的经验做法，基于国际视角梳理形成中国减贫经验分享的知识产品。

　　"国际乡村发展经验分享系列"聚焦国际乡村发展历程、政策和实践，比较中外乡村发展经验和做法，为全球乡村发展事业提供交流互鉴的知识产品。该系列主要包括"国际乡村振兴年度报告""乡村治理国际经验比较分析报告""县域城乡融合发展与乡村振兴"等研究成果。

　　"中国乡村振兴经验分享系列"聚焦讲好中国乡村振兴故事，及时总结乡村振兴经验、做法和典型案例，为国内外政策制定者和研究者提供参考。该系列主要围绕乡村发展、乡村规划、共同富裕等议题，梳理总结有关政策、经验和实践，基于国际视角开发编写典型案例等。

　　最后，感谢所有为系列图书顺利付梓付出辛勤汗水的相关项目组、出版社和编辑人员，以及关心和支持中国国际减贫中心的政府机构、高校和科研院所、社会组织和各界朋友。系列书籍得到了比尔及梅琳达·盖茨基金会的慷慨资助以及盖茨基金会北京代表处的悉心指导和帮助，在此表示衷心感谢！

　　全球减贫与乡村发展是动态的、不断变化的，书中难免有挂一漏万之处，敬请读者指正！

刘俊文

中国国际减贫中心主任

2024年1月

过去20年来，人类发展方面取得显著成就：全球绝对贫困人口显著减少、人类健康状况明显改善，受教育机会不断增大，人们生活更加便捷。但摆脱贫困仍然是全人类社会共同面对且亟待解决的重要议题。新冠疫情逆转了全球20年的减贫成果，导致数千万人重新陷入极端贫困，为全球减贫带来了前所未有的挑战。为落实全球发展倡议，推动构建没有贫困、共同发展的人类命运共同体，中国国际减贫中心编撰了《国际减贫年度报告2024》，梳理新冠疫情后全球减贫进展，持续跟踪全球减贫事业进展，促进国际减贫交流与合作。

报告认为：

1.**全球减贫进程恢复至疫情前水平。**2.15美元标准下，2022年全球贫困发生率从2020年的9.3%降至8.4%，贫困人口从2020年的7.19亿人降至2022年的6.67亿人，可持续发展目标的首要目标——消除贫困（SDG1）得分上升至79.8，恢复至疫情前状态。2023年全球多维贫困人数和多维贫困发生率分别为11亿人和18.3%，低于2019年疫情前的13亿人和23.1%。在过去15年间，近三分之一的国家实现了多维贫困指数减半。

2.**主要减贫议题实施情况整体向好。**全球经济复苏，但人均GDP差异扩大，2022年全球GDP达到101万亿美元，较2021年增长3.08%，失业率为5.77%，恢复至疫情前水平，高收入国家与低收入国家的人均GDP差异高达66.68倍。教育发展逐步恢复，但不平等问题依旧突出，超过60%的国家进行了社区复学动员，近二分之一的国家现金支持家庭经济困难学生恢复教育，高收入国家的基础教育普及率维持在较高的水平，除此之外的非高收入国家停滞不前。营养健康水平取得显著提升，新生儿死亡率从2000年的23.01‰下降到2021年的12.14‰，但低收入国家新生儿死亡率是高收入国家的8倍，疫情和日益严重的粮食不安全问题进一步阻碍了改善儿童营养不良方面的进展。全球基础设施持续改善，但贫困国家仍然有较大提升空间，清洁饮用水人口比例从2000年75.5%上升到2020年的88.32%，使用互联网的人口比例在2021年增长至69.44%，但非洲一些国家仍面临基础设施短缺、融资困难等问题。自然灾害分布区域广、受灾人数多、经济损失巨大。2000~2022年，亚洲遭受的自然灾害种类多，且发生更频繁，而非洲由于气候条件变化、医疗卫生水平和土地退化，受损总额最高，达到19384.83亿美元，阻碍了减贫进展。

3.国家政策的制定实施有效助力减贫。到2030年基本消除全球极端贫困依旧是当今世界面临的最大挑战。为此，众多发展中国家和新兴经济体分别制定和实施了一系列减贫战略、政策和措施。亚洲尝试收紧货币政策，积极优化贫困识别，通过实施公共服务项目推进减贫治理；非洲推进贫困地区基础设施和公共服务升级，努力提升减贫财政开支的使用效率，并依托青年就业创业促进社会凝聚包容；拉丁美洲及加勒比地区通过融资引资促进经济恢复，积极挖掘特殊就业项目潜力，发展家庭农业及生态农业，针对脆弱群体持续提供财政支持；大洋洲推出数字经济战略，通过经济转型减贫，重启旅游业并大力发展蓝色经济；北美洲制定气候和能源转型战略，创造全新就业机会，推出差别化的减贫政策，持续采取扩张性财政政策；欧洲积极推进普惠性的社会保障全覆盖，努力完善多样化的就业培训与扶助政策。此外，联合国、世界银行、国际货币基金组织和诸多发达国家也提供了形式多样的援助支持以助力全球减贫。

4.中国脱贫攻坚战取得全面胜利后，巩固拓展脱贫攻坚成果同乡村振兴有效衔接工作取得新进展。防止返贫动态监测和帮扶机制健全完善并有效运转，在农村产业发展、扩大就业、壮大新型农村集体经济等方面持续发力，不断增强脱贫地区和脱贫群众内生动力，脱贫攻坚成果得到进一步巩固拓展，守住了不发生规模性返贫的底线。乡村全面振兴见实效，扎实推进了乡村发展、乡村建设、乡村治理，接续推进乡村振兴，推动巩固拓展脱贫攻坚成果上台阶。

5.国际减贫合作已成为重要的全球共识。加强各国间的减贫合作与交流将有助于各国减少贫困人口，提高人民生活水平，有利于全球减贫目标实现，同时可以促进资源和技术的共享，共同推动经济发展和社会进步。多年来，联合国、世界银行等国际组织与机构通过提供资金、技术和人力资源等方面的支持，有效促进了欠发达国家的减贫进程。各国之间积极开展双边与多边合作，分享减贫政策和措施，共同推动实现2030年可持续发展目标进程。2021年9月21日，中国国家主席习近平在第七十六届联合国大会上提出全球发展倡议，指出中国将"携手应对全球性威胁和挑战，推动构建人类命运共同体，共同建设更加美好的世界"。2022年4月，习近平主席在博鳌亚洲论坛再次重申，"人类是休戚与共的命运共同体，各国要顺应和平、发展、合作、共赢的时代潮流，向着构建人类命运共同体的正确方向，携手迎接挑战、合作开创未来"。当前，在新冠疫情和经济复苏缓慢等多重因素影响下，加强国际减贫合作，共同推动减贫目标实现，已经成为国际社会的重要共识。

报告共分为五章：第一章是全球减贫进展，第二章是主要减贫议题实施情况，第三章是世界主要地区及典型国家推进减贫的政策供给与实施成效，第四章是中国巩固拓展脱贫攻坚成果同乡村振兴有效衔接政策和实践，第五章是全球减贫展望。

报告所采用主要数据来源包括：联合国《可持续发展报告2022》《可持续发展报告2023》；《全球多维贫困指数2019》《全球多维贫困指数2023》；世界银行贫困与不平等平台数据、《贫困与共享繁荣2022》；世界银行等关于因疫情关闭学校的教育应对调查数据库；联合国经济和社会事务部数据库等。

目录

Contents

第一章
全球减贫进展

本章要点

新冠疫情导致数千万人重新陷入极端贫困，为全球减贫带来前所未有的挑战。国际社会采取了经济刺激、社会投入、健康保障、教育普及等一系列积极措施，以应对新冠疫情冲击，重启减贫进程。2022年全球在减少绝对贫困和多维贫困方面都取得了良好进展，全球减少多维贫困的情况优于疫情前，但全球减贫进程存在区域差异，部分国家的绝对贫困尚未恢复到疫情前水平，不同收入组别国家的多维贫困人口结构变化也存在差异。展望未来，受经济增速放缓、地缘政治冲突和气候风险影响，新冠疫情后全球减贫进程仍面临多重挑战；多重危机影响多维贫困的减贫进程，但部分国家在减少多维贫困方面进展良好。

一、减贫概况

过去20年来，人类发展方面取得了显著成就：全球绝对贫困人口显著减少、人类健康状况明显改善，受教育机会不断增加，人们生活更加便捷。但摆脱贫困仍然是全人类社会共同面对的且亟待解决的重要议题。新冠疫情（以下简称"疫情"）的发生逆转了全球20年的减贫成果，导致数千万人重新陷入极端贫困，为全球减贫带来了前所未有的挑战。为了应对疫情冲击，国际社会采取了一系列包括经济刺激、社会投入、健康保障、教育普及等在内的积极举措，重启减贫进程。值得注意的是，经过不懈努力，到2022年疫情影响已逐渐减弱，全球贫困发生率已重新恢复到疫情前的水平。

2022年全球贫困发生率已恢复至疫情前水平。根据《贫困与共享繁荣

2022》，2.15美元标准下，2022年全球贫困发生率从2020年的9.3%降至8.4%，贫困人口数量从2020年的7.19亿人降至2022年的6.67亿人，已低于2019年疫情前的水平。"消除贫困"是2030年可持续发展议程的首要目标，根据《可持续发展报告2023》，2015~2019年可持续发展目标的首要目标——消除贫困（SDG1）[1]的得分从74.7上升至78.5，全球减贫进程取得良好发展。受疫情影响，SDG1得分在2020年降至77.1，2022年上升至79.8，减贫方面的进展超过2019年疫情前的水平。

受多重冲击影响，2023年全球经济复苏放缓，为减贫带来严峻挑战。根据联合国《2024年世界经济形势与展望报告》，受疫情、粮食和能源危机、通货膨胀飙升、债务收紧以及气候紧急状况等系列冲击影响，世界经济遭受重创，2023年全球经济增速为2.7%，预计2024年将继续放缓至2.4%，低于疫情前的水平（3%），世界经济将面临长期低增长的风险，为全球减贫进程带来挑战。

二、减贫进程

为监测全球范围内绝对贫困和多维贫困的变化情况，报告采用了联合国2019~2023年《可持续发展报告》、《全球可持续发展报告2019》、2019~2023年《全球多维贫困指数》和《2023世界经济形势与展望》，世界银行《贫困与共享繁荣2022》《世界经济展望2023》和《全球贫困展望2023》等提供的数据进行综合分析。

（一）绝对贫困

1.各国政府积极采取措施，2022年全球减贫进程已恢复至疫情前的状态

2021年以来，全球贫困发生率和贫困人口数量持续降低。疫情使全球减贫进程逆转，2020年贫困发生率和贫困人口数量为30多年来的最大增幅，但各国政府采取积极的财政政策、货币政策等，以降低疫情对贫困人口的影响，推动减贫事业不断向前推进，2022年全球减贫进程已恢复到正常路径（见图1.1）。根据世界银行贫困与不平等平台的数据[2]，2.15美元标准下全球贫困发生

---

① 2015年9月，世界各国领导人在联合国峰会上通过了"2030年可持续发展议程"，提出17项可持续发展目标（SDGs），呼吁所有国家（不论该国是贫穷、富裕还是中等收入）行动起来，在促进经济繁荣的同时保护地球。新目标指出，消除贫困必须与一系列战略齐头并进，包括促进经济增长，解决教育、卫生、社会保护和就业机会的社会需求，遏制气候变化和保护环境。其中，可持续发展目标1（SDG1）为"消除贫困"。可持续发展目标总得分是17项可持续发展目标得分的平均，得分计算方法详见《可持续发展报告2023》，得分越高表示减贫效果越好。

② 参见：https://pip.worldbank.org/home。

率从1990年的37.89%降至2019年的8.51%，贫困人口从20.06亿人下降至6.59亿人^①，整体呈现持续递减趋势；受亚洲金融危机等因素影响，1998年，2.15美元标准下全球贫困发生率增加0.21%，但在2020年，2.15美元标准下全球贫困发生率比2019年增加0.79%，增幅约为1998年的3.7倍。根据《贫困与共享繁荣2022》，2.15美元标准下2020~2022年全球贫困发生率分别为9.3%、8.8%和8.4%，贫困人口数量分别为7.19亿人、6.9亿人和6.67亿人，贫困水平恢复至疫情前水平。

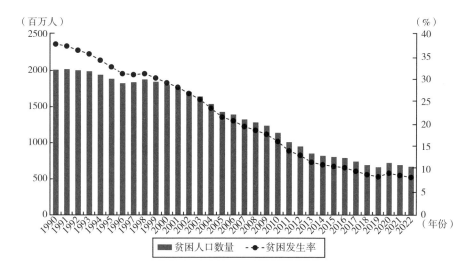

图1.1　1981~2022年2.15美元标准下的全球贫困人口数量和贫困发生率

资料来源：1990~2019年的数据来自世界银行的贫困与不平等平台，2020~2022年的数据来自《贫困与共享繁荣2022》。

消除贫困的进程重启，全球减贫进程持续向前推进。根据联合国《可持续发展报告2023》，2015~2019年可持续发展首要目标——消除贫困（SDG1）的得分年均增速为1.25%；受疫情影响，SDG1的得分从2019年疫情前的78.5降至2020年的77.1，降低了1.78%，2022年恢复到79.8，2020~2022年年均增速为1.74%，超过2019年疫情前的水平（见图1.2）。然而，全球经济复苏仍受通货膨胀、政策的不确定性以及劳动力市场挑战等多方面的影响，世界银行《贫困与共享繁荣2022》报告显示，到2022年底，全球仍有6.85亿人生活在绝对

---

① 该数据是2023年7月的最新估算结果，略高于《贫困与共享繁荣2022》的估算。根据《贫困与共享繁荣2022》，2019年全球贫困发生率为8.4%，贫困人口数量为6.48亿人。

贫困之中，预计到2030年，全球仍有6.8%的人口（约5.74亿人）仍然生活在绝对贫困中，远低于2030年全球绝对贫困发生率降至3%的目标，2030年全球消除绝对贫困的目标或无法实现，全球减贫进程有待加快推进。

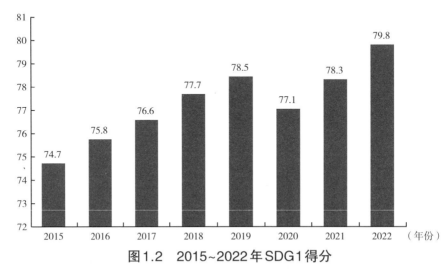

图1.2　2015~2022年SDG1得分

资料来源：根据《可持续发展报告2023》的数据绘制，为保持数据可比性，选取2015~2022年的数据。

2.减贫进程存在区域差异，部分国家尚未恢复到疫情前水平

疫情后，减贫进程不仅在区域间，而且在区域内各国之间也存在差异。与2019年疫情前相比，2022年各区域既有减贫进程强力恢复的国家，也有减贫进程受阻、停滞不前甚至衰退的国家。根据《可持续发展报告2023》，受疫情影响，2020年超过70%的国家的贫困发生率增加，仅少数国家受疫情冲击较小，如圭亚那、巴西、埃塞俄比亚、吉布提和塞拉利昂等国家的2.15美元标准下的贫困发生率较2019年降低了至少1%。2020年，有统计数据的159个国家中，114个国家的贫困发生率增加，其中41个国家的贫困发生率增幅超过1%。到2022年，东欧和中亚地区、撒哈拉以南非洲地区分别有63.64%和51.06%的国家的2.15美元标准下的贫困发生率较2019年疫情前有所降低，而大洋洲、拉丁美洲和加勒比地区分别有66.67%和55%的国家尚未恢复到疫情前的水平（见图1.3）。此外，东欧和中亚地区超过90%的国家的贫困发生率降低或不变，快速了摆脱疫情影响，减贫进程持续推进。约20%的经济合作与发展组织（OECD）国家的贫困发生率增加，但除哥伦比亚（3.59%）、哥斯达黎加（0.89%）和墨西哥（0.76%）以外，其他国家的贫困发生率增幅不超过0.02%。

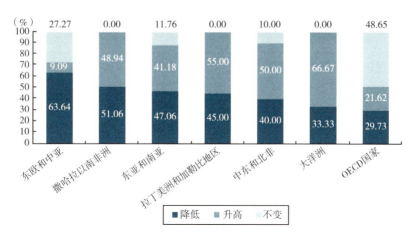

图1.3　2019~2022年2.15美元标准下主要区域贫困发生率变化的国家占比

资料来源：根据联合国《可持续发展报告2023》数据计算和绘制。区域划分标准参照《可持续发展报告2023》。

不同收入组别国家在减贫进程恢复方面存在差异，低收入国家的减贫进程恢复相对较弱。 根据《可持续发展报告2023》，80%的高收入国家的贫困发生率已经低于2019年的水平或与之持平，然而低收入国家中仍有60%的国家的减贫事业受疫情冲击仍未恢复至之前的水平（见图1.4）。收入水平越高，受疫情等冲击后越容易快速恢复减贫进程，而收入水平越低，贫困水平的复原能力越弱。

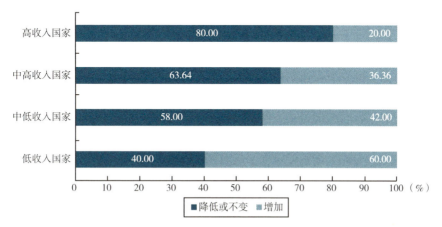

**图1.4　2019~2022年2.15美元标准下不同收入组别国家
贫困发生率变化的国家占比**

资料来源：根据联合国《可持续发展报告2023》数据计算和绘制。收入组别划分标准参照世界银行2022财年的收入分组。

3.国际贫困线调整对全球贫困发生率的影响较小，对不同区域的影响存在差异

国际贫困线调整对全球绝对贫困发生率和贫困人口数量影响较小，疫情后2.15美元标准下全球贫困发生率和贫困人口略高于1.9美元标准（见图1.5）。无论是1.9美元标准还是2.15美元标准，1990~2022年全球贫困发生率和贫困人口数量的变化趋势均相似。1.9美元标准和2.15美元标准的全球贫困发生率的相关系数为0.9998，全球贫困人口数量的相关系数为0.9997，两种标准的贫困特征几乎一致。2020年，1.9美元标准和2.15美元标准下全球贫困进展都大幅逆转，2.15美元标准下全球贫困发生率的增幅更大，全球贫困水平在2021年和2022年持续降低。

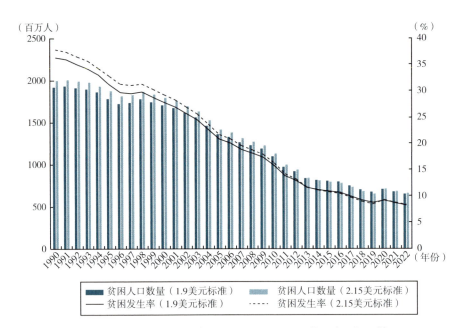

图1.5　1990~2022年1.9美元和2.15美元标准下的全球贫困人口数量和贫困发生率

资料来源：1990~2019年1.9美元和2.15美元标准下的全球贫困人口数量和贫困发生率数据来自世界银行贫困与不平等平台2023年7月的最新测算，2020~2022年1.9美元标准的全球贫困人口数量和贫困发生率根据联合国《可持续发展目标报告2022》计算并绘制，2020~2022年2.15美元标准下的全球贫困人口数量和贫困发生率根据世界银行《贫困与共享繁荣2022》计算并绘制。

国际贫困线调整对不同区域的贫困发生率的影响存在差异。根据世界银行

贫困与不平等平台的数据测算，与2.15美元标准相比，2019年以1.9美元标准计算的西非和中非、撒哈拉以南非洲的贫困发生率下降和贫困人口减少，东亚和太平洋地区、欧洲和中亚，以及拉丁美洲和加勒比地区的贫困发生率上升和贫困人口显著增加，而南亚的贫困情况差异不大（见图1.6）。

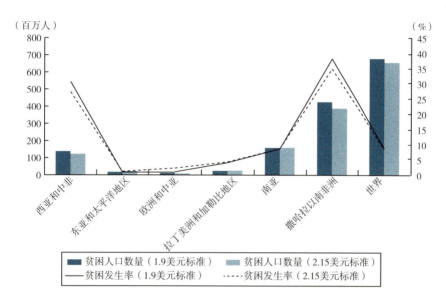

图1.6 2019年1.9美元和2.15美元标准下主要区域的贫困人口数量和贫困发生率

资料来源：根据世界银行贫困与不平等平台2023年7月的最新测算数据绘制。

（二）多维贫困

1.全球多维贫困改善状况优于疫情前，但存在区域差异

根据《全球多维贫困指数2019》和《全球多维贫困指数2023》，2023年全球多维贫困人口数量和多维贫困发生率分别为11亿人和18.3%，低于2019年疫情前的13亿人和23.1%。2019~2023年，撒哈拉以南非洲的多维贫困指数（MPI）[①]降幅最大，南亚次之，随后是拉丁美洲和加勒比地区，而欧洲和中亚的MPI有所升高；南亚的多维贫困发生率降幅最大，撒哈拉以南非洲次之，随

[①] 多维贫困指数（MPI）是一种超越收入的指标，包括获得安全饮用水、教育、电力、食品以及其他六项指标。该指标由联合国开发计划署和牛津贫困与人类发展倡议（Oxford Poverty and Human Development Initiative）共同制定。MPI既能反映多维贫困发生率（H），也能反映多维贫困发生的强度（A），同时还能反映个人或家庭的被剥夺量。其中，MPI=H×A。

后是拉丁美洲和加勒比地区（见图1.7）。总的来看，撒哈拉以南非洲和南亚在降低多维贫困方面均进展良好。

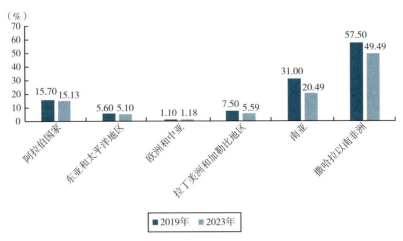

图1.7　2019年和2023年各区域多维贫困发生率

资料来源：根据《全球多维贫困指数2019》和《全球多维贫困指数2023》的数据计算并绘制。

2.不同收入组别国家的多维贫困人口结构变化存在差异，仍需持续关注儿童贫困

根据《全球多维贫困指数2019》和《全球多维贫困指数2023》，2019~2023年中低收入国家贫困人口占比从59.73%降至57.26%，然而低收入国家和中高收入国家的贫困人口占比呈现升高态势。《全球多维贫困指数2023》报告显示，全球儿童多维贫困人口占总贫困人口的比例仍超过50%。儿童多维贫困指数和多维贫困发生率的下降速度显著低于成人，2019~2023年儿童多维贫困发生率年均降幅为4.85%，远低于成人6.46%的年均降幅。根据《全球多维贫困指数2023》，全球5.66亿儿童陷入多维贫困，比2019年减少了0.97亿人。值得注意的是，儿童贫困不仅是当前的问题，还将产生长期持续的影响，降低儿童贫困水平应受到持续关注。

3.近三分之一国家的多维贫困指数减半

根据《全球多维贫困指数2023》，在过去15年间，具有长期可比数据的81国家中有25个国家成功将多维贫困指数减半，20个国家多维贫困指数年均降幅超过10%，中国和吉尔吉斯斯坦的多维贫困发生率年均降幅分别为18.46%和15.77%（见图1.8）。

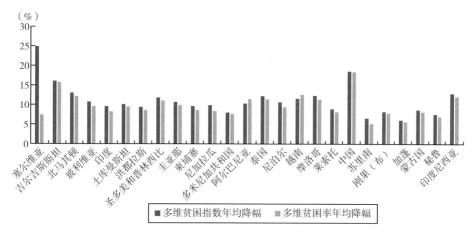

图1.8 2000~2022年部分国家多维贫困指数和多维贫困率年均降幅

资料来源：根据《全球多维贫困指数2019》和《全球多维贫困指数2023》的数据计算并绘制。

三、减贫展望

（一）全球减贫展望

受经济增速放缓、地缘政治冲突和气候风险影响，疫情后全球减贫进程仍面临多重挑战。联合国《2023年世界经济形势与展望》显示，世界经济面临长期低增长的风险，2023年许多国家面临经济衰退风险。根据联合国的《2024年世界经济形势与展望》，全球经济增长将从2023年的2.7%放缓至2024年的2.4%。根据《可持续发展报告2023》，自2020年全球贫困发生率（2.15美元标准）大幅上升以来，减贫进程持续推进，2023年全球贫困发生率从2022年的8.4%降至7.5%。同时，2023年SDG1得分估计会上升至80，比2022年增加0.25%，增速放缓。

多重危机影响多维贫困进程，但部分国家多维贫困方面的进展良好。疫情前，2019年全球多维贫困指数涵盖的81个国家当中，有72个国家的MPI值在统计上显著下降。然而，疫情给全球多维贫困带来了严重的冲击。根据《全球多维贫困指数2022》，约有12亿人生活在多维贫困中（约占19.1%）。联合国开发计划署估计，疫情对健康、教育和收入的影响相当于人类发展指数倒退6年、减贫进程倒退9年，使70个国家陷入多维贫困的人口新增4.9亿人。但总的来看，部分国家仍呈现了较好的减贫态势。根据《全球多维贫困指数2023》，在具有可比数据的81个国家中，柬埔寨、中国、刚果（布）、洪都拉斯、印度、印度尼西亚、摩洛哥、塞尔维亚和越南等25个国家在4~12年的时间内成功实现MPI减半。

（二）区域减贫展望

参照《可持续发展报告2023》的区域划分标准，本部分将193个经济体划分为撒哈拉以南非洲、大洋洲、东欧和中亚、中东和北非、拉丁美洲和加勒比地区、东亚和南亚，以及OECD国家七个区域。

1.撒哈拉以南非洲

撒哈拉以南非洲的经济增长放缓。世界银行《全球经济展望2023》预计，2023年撒哈拉以南非洲的经济增速降至3.2%，2024年将升至3.9%。持续的经济增长是推动减贫的重要动力之一。根据《可持续发展报告2023》，撒哈拉以南非洲的贫困发生率（2.15美元标准）为32.10%，仍是全球贫困发生率最高、贫困人口数量最多的区域。世界银行《宏观贫困展望2023》估计，疫情暴发以来全球贫困人口增幅最大的10个国家中，有八个位于撒哈拉以南非洲。

撒哈拉以南非洲的减贫进程持续推进。根据《可持续发展报告2023》，2020~2023年，在撒哈拉以南非洲，贫困发生率恢复至疫情前水平的国家不断增多，从11个增加到34个（见图1.9）。其中，与2019年相比，2023年撒哈拉以南非洲的贫困发生率（2.15美元标准）降幅超过3%的国家有塞拉利昂、埃塞俄比亚、贝宁、尼日利亚、吉布提、刚果（金）、多哥和布基纳法索等。然而，面对疫情等挑战，部分撒哈拉以南非洲国家的贫困发生率仍未恢复到疫情前水平，其中索马里、乍得、中非共和国、马拉维和苏丹五个国家2023年的贫困发生率比2019年增加了1%以上。

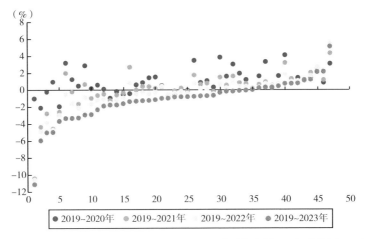

图1.9 与2019年相比，2020~2023年撒哈拉以南非洲各国的
贫困发生率变化情况

资料来源：根据联合国《可持续发展报告2023》的数据计算并绘制。

　　撒哈拉以南非洲的可持续发展的首要目标——消除贫困（SDG1）和总目标都进展良好。2015年联合国提出的可持续发展目标（SDG）旨在从2015年到2030年以综合方式彻底解决社会、经济和环境三个维度的发展问题，可持续发展目标得分反映一个国家在可持续发展道路上的进展情况。根据《可持续发展报告2023》和《2023可持续发展目标报告》，2015~2023年撒哈拉以南非洲的可持续发展目标不断向前推进，但受疫情影响，2022年和2023年可持续发展目标进展暂时停滞。2015~2019年SDG1进展良好，2020年SDG1得分降至2017年的水平，但自2021年以来又开始随着疫情消退而升高（见图1.10）。SDG1方面的进展速度快于可持续发展总目标。

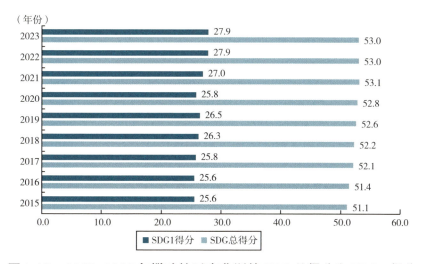

图1.10　2015~2023年撒哈拉以南非洲的SDG总得分和SDG1得分

资料来源：根据联合国《可持续发展报告2023》的数据绘制。

2. 东欧和中亚

　　受疫情等的影响，东欧和中亚的经济增长放缓，但有所回升。根据世界银行2023年6月公布的《全球经济展望》，2022年欧洲和中亚的经济增长跌至1.2%，东欧的产出下降了20.2%，但将欧洲和中亚的经济增长预期从0.1%提高到1.4%，预计2024~2025年经济增长将恢复至2.7%。

　　东欧和中亚区域内贫困水平存在较大差异。根据《可持续发展报告2023》，2023年东欧和中亚的贫困发生率（2.15美元标准）为7.06%；在有统计数据的22个国家中，除格鲁吉亚和阿富汗以外，20个国家的贫困发生率均低于3%。2023年，除阿富汗以外，其他21个国家的贫困发生率已经降至2019年水平以下。近年来，塔吉克斯坦的经济持续快速增长，推动贫困发生率不断降低，2023年的贫困发生率（2.15美元标准）降至2.51%，比2019年下降了约50%。

东欧和中亚的可持续发展目标（SDG）进展缓慢。2019年疫情前东欧和中亚的SDG总得分和SDG1得分稳步提高（见图1.11），与2015年相比，SDG1得分年均增速为0.75%，远高于SDG总得分的年均增速（0.44%）。受疫情等影响，相比2019年，预计2023年SDG1得分略微上升，提高了0.42%，然而SDG得分降低了5.37%。

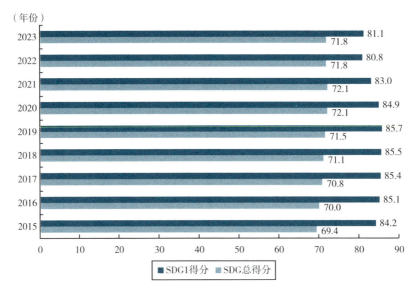

图1.11　2015~2023年东欧和中亚的SDG总得分和SDG1得分

资料来源：根据联合国《可持续发展报告2023》的数据绘制。

　　总体来看，疫情使东欧和中亚经济增速放缓，减贫进程逆转，目前经济复苏还受通货膨胀加剧、供应链中断、政策的不确定性以及劳动力市场的挑战等多方面影响，该地区的减贫进程尚未恢复至疫情前状态。

3.中东和北非

中东和北非的经济增长不及预期，通货膨胀居高不下，粮食安全风险增加。根据2023年5月国际货币基金组织（IMF）发布的《中东和中亚地区经济展望》，尽管2022年受到全球冲击，但中东和北非国家因国内需求强劲和石油产量反弹，其增长仍高于预期，实际GDP增长了5.3%。根据2024年4月世界银行发布的《中东和北非的冲突和债务》，2023年中东和北非地区的经济增长率为1.9%，预计2024年将增长2.7%。由于中东地区的冲突导致增长乏力、债务增加和不确定性加剧，该地区回到了疫情前十年的低增长水平。根据2023年4月世界银行发布的《动荡的命运：物价上涨、粮食安全问题对中东和北非地区的长期影响》，2023年该地区通货膨胀率保持在14.8%的高位，2024年略微下降，预计通货膨胀高企将使该地区的粮食安全风险增加24%~33%，使约五分之一的人口可能面临粮食安全风险，800万5岁以下儿童面临饥饿。

中东和北非的减贫进展已恢复至疫情前水平，但进展缓慢。根据联合国的《可持续发展报告2023》，估计2023年埃及、伊朗、约旦和阿尔及利亚的贫困发生率低于疫情前。然而，由于物价高企、宏观政策收紧、地区冲突等，中东部分地区的贫困发生率仍高于2019年疫情前水平。根据世界银行的数据，中东和北非2019~2022年绝对贫困人口持续小幅增加，从2019年的3300万人上升至2022年的3690万人，新增330万绝对贫困人口。从可持续发展目标进展来看，一方面，2015~2023年可持续发展目标持续向好，受疫情影响，2020年首次降低，此后可持续发展进程不断恢复，但进展缓慢；另一方面，SDG1进程恢复不及可持续发展目标，2023年SDG1的得分比2020年分别增加了1.1%和0.3%（见图1.12）。

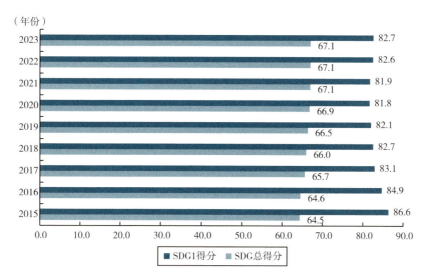

图1.12　2015~2023年中东和北非的SDG总得分和SDG1得分

资料来源：根据联合国《可持续发展报告2023》的数据绘制。

4.拉丁美洲和加勒比地区

拉丁美洲和加勒比地区的经济增速放缓。根据2024年4月国际货币基金组织（IMF）发布的《世界经济展望》，2023年拉丁美洲和加勒比地区经济增长2.3%，预计2024年和2025年该地区的经济增速分别为2%和2.5%。

拉丁美洲和加勒比地区的贫困水平持续下降。自1990年以来，拉丁美洲和加勒比地区的贫困发生率稳步降低。根据世界银行贫困与不平等平台的数据，拉丁美洲和加勒比地区1.9美元标准和2.15美元标准下的贫困发生率变化趋势相似，2.15美元标准下的贫困发生率略高于1.9美元标准，2021年该地区2.15美元标准下的贫困发生率比2019年高0.37%（见图1.13）。根据联合国《可持续发展报告2023》，2023年拉丁美洲和加勒比地区2.15美元标准下的贫困发生率为6.1%。

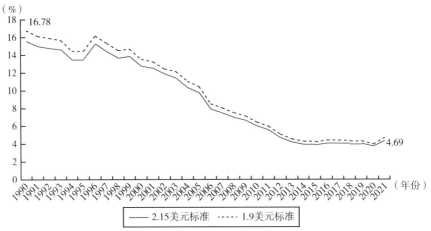

图1.13　1990~2021年拉丁美洲和加勒比地区的贫困发生率

资料来源：根据世界银行贫困与不平等平台的数据绘制。

拉丁美洲和加勒比地区内各国的减贫恢复情况存在差异。根据联合国《可继续发展报告2023》，与2019年相比，2023年圭亚那、巴西、尼加拉瓜、洪都拉斯的贫困发生率（2.15美元标准）的降幅均超过1%，分别为6.56%、3.98%、1.89%和1.59%。然而，受地区冲突和疫情影响，2023年厄瓜多尔、海地和委内瑞拉的贫困状况仍未恢复至2019年水平。

拉丁美洲和加勒比地区的可持续发展目标及其首要目标虽进展缓慢，但持续向好。根据《可持续发展报告2023》，SDG总得分从2019年的69.4增加到2023年的70.2，SDG1得分从2019年的80.8增加到2023年的84，这表

明拉丁美洲和加勒比地区的SDG1进展速度快于可持续发展总目标（见图
1.14）。

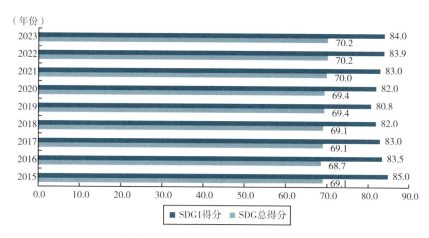

图1.14　2015~2023年拉丁美洲和加勒比地区的SDG总得分和SDG1得分

资料来源：根据联合国《可持续发展报告2023》的数据绘制。

5. 东亚和南亚

东亚和南亚经济增长加速，减贫进程快速恢复。根据世界银行2023年4
月发布的《东亚和太平洋地区经济半年报》，东亚和太平洋地区大多数发展中
国家的经济活动已从疫情冲击中复苏。根据亚洲开发银行2024年4月发布的
《2024年亚洲发展展望》，随着疫后持续复苏，亚洲和太平洋地区的前景依然
强劲，预计2024年和2025年的增长率为4.9%，其中，东亚的GDP增速从2022
年的2.9%反弹至2023年的4.7%，预计2024年为4.3%；南亚2023年GDP增速
为5.4%，预计2024年为5.8%。

**南亚是遭受疫情冲击最为严重的地区之一，但大部分南亚国家的贫困水
平已低于疫情前。**该地区是全球总人口和贫困人口密度最稠密的地区之一，极
高的人口密度和贫困人口密度加大了南亚经济复苏和减贫的压力。联合国的
《可持续发展报告2023》指出，2023年南亚的贫困发生率（2.15美元标准）为
2.41%，绝大多数南亚国家的贫困发生率将降至2019年水平以下。根据《可持
续发展报告2023》，与2019年相比，2023年孟加拉国、印度尼西亚、尼泊尔
和巴基斯坦的贫困发生率的降幅分别为5.56%、1.595%、1.06%和1%，然而，
2023年斯里兰卡、东帝汶和缅甸的贫困发生率仍高于2019年。

东亚和南亚可持续发展目标进展持续向好，SDG1得分持续提高。根据《可持续发展报告2023》，2015~2023年东亚和南亚的SDG1得分持续提高，从63增加到67.2。受疫情影响，2020年SDG1得分降低至2018年的水平，2023年增加到89.7，比2022年略有增加。分国家来看，绝大部分东亚和南亚国家的减贫水平已经好于2019年，但老挝、斯里兰卡、缅甸和蒙古国的减贫成果有待进一步巩固（见图1.15）。

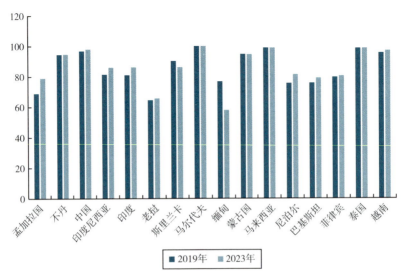

图1.15　2019年和2023年东亚和南亚国家的SDG1得分

资料来源：根据联合国《可持续发展报告2023》的数据绘制。

6.OECD国家

经济合作与发展组织（OECD）国家经济基础较好，但疫情后复苏仍然脆弱。根据2023年6月OECD国家的《经济展望》，预计2024年OECD国家的GDP增速为1.4%，由于货币政策收紧、能源和食品价格下降，以及供应"瓶颈"减少，通货膨胀将从2022年的9.4%下降至2023年的6.6%，并在2024年降至4.3%。

OECD国家绝对贫困水平整体很低。根据世界银行最新的收入组划分标准，38个OECD成员国中有34个属于高收入国家，仅有哥斯达黎加、土耳其、哥伦比亚和墨西哥属于中高收入国家，整体经济发展水平较高。根据联合国的《可持续发展报告2023》，2023年OECD国家2.15美元标准和3.65美元标准下的贫困发生率分别为1.3%和2.2%，均低于3%。从可持续发展目标来看，OECD国家的SDG1得分位居各区域之首，并且远远领先其他目标，2023年SDG总得分增至77.8。疫情前2019年OECD国家的SDG1得分已经高达97.3，2020年降为96.5，2023年恢复到97。2015~2023年，OECD国家的可持续发展总目标持续改善，但受疫情影响，2021年和2022年进展缓慢（见图1.16）。

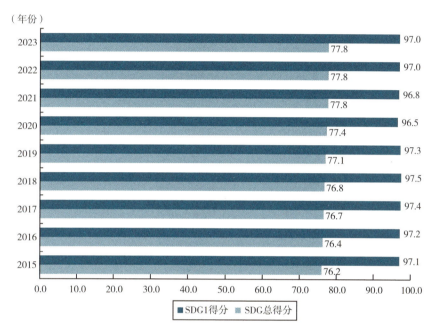

（年份）

图1.16　2015~2023年OECD国家的SDG总得分和SDG1得分

资料来源：根据联合国《可持续发展报告2023》的数据绘制。

OECD国家之间的绝对贫困水平存在差异。根据联合国的《可持续发展报告2023》，OECD高收入国家2.15美元标准下的贫困发生率介于0.01%和1.13%，3.65美元标准下的贫困发生率介于0.01%和3.75%，然而OECD中高收入国家2.15美元标准下的贫困发生率和3.65美元标准下的贫困发生率分别介于0.76%~9.725%和1.39%~16.06%（见表1.1）。OECD国家的SDG1得分很高。2023年，OECD高收入国家中，智利的SDG1得分最低（96.4），25个OECD高收入组国家的SDG1得分高于99。2023年，OECD中高收入国家中，哥伦比亚、墨西哥、哥斯达黎加和土耳其的SDG1得分分别为77.7、86.3、93.8和98.1。

表 1.1   2023 年 OECD 国家的贫困水平

国家代码	国家	收入组	2.15 美元标准的贫困发生率（%）	3.65 美元标准的贫困发生率（%）	SDG1得分
AUS	澳大利亚	高收入	0.34	0.43	99.30
AUT	奥地利	高收入	0.29	0.36	99.50
BEL	比利时	高收入	0.23	0.40	99.50
CAN	加拿大	高收入	0.20	0.27	99.60
CHE	瑞士	高收入	0.23	0.39	99.50
CHL	智利	高收入	0.01	3.75	96.40
CZE	捷克	高收入	0.05	0.07	99.90
DEU	德国	高收入	0.26	0.32	99.50
DNK	丹麦	高收入	0.35	0.56	99.20
ESP	西班牙	高收入	0.59	0.88	98.70
EST	爱沙尼亚	高收入	0.01	0.01	100.00
FIN	芬兰	高收入	0.18	0.31	99.60
FRA	法国	高收入	0.14	0.18	99.70
GBR	英国	高收入	0.50	0.72	99.00
GRC	希腊	高收入	0.27	0.60	99.00
HUN	匈牙利	高收入	0.47	0.77	98.90
IRL	爱尔兰	高收入	0.02	0.04	99.90
ISL	冰岛	高收入	0.07	0.09	99.90
ISR	以色列	高收入	0.67	0.94	98.60
ITA	意大利	高收入	1.13	1.77	97.50
JPN	日本	高收入	0.36	0.47	99.30
KOR	韩国	高收入	0.25	0.36	99.50
LTU	立陶宛	高收入	0.01	0.01	100.00
LUX	卢森堡	高收入	0.01	0.02	100.00
LVA	拉脱维亚	高收入	0.01	0.01	100.00
NLD	荷兰	高收入	0.32	0.53	99.30
NOR	挪威	高收入	0.34	0.56	99.30
NZL	新西兰	高收入	—	—	—
POL	波兰	高收入	0.42	0.69	99.00
PRT	葡萄牙	高收入	0.02	0.05	99.90
SVK	斯洛伐克	高收入	0.37	0.61	99.20
SVN	斯洛文尼亚	高收入	0.25	0.44	99.40

续表

国家代码	国家	收入组	2.15美元标准的贫困发生率（%）	3.65美元标准的贫困发生率（%）	SDG1得分
SWE	瑞典	高收入	0.50	0.79	98.90
USA	美国	高收入	0.55	0.78	98.90
COL	哥伦比亚	中高收入	9.72	16.06	77.70
CRI	哥斯达黎加	中高收入	2.19	4.86	93.80
MEX	墨西哥	中高收入	5.76	10.06	86.30
TUR	土耳其	中高收入	0.76	1.39	98.10

资料来源：贫困数据来自《可持续发展报告2023》，收入组别划分标准参照世界银行2022财年的收入分组。"—"表示数据缺失。

OECD国家的相对贫困水平存在差异。不同于中等收入和低收入国家，高收入国家的贫困主要表现为相对贫困。根据联合国的《可持续发展报告2023》，OECD国家的相对贫困发生率（经税收和转移支付调整后贫困发生率）高低不一（见图1.17）。2023年，在高收入组别中，冰岛的相对贫困发生率最低（4.9%），拉脱维亚的相对贫困发生率最高（17.3%），34个高收入国家相对贫困发生率的中位数为10.25%；2023年，在中高收入组别中，土耳其、墨西哥和哥斯达黎加的相对贫困发生率分别为15%、16.6%和20.3%。

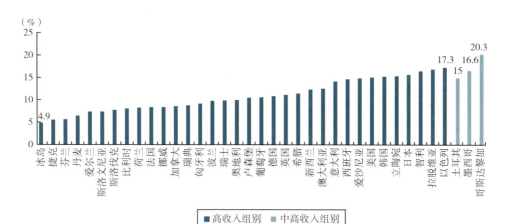

图1.17　2023年OECD国家的相对贫困发生率

资料来源：相对贫困数据来自《可持续发展报告2023》，收入组别划分标准参照世界银行2022财年的收入分组。哥伦比亚的数据缺失。

7.大洋洲

大洋洲国家贫困分化，国家之间存在较大差异，贫困人口集中，减贫进展快慢不一。 大洋洲国家绝对贫困主要集中在美拉尼西亚区域，占贫困人口的90%以上。根据联合国的《可持续发展报告2023》，相对其他区域，大洋洲的可持续发展目标尚有较大提升空间，SDG1得分不足SDG总得分的七成。疫情前后，SDG1得分在波动中改善，但受疫情影响，2020年SDG1得分比2019年下降13.6%，从37.8降至32.6，而且2021年继续降至32，2023年恢复至35.6（见图1.18）。

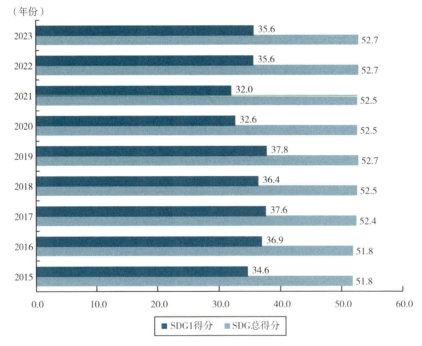

图1.18 2015~2023年大洋洲的SDG总得分和SDG1得分

资料来源：根据联合国《可持续发展报告2023》的数据绘制。

大洋洲中高收入国家的绝对贫困发生率较低，中低收入国家的绝对贫困发生率整体较高，但也有例外。 根据联合国的《可持续发展报告2023》，2023年大洋洲的两个中高收入国家——汤加和斐济2.15美元标准下的贫困发生率分别为1.02%和2%，均低于3%；此外，虽然萨摩亚属于中低收入国家，但是其2.15美元标准下的贫困发生率为1.23%，远低于3%（见图1.19）。

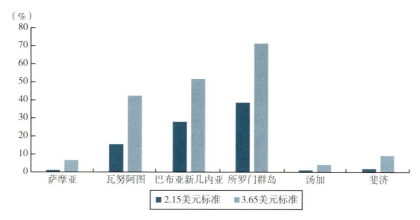

图1.19 2023年大洋洲国家的绝对贫困发生率

资料来源：根据联合国《可持续发展报告2023》的数据绘制。

总体来看，2015~2023年OECD国家、东亚和南亚的贫困水平较低，且东亚和南亚的减贫幅度最大，虽然撒哈拉以南非洲和大洋洲的贫困程度较高，但是撒哈拉以南非洲减贫幅度仅次于东亚和南亚。东欧和中亚、中东和北非、拉丁美洲和加勒比地区、东亚和南亚，以及OECD国家五个区域的SDG1进展均好于可持续发展总目标，然而消除贫困仍是撒哈拉以南非洲和大洋洲需要重点关注的可持续发展目标之一。根据联合国的《可持续发展报告2023》，从SDG1得分来看，东亚和南亚的得分从2015年的78.5提高到2023年的89.7，上涨幅度高达14.32%，贫困水平仅次于OECD国家，而撒哈拉以南非洲的得分从2015年的25.6提高到2023年的27.9，提高了9.07%，仍有很大的减贫空间（见图1.20）。

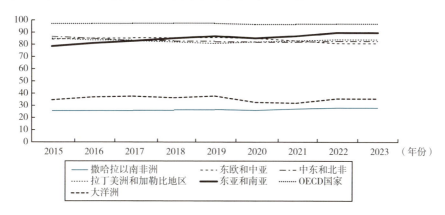

图1.20 2015~2023年主要区域的减贫趋势

资料来源：根据联合国《可持续发展报告2023》的数据绘制。

第二章
主要减贫议题实施情况

本章要点

　　本章延续2021年和2022年《国际减贫年度报告》对主要减贫议题实施情况的梳理和跟踪，讨论经济从新冠疫情冲击中缓慢复苏的背景下，教育发展、营养健康、基础设施、自然灾害和地区冲突五大跨领域议题的实施情况。议题与贫困相互交织、相互影响，回顾其取得的进展，有助于更深刻地理解全球减贫的进程，为促进减贫提供启示。

　　疫情后，各国积极采取措施，推动教学活动和质量的恢复，但全球范围内的教育不平等问题进一步加剧；疫情和日益严重的粮食不安全问题加重了贫困人口的营养健康危机；基础设施的恢复和改善同样具有区域差异性，具备韧性的基础设施对应对疫情冲击和重建更美好的家园具有重要意义；自然灾害的发生分布区域广，受灾人数多，经济损失大，增加了贫困人口的脆弱性，国际援助是应对灾害和减贫的重要力量；地区冲突的发生和伤亡人员分布集中，影响减贫进程，实现区域和平稳定是促进减贫的关键所在。

一、经济复苏

　　（一）尽管全球GDP增速和失业率恢复到疫情前水平，但经济前景仍存在不确定性

　　2022年全球GDP达到101万亿美元，较2021年增长了3.08%，全球经济从疫情的巨大冲击中复苏。受疫情影响，2020年全球GDP增长率为−3.07%，呈现了较大幅度的负增长状态。2021年世界经济实现了恢复性反弹，GDP增长率达到6.02%。2020~2022年三年的平均增速为2.01%，GDP增速逐渐回到疫情前水

平（见图2.1）。但受多重危机的影响，世界经济前景暗淡且存在不确定性。

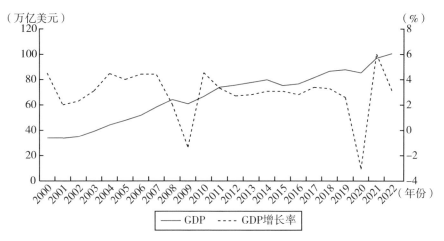

图2.1　2000~2022年全球GDP和GDP增长率

资料来源：世界银行，《世界发展指标》。

2022年全球失业率为5.77%，尽管仍略高于疫情前（2019年）的5.54%，但较2020年的6.9%和2021年的6.2%已显著下降（见图2.2）。新冠疫情仍具有不确定性，地区局势紧张，气候变化日益恶化，企业面临关闭危机，投资减少，导致就业增长的潜力不足。另外，自动化和人工智能技术的发展给全球劳动力市场带来新的挑战。

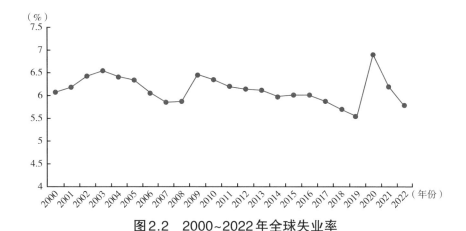

图2.2　2000~2022年全球失业率

资料来源：世界银行，《世界发展指标》。

　　失业率的国别差异和区域差异显著。高收入、中高收入、中低收入和低收入国家之间失业率存在差异，高收入国家平均失业率最高且变动幅度较大，中低收入国家失业率次之，低收入国家平均失业率最低，这可能与低收入国家的失业率数据统计的质量有关。如图2.3所示，除了低收入国家，其他收入水平国家的失业率都在2008年金融危机中有所提高，其中高收入国家的上升幅度最大，从2008年的5.87%上升到2009年的7.95%。在2010年之后，高收入国家的失业率显著下降，其他国家则保持相对稳定。与2008年金融危机的影响类似，在2019年疫情发生之后，不同收入水平国家的失业率都显著上升。其中，低收入国家的失业率从2019年的5.14%上升到2020年的5.9%，之后缓慢下降，分别下降到2021年的5.6%和2022年的5.52%。中低收入国家的失业率从2019年的5.73%上升到2020年的7.78%，之后下降到2021年的6.79%和2022年的6.46%。中高收入国家的失业率从2019年的5.81%上升到2020年的6.52%，之后下降到2021年的6.09%和2022年的5.83%。高收入国家则从2019年的4.77%快速上升到2020年的6.51%，之后下降到2021年的5.61%和2022年的4.51%。

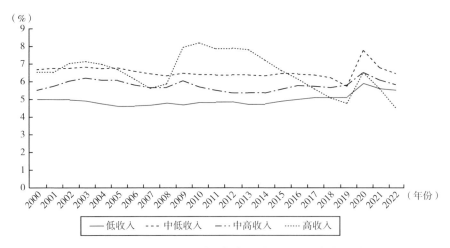

图2.3　2000~2022年按收入水平划分的失业率

资料来源：世界银行，《世界发展指标》。

　　失业率的区域差异体现了区域经济发展不平衡和劳动力市场的区域差异。如图2.4所示，中东和北非的失业率最高，但呈现下降趋势，从2000年的11.92%下降至2019年的9.33%，受疫情影响，2020年有所提升，为10.03%，随后缓慢下降，2022年为9.63%；而东欧和中亚、拉丁美洲和加勒比地区的失业率次之，分别从2000年的9.79%和9.33%下降至2019年的6.64%和7.98%，受疫情影响，2020年这两个地区的失业率都有所提升，分别为7.08%和10.2%，随后下降至2022年的6.27%和7.02%。大洋洲的失业率相对最低，2000~2022年的变化幅度也相对平缓，从2000年的3.67%下降至2019年的3.02%，2020年上升至3.29%，随后在2021年和2022年都有小幅度上升，分别为3.38%和3.39%。

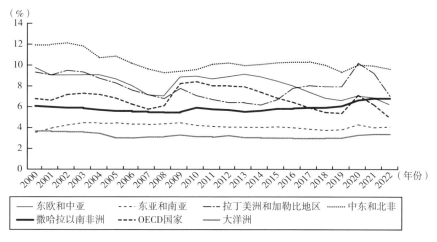

图2.4　2000~2022年全球各区域失业率

资料来源：世界银行，《世界发展指标》。

（二）人均GDP区域差异进一步扩大

经济发展区域不平衡不断加剧。2010年，高收入国家的人均GDP是低收入国家的33.47倍；在2021年和2022年，高收入国家与低收入国家的人均GDP的差异高达70.81倍和66.68倍。从高收入水平国家来看，OECD国家的人均GDP水平及增速都较高，2000年人均GDP为23026.18美元，2019年达到39531.43美元，受疫情影响，2020年微降至38341.32美元，2022年快速升至43260.7美元，近三年年均增速达9.63%。而从低收入水平国家来看，撒哈拉以南非洲的人均GDP最低且增速较慢，2000年为632.35美元，2019年增加至1625.76美元，受疫情影响，2020年下降至1488.8美元，2022年升至1690.39美元，近三年年均增速为4.77%，较OECD国家低5个百分点。

高收入、中高收入、中低收入和低收入国家之间人均GDP差异显著，且呈现明显的上涨趋势。在21世纪初，高收入国家的人均GDP是低收入国家的50

倍左右。在21世纪第一个十年，人均GDP的国别差异逐渐缩小，2010年高收入国家的人均GDP是低收入国家的33.47倍。但是，自2010年以来，人均GDP的国别差异又显著扩大，尤其是疫情发生以后，2021年高收入国家与低收入国家的人均GDP的差异高达70.81倍，这一数字在2022年有所下降，为66.68倍。

如图2.5所示，低收入国家的人均GDP在疫情后呈现复苏趋势，但增长缓慢。受疫情冲击，低收入国家的人均GDP从2019年的681.75美元下降至2020年的653.67美元，之后缓慢上升，2021年和2022年的人均GDP分别为682.78美元和741.24美元。中低收入国家的人均GDP从2019年的2411.33美元下降至2020年的2285.71美元，2021年又恢复至2581.86美元，2022年降至2542.20美元。中高收入国家的人均GDP从2019年的9548.2美元下降至2020年的9166.46美元，但在2021年又迅速恢复至10835.52美元，2022年进一步提升至10953.19美元。高收入国家的人均GDP从2019年的44744.78美元下降至2020年的43282.42美元，2021年迅速恢复至47886.78美元，2022年进一步提升至49430.33美元。

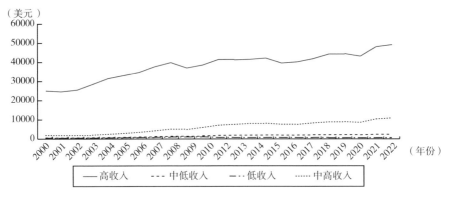

图2.5　2000~2022年按收入水平划分的人均GDP

资料来源：世界银行，《世界发展指标》。

人均GDP的区域差异也呈现逐步扩大趋势，体现了区域经济发展不平衡的情况加剧。如图2.6所示，OECD国家不仅人均GDP水平最高且增速也快，体现了迅速的经济发展，其人均GDP从2000年的23026.18美元一路快速上涨至2019年的39531.43美元，受疫情影响，2020年略有下降，为38341.32美元，而后逐步增长，2022年升至43260.7美元。人均GDP次高的地区是东欧和中亚，其人均GDP从2000年的11667.34美元上涨至2019年的24870.58美元，受疫情影响，2020年略有下降，为23995.15美元，而后逐步增长，2022年升至27363.87美元。而撒哈拉以南非洲的人均GDP最低且上涨幅度极小，从2000年的632.35美元上升到2019年的1625.76美元，2020年下降为1488.8美元，而后逐步增长，2022年升至1690.39美元，增长幅度较小。

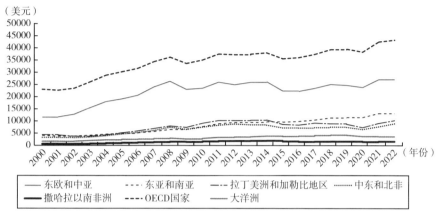

图2.6　2000~2022年全球各区域人均GDP

资料来源：世界银行，《世界发展指标》。

二、教育发展

（一）全球基础教育的普及率维持稳定，高等教育普及率继续提高

尽管在过去20年全球的教育情况不断得到改善，教育普及尤其是基础教育的普及率提高到了一个较高的水平，高等教育不断发展，但近几年基础教育的普及率有所下降，高等教育继续发展。《可持续发展报告2023》的数据显示，全球小学净入学率在2021年有下降趋势，从2019年的94.76%和2020年的95.54%下降至2021年的92.54%；中等教育完成率具有同样的趋势，从2019年的84.44%和2020年的87.17%下降至2021年的77.33%；全球范围内的高等教育继续改善，从2019年的41.61%和2020年的42.65%提高至2021年的45.06%。

国家、区域之间教育发展更加不平衡。根据《可持续发展报告2023》的数据，高收入国家的基础教育普及率维持在较高的水平且高等教育程度继续提高，而其他收入水平国家的基础教育和高等教育发展都停滞不前。高收入国家的小学净入学率维持在98%左右，2021年降至96.57%；中等教育完成率从2018年的98.66%上升至2021年的98.78%；高等教育程度从2019年的46.98%上升至2021年的48.91%。中高收入国家的小学净入学率从2019年的96.2%降至2021年的93.34%；中等教育完成率从2018年的86.03%上升至2021年的

86.92%；高等教育程度从2019年的29.87%下降至2021年的28.29%。中低收入国家的小学净入学率从2019年的92.75%至2021年的92.75%，几乎不变；中等教育完成率从2020年的67.45%上升至2021年的72.26%。低收入国家的小学净入学率从2020年的98.78%降至2021年的84.91%；中等教育完成率从2019年的41.04%下降至2021年的40.35%。

（二）通过积极动员和现金补贴等方式，有效推动教学恢复

1.疫情期间，大部分国家都采取了关闭学校的措施，疫情后教育恢复和转型的规划及措施存在区域差异

新冠疫情对全球教育造成重击，由于教学中止以及对于创新教育方式和恢复学校开放态度和措施存在国别和区域差异，进一步扩大了全球教育发展的不均衡。世界银行展开了四轮关于因疫情关闭学校的教育应对调查，调研各个国家教育部门为应对疫情而关闭学校以及后疫情时代恢复教育水平、创新教育方式等问题的观点及做法。

世界银行关于因疫情关闭学校的教育应对调查的前三轮分别于2020年5月至6月、2020年7月和2021年2月至6月实施，调查问卷所涉问题主旨相近。第一轮调查涵盖了118个国家在疫情暴发前期教育对策的三个主要方面：教育战略、教育参与者，以及对学习成果的影响，共包括八个主题：复课计划、校历调整、远程教育系统、在线远程学习方法、教师状态、学生状态、家长/看护人态度、学习进度及质量、考试及教学评估的执行。第二轮调查在第一轮调查的基础上添加了对各国教育财政水平以及未来支出规划的调查，如未来一年的教育财政预算、对于疫情期间家庭教育的融资支持力度、对教师薪资发放的资金支持等，调研了149个国家。第三轮问卷共有143个国家参与调查，其设计目的倾向于为全球重新开放学校做好准备，问卷设计在前两轮的核心模块基础上增添了对各国学生健康及卫生情况、2021年教育恢复计划、国际学生流动情况的调研。第四轮调查历时近一年，数据收集截至2022年7月。相比前三轮调查，第四轮调查在全球几乎所有学校重新开放，各国政策制定者开始规划如何恢复教育水平的背景下，所涉问题发生显著调整，主要围绕着减少未来全球教育系统的不均衡性，实现教育的可持续发展目标展开。其问题涉及核心模块中的复学缺勤情况、学生健康、评估疫情的影响、教育水平恢复策略、教育财政融资、数字化教育转型六大类问题，后由经合组织补充了关于高等教育恢复及发展的相关问题。

该调研数据显示，虽然全球大多数国家在疫情期间均采取了关闭学校的措施，各地区在疫情期间关闭学校的情况并不均衡，如图2.7所示。如今，随着

疫情后学校重新开放，各国对于教育恢复和转型的规划及措施也各不相同。

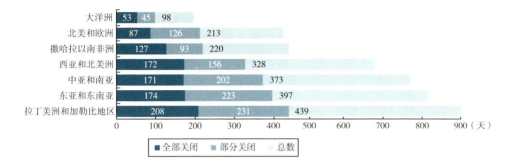

图2.7　各地区在新冠疫情期间平均学校关闭天数

注：统计期间为2020年2月16日至2022年4月30日。
资料来源：世界银行关于因疫情关闭学校的教育应对调查。

2. 各国通过动员、现金补贴和改善卫生措施等方式激励学生返校

疫情期间全球大多数国家经历了持续的学校关闭，导致恢复教学后学生的缺勤率大幅上升。如图2.8所示，在不同的学习阶段，均有80%以上的中高收入国家的学生缺勤率上升，说明中高收入国家的学生更易受疫情期间学校关闭的影响而选择辍学或因故无法返校学习。相比之下，低收入国家、中低收入国家和高收入国家受到的影响较小，各约有一半国家的学生缺勤率上升。

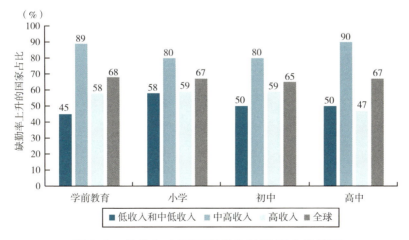

图2.8　各收入水平国家学生缺勤率上升情况

资料来源：世界银行关于因疫情关闭学校的教育应对调查。

　　为促进学生返校，各国积极采取社区动员和财政补贴等手段。如图2.9所示，返校社区动员是大多数低收入和中低收入国家的激励手段，2022年约61%的受访国家对学前教育适龄儿童采取了复学社区动员，另有68%的国家在小学至初中学生群体的教育方面也实施了这项措施。相比之下，高收入国家较少使用此类激励措施。图2.10显示了政府对贫困家庭学生复学提供现金支持的情况，低收入、中低收入和中高收入国家均有近半数以财政支持手段支持经济困难家庭的学生恢复学校教育。此外，智利、罗马尼亚等国表示在疫情后学生复学方面建立了早期预警措施，查明不同阶段学生返校障碍，以便后期针对可能出现高缺勤率的群体采取返校激励措施。

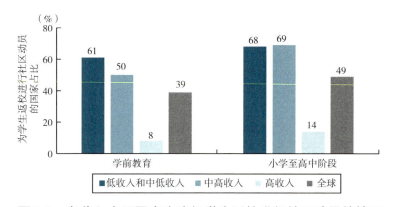

图2.9　各收入水平国家为确保学生返校进行社区动员的情况

资料来源：世界银行关于因疫情关闭学校的教育应对调查。

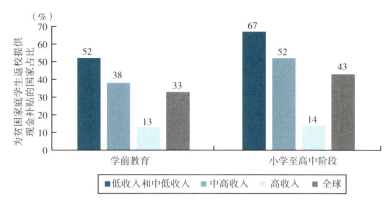

图2.10　各收入水平国家为确保学生返校进行现金补贴情况

资料来源：世界银行关于因疫情关闭学校的教育应对调查。

导致各国学生不能如常返校的因素不仅是家庭经济困难，很多父母担心孩子重返校园的健康问题。根据联合国教科文组织的数据，在法国、科威特和哥伦比亚，超过80%的家长对送孩子上学表示担心。因此，采取一定的卫生方案和预防措施有利于促进儿童和青少年尽快回归正常的教育生活，降低辍学率。如图2.11所示，全球范围内最广泛采取的卫生措施包括在校内提倡勤洗手和加强消毒/清洁，强制教师佩戴口罩授课等。中高收入和高收入国家更多鼓励调整校内的卫生健康基础设施（例如，进一步改善通风、改善空气质量和更灵活的教学空间），超81%的中高收入国家做出了调整。较低收入水平国家更多采取疫苗接种等强制性措施，约有72%的低收入和中低收入国家强制教师接种疫苗，约半数低收入国家要求返校学生必须接种疫苗。

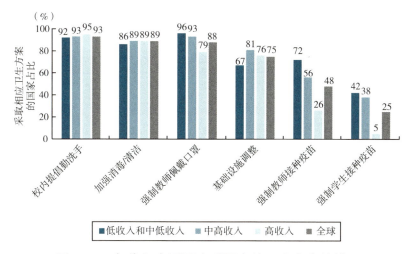

图2.11　各收入水平国家采取在校卫生方案的情况

资料来源：世界银行关于因疫情关闭学校的教育应对调查。

（三）通过调整教学内容和教学方式，恢复教学质量

1.调整学习内容及强度，恢复教学质量

疫情期间，各国在校教学时间的缺失和远程教育质量欠佳使全球大量学生的知识水平低于实际教育阶段的要求。这种影响涉及阅读、数学等基础学科，也涉及社交技能、心理情感等方面的能力。各国积极通过调整教学内容和强度、提高教师教学能力、提供心理辅导等方式来恢复教学质量。

正式考试和教学评估在衡量教育质量方面发挥了重要作用，大部分高收入国家表示将在各个教学阶段重新恢复标准化的大型教学考试以更好地监测学

生的学习进度和学习质量。低收入和中低收入国家在恢复考试方面的态度并不积极。同时，各国不断调整教学内容和课程设计。世界银行关于因疫情关闭学校的教育应对调查第三轮和第四轮调查数据显示，近半数的国家表示在2021~2022学年曾对至少一个教育阶段的学科或年级的课程进行了调整，超三分之一的国家表示会在2022~2023学年持续地调整教学内容。

如图2.12所示，恢复标准化考试在高收入国家更为普遍，分别有93%、89%、88%和85%的高收入国家表示会在学前教育、小学、初中和高中教学中重新恢复标准化的大型教学考试，以更好地监测学生的学习进度和学习质量。低收入和中低收入国家在恢复考试方面态度并不积极，以小学教育为例，仅有37%的受访国家表示会立刻恢复教学评估测试。

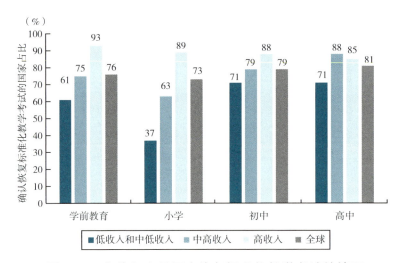

图2.12　各收入水平国家恢复标准化教学考试的情况

资料来源：世界银行关于因疫情关闭学校的教育应对调查。

在校教学时间的缺失和远程教育质量欠佳使大量学生在阅读、数学等基础学科以及社交技能、心理情感等方面的水平低于实际教育阶段的要求，从而增加了复学后的课程负荷，而课程超负荷会导致学生的学习质量下降。专家指出，各国应该将各学科的教学内容和课程进度进行调整，重新设计教学校历。事实上，在2021年的第三轮问卷调查中，全球约有五分之二的国家提出会实施课程调整，如图2.13所示，其形式主要包括减少教学科目或删减各科实际教学内容等。

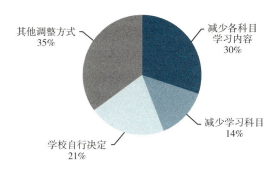

图2.13 调整教学内容方式

资料来源：世界银行关于因疫情关闭学校的教育应对调查第三轮调查。

在第四轮调查中，有更多的国家在实施课程调整。其中，近半数的国家表示在2021~2022学年曾对至少一个教育阶段的学科或年级的课程进行了调整，超三分之一的国家表示会在2022~2023学年持续地调整教学内容。如图2.14所示，课程调整措施的实施随教育阶段和国家收入水平而异。高收入国家群体并不倾向于调整教学内容，仅8%的国家在2022学年调整了学前教育内容，19%的国家调整了小学至高中阶段的教学内容。相比之下，超过半数的低收入和中低收入、中高收入国家已经调整了教学内容。计划在2023学年持续调整教学目录的国家比例下降，尤其是小学至高中教育的下降比例更大，说明此阶段教育的教学内容不会持续大幅调整。

图2.14 教学内容调整的情况

资料来源：世界银行关于因疫情关闭学校的教育应对调查第四轮调查。

2.提升教师的教学能力，改善教学质量

提高教师的教学能力也是恢复教育质量的重要途径。为教师提供教学指导、结构化教学计划、课程培训等，都可以提升教师的教学能力，从而改善教学质量。其中，为教师提供结构化教学计划的方式是全球各国短期内提升教师教学质量的最有效措施之一，在低收入和中高收入国家大规模施行。如图2.15所示，全球分别有73%和64%的受访国家表示在2021~2022学年实施了为学前教育以及小学至高中阶段的教师提供结构化教育方案的政策，特别是88%的中高收入国家已经要求小学至高中阶段教师进行结构化教学。但预计未来几年，各收入水平国家在结构化教学的实施计划方面并无显著变化，这意味着至少有四分之一的受访国家并未在教学方案上为教师提供支持和培训。

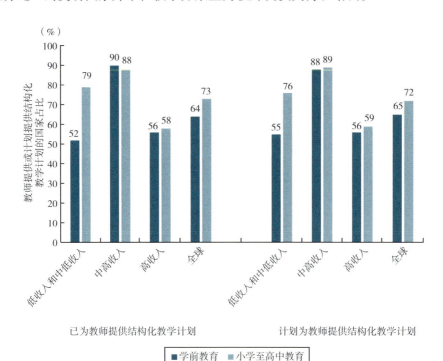

图2.15　不同收入组别国家为教师提供结构化教学计划的情况

资料来源：世界银行关于因疫情关闭学校的教育应对调查。

在疫情期间，全球大多数国家将教学方式转为线上教学，对于教师的远程通信技术运用能力提出新挑战。加强教师在职或入职前数字技术使用技能培训有利于提升未来的教育稳定性和教学质量。如图2.16所示，疫情后全球超半数

的国家对不同教学阶段的在职或入职前教师进行了数字技术使用技能方面的培训。各国都格外重视高中教师使用远程通信技术的能力，82%的国家对高中教师进行了在职培训，69%的国家同时实施了入职前培训。相比之下，仅有57%及70%的国家针对学前教育教师展开入职前培训及在职培训，这一差异或与不同阶段的教学内容和教学方式有关。

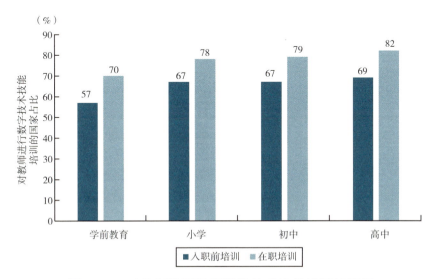

图2.16　对教师使用远程通信技术进行培训的情况

资料来源：世界银行关于因疫情关闭学校的教育应对调查。

　　教师短缺始终是全球教育面临的一大问题，在疫情期间更是有近半数的受访国家表示缺勤教师人数增加。面对疫情后教师短缺带来的挑战，各国采取了多样化策略，如招聘临时教师，将缺勤教师的学生分配到其他班级，监督非教学人员到校授课等。如图2.17所示，应对教师资源短缺的措施在疫情发展的不同时期存在差异。在2020年学校首次关闭之前，分别有45%、15%、4%和9%的受访国家表示会采取使用原有备用教师资源、将缺乏教师的学生分配到其他班级、由非专业教学人员授课、中止学生课程等方式来应对教师缺勤的状况。而在疫情期间，全球有24%的国家选择聘请临时教师进行教学，监督非专业教师授课的措施在国际上也更为普遍。调查显示，在后疫情时代，有44%的国家有备用教师资源来替代缺勤教师，18%的国家计划寻找临时教师，13%的国家会对学生进行重新分配，分别有4%和6%的国家选择由非专业教师进行教学或暂时中止学生课程。为了长期维持有效的教学工作，各国还必须重视与教育提供者（包括教师工会和协会）的交流及支持。教师处于教育政策实施的第一线，确保他们的意见被纳入其中，对制定影响教师和教学的政策至关重要。

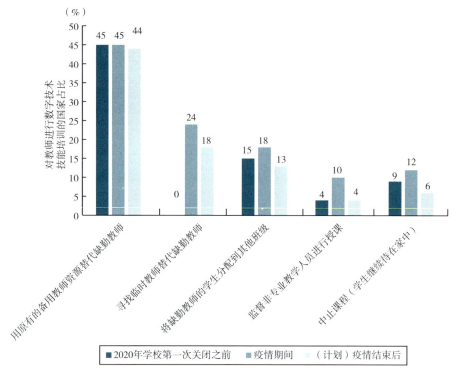

图2.17　应对教师缺勤情况所采取的措施

资料来源：世界银行关于因疫情关闭学校的教育应对调查。

3.通过提供心理辅导提高学生的心理健康

心理健康与营养、水、环境卫生和个人卫生等一样，对于支持学生的正常出勤和学习效率至关重要。如图2.18所示，为确保学生能在学校获得全面的支持和服务，全球分别有约62%及41%的国家表示已经为小学至高中阶段和学前阶段的学生提供心理咨询等心理健康支持，分别有35%和29%的国家通过招募心理学家及辅导员的方式来为小学至高中阶段以及学前阶段学生提供心理健康支持，同时超半数的国家对教师进行心理支持辅导以帮助其更好地为学生提供心理健康支持。低收入和中低收入国家提供这种支持的可能性显著低于中高收入和高收入国家。

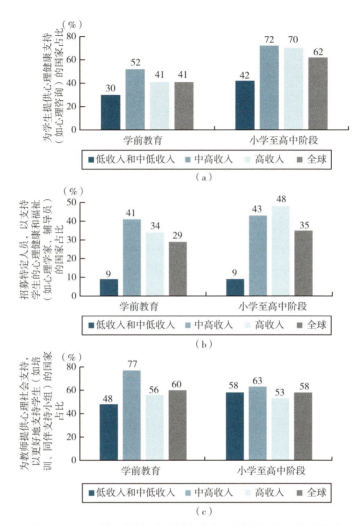

图2.18 为学生提供心理援助支持的具体形式及分布

资料来源：世界银行关于因疫情关闭学校的教育应对调查。

（四）全球范围内的教育不平等问题进一步恶化

不管是疫情期间的教育应对措施，还是疫情后的教育恢复措施，均存在巨大的国别差异。疫情危及了全球教育，因此有必要扩大教育预算，以确保全球学生尽可能全面回归学习[①]。然而，各国在教育方面的财政投入存在很大差异，

① 参见联合国教育、科学及文化组织统计司、联合国儿童基金会、世界银行和经合组织于2022年发布的《从恢复学习到教育转型：世界银行关于因疫情关闭学校的教育应对调查（第四轮）的见解和思考》。

教育不平等问题将持续并进一步恶化。

2020年，新冠疫情暴发后，很多国家减少了政府教育财政支出，如40%的中低收入国家减少了实际教育支出，相比2019年，2020年平均下降13.5%[①]。2020~2021年，大多数国家维持或增加了教育财政支出，但不同收入组别国家之间存在很大差异。如图2.19所示，在全球范围内，在小学至高中阶段，超70%的受访国家在2021年增加了政府预算，减少预算的国家仅占7%，在学前教育阶段减少财政预算的国家仅占4%。从不同收入组别国家之间的差异来看，中低收入国家、中高收入国家与高收入国家之间的差异很明显。以小学至高中阶段教育财政支出变化为例，超过90%的高收入国家和超过80%的中高收入国家增加了小学至高中教育的预算，但是不足50%的中低收入水平国家实现了教育财政投入的增长（见图2.20）。这说明，后疫情时代全球各国所处的收入水平会显著影响其在未来通过财政投入支持本国教育水平恢复和进一步提升的能力。

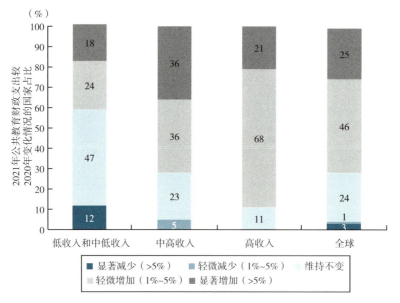

图2.19 2021年全球学前教育公共教育财政支出较2020年的变化情况

资料来源：世界银行关于因疫情关闭学校的教育应对调查。

---

① 参见世界银行、全球教育监测报告（Global Education Monitoring Report 和 GEM）和联合国教科文组织统计研究所（UNESCO Institute for Statistics，UIS）于2022年联合发布的《2022年教育财政观察》。

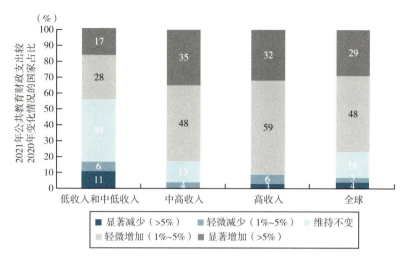

图2.20 2021年全球小学至高中公共教育财政支出较2020年的变化情况

资料来源：世界银行关于因疫情关闭学校的教育应对调查。

三、营养健康

（一）孕产妇和儿童健康方面取得了进展，但地区差异显著

全球范围内的营养健康问题继续得到改善，包括儿童营养状况、医疗保健服务覆盖面和服务水平不断提高。《可持续发展报告2023》的数据显示，营养不良发生率从2000年的16.87%下降到2017年的12.49%、2019年的9.98%和2020年的9.79%；五岁以下儿童发育迟缓的患病率从2000年的26.07%下降到2019年的18.05%、2020年的17.67%、2021年的17.32%和2022年的17.01%；新生儿死亡率从2000年的23.01‰下降到2019年的12.7‰、2020年的12.42‰和2021年的12.14‰；五岁以下儿童死亡率从2000年的69.54‰下降到2019年的27.9‰、2020年的27‰和2021年的26.22‰。全民健康服务覆盖指数（UHC）和由熟练医护人员接生的婴儿比例从2000年的41.18%和71.33%分别提高到2017年的60.83%和83.73%，2019年分别达到64.37%和93.06%。

不同收入水平国家之间的营养健康问题差异仍然显著。根据《可持续发展报告2023》，2021年低收入国家的食物不足发生率和五岁以下儿童发育迟缓的患病率分别是高收入国家的12倍和7倍，低收入国家新生儿死亡率是高收入国家的8倍，低收入国家五岁以下儿童死亡率是高收入国家的12倍。2019年，高收入国家的全民健康服务覆盖指数（UHC）和由熟练医护人员接生的婴儿比例

比低收入国家分别高37.66个百分点和15个百分点。

在高收入国家，从2000年开始，其营养不良发生率一直维持在4%左右，2020年为2.91%；五岁以下儿童发育迟缓的患病率从2000年的6.77%下降至2019年的5.03%，随后提升至2021年的5.28%和2022年的5.22%；新生儿死亡率和五岁以下儿童死亡率从2000年的5.89‰和10.92‰分别下降至2019年的3.56‰和6.15‰，随后分别降至2021年的3.33‰和5.72‰。高收入国家的全民健康服务覆盖指数（UHC）从62.98稳步增长至78.88，2019年提升至79.96；由熟练医护人员接生的婴儿比例一直稳定在98%以上。

在中高收入国家，2001~2018年，营养不良发生率下降了3个百分点，从9.68%下降至6.46%，而后在2020年上升至6.97%；2000~2019年，五岁以下儿童发育迟缓的患病率下降了5个百分点，从19.31%下降至14.11%，而后在2021年和2022年分别降至11.36%和11.19%；新生儿死亡率下降了6个千分点，从16.4‰下降到9.99‰，2021年降至9.24‰；五岁以下儿童死亡率下降了17个千分点，从36.25‰下降到18.84‰，2021年下降至17.01‰；同期，中高收入国家的全民健康服务覆盖指数（UHC）从46.79增长至2017年的68.83，随后下降至2019年的68.68；由熟练医护人员接生的婴儿比例从91.8%稳步增长至2018年的98.37%，随后增长至2020年的99.04%，接近高收入国家水平。

在中低收入国家，2001~2018年，营养不良发生率下降了6个百分点，从19.05%下降到12.96%，随后在2020年降至11.7；2000~2019年，五岁以下儿童发育迟缓的患病率下降了8个百分点，从34.97%下降到27.12%，随后在2021年和2022年分别下降至21.47%和21.02%；新生儿死亡率下降了10个千分点，从28.93‰下降到18.61‰，而后下降至2021年的17.06‰；五岁以下儿童死亡率下降了约一半，从82‰下降至40.26‰，随后在2021年下降至35.55‰；同期，中低收入国家的全民健康服务覆盖指数（UHC）从33.72增长至2017年的55.61，随后上升至2019年的56.59；由熟练医护人员接生的婴儿比例从63.49%稳步增长至2015年的85.95%，而后下降，2018年仅为65.52%，之后提升至2020年的87.88%。

在低收入国家，营养不良发生率在2000年为34.59%，2013年下降了9.57个百分点，为25.02%，而后开始逐渐上升，2018年为26.58%，2020年上升至31.42%；五岁以下儿童发育迟缓的患病率在2000年为43.22%，2019年仍高达37.14%，2021年和2022年分别下降至31.82%和31.3%；新生儿死亡率和五岁以下儿童死亡率分别从2000年的40.82‰和148.97‰下降至2019年的26.78‰和

69.96‰，随后在2021年降至26.44‰和68.97‰，但仍然处于一个很高的水平；同期，全民健康服务覆盖指数（UHC）从2000年的21.22上升至2017年的40，2019年上升至42.3；由熟练医护人员接生的婴儿比例从2000年的31.23%上升至2018年的55.3%，随后上升至2020年的84.12%。

（二）疫情和日益严重的粮食不安全问题加重了贫困人口的营养健康危机

尽管全球范围内的营养健康问题继续得到改善，但贫困国家的贫困人口的营养健康危机仍然严重。疫情和日益严重的粮食不安全问题可能进一步阻碍在改善儿童营养不良方面本已缓慢的进展[①]。疫情加剧了贫困国家本已严重的营养挑战，尤其是穷人和儿童等弱势群体。疫情导致失业和收入减少，尤其是非正规部门的失业和收入下降，使许多家庭难以负担营养食品。疫情的经济影响使许多坦桑尼亚家庭买不起粮食，玉米和豆类等主要主食的价格在一些地区上涨了30%[②]。此外，粮食供应链中断以及对人口流动和贸易的限制也可能导致粮食短缺和粮食价格上涨，特别是在农村地区。对于严重依赖市场购买食品的弱势群体来说，这个问题尤其严重。为了控制病毒传播而采取的学校关闭措施也对营养健康方面产生了负面影响，尤其是对那些每天大部分营养摄入都依赖学校膳食的学龄儿童。学校供餐计划暂停可能导致营养食品消费减少，特别是对于那些无法获得替代食品来源的贫困家庭儿童而言。

全球抗击粮食危机网络（Global Network Against Food Crises，GNAFC）于2023年5月3日发布的《2023年全球粮食危机报告》显示，2022年面临重度粮食不安全的人口连续第四年增长[③]，超过2.5亿人面临严重饥饿，七个国家的民众即将陷入饥荒。报告分析了42个遭受粮食危机的主要地区，其中30个地区有超过3500万五岁以下儿童患有消瘦或重度营养不良，其中920万儿童严重消瘦（这种形式的营养不良最为危险，它是导致儿童死亡率上升的主要原因）。报告指出，疫情造成的经济影响引发的连锁反应也是导致粮食不安全问题的主要原因。高度依赖进口粮食和农业投入品的低收入国家首当其冲，因为疫情严重破坏了这些国家的经济韧性，使其更容易受到全球粮食价格的冲击。

---

① 参见：《可持续发展报告2022》。
② UNICEF Tanzania.COVID-19 Response：Nutrition，2020.
③ 《全球粮食危机报告》将粮食不安全问题按照从轻到重划分为五个等级，等级1~5分别对应轻微（none/minimal）、有压力（stressed）、危机（crisis）、紧急（emergency）和灾难（catastrophe/famine）级别，处于危机以上级别为重度粮食不安全状况。

2023年7月由五家联合国专门机构^①联合发布的《世界粮食安全和营养状况》报告显示，2022年全世界有6.91亿~7.83亿人面临饥饿^②，较疫情暴发前的2019年，全球饥饿人口增加了1.22亿人。报告指出，如果放任态势发展，世界各国无法如期实现到2030年消除饥饿的可持续发展目标，且到2030年全世界预计仍将有近6亿人面临饥饿。报告建议，为有效加强粮食安全、改善营养状况，必须推动农业粮食体系转型，全面把握城乡辐射区域与农业粮食体系之间复杂多变的关系，为政策干预、行动和投资奠定基础。

案例：坦桑尼亚——应对疫情的社会保护计划

坦桑尼亚启动了多项社会保护计划，为弱势群体提供食物、医疗保健等基本资源，以改善他们的福祉，并确保这些计划有效地实施，从而惠及最需要的人群。具体计划包括：

现金转账方案：通过现金转移计划，包括生产性社会安全网和坦桑尼亚社会行动基金等，定期向符合条件的家庭提供现金转移，帮助他们满足基本需求，包括食品、医疗保健和教育。现金转移计划在减少贫困和改善粮食安全方面是有效的，特别是对穷人、妇女和儿童等弱势群体。

学校供餐计划：实施全国学校供餐计划，为学龄儿童提供免费或补贴膳食，以帮助改善他们的营养并支持他们接受教育。学校供餐计划在提高入学率和学习成绩以及减少营养不良方面效果显著。

健康保险计划：实施国家健康保险基金，为正规部门雇员及其家属提供健康保险，使他们能够在不面临经济困难的情况下获得基本的医疗保健服务。健康保险计划已被证明在改善健康结果和减少贫困方面是有效的，特别是对弱势群体。

公共工程项目：通过公共工程项目，包括坦桑尼亚社会行动基金公共工程项目，为符合条件的家庭提供临时就业机会，使他们能够获得收入，同时为公共基础设施和服务的发展作出贡献。

---

① 这五家联合国专门机构分别为联合国粮食及农业组织、国际农业发展基金、联合国儿童基金会、世界卫生组织和世界粮食计划署。

② 《世界粮食安全和营养状况》中的饥饿是指由膳食能量摄入不足引起的一种不舒适或痛苦的身体感觉，以食物不足发生率来衡量。

四、基础设施

（一）全球基础设施持续改善

全球范围内的水资源基础设施、能源基础设施、互联网基础设施和交通基础设施均持续得到改善。《可持续发展报告2023》的数据显示，获得清洁饮用水的人口比例从2000年的75.5%上升到2017年的83.3%、2019年的88.13%和2020年的88.32%；获得清洁燃料的人口比例从2000年的48.28%上升到2016年的57.2%、2019年的67.04%和2020年的67.4%；用电人口比例从2000年的62.73%上涨到2017年的77.05%、2019年的84.73%和2020年的85.47%；使用互联网的人口比例从2000年的6.65%上涨到2017年的46.87%、2019年的61.07%、2020年的64.72%和2021年的69.44%；物流网指数[1]从2010年的2.53稳步增长到2016年的2.64、2018年的2.71。

不同收入水平国家在基础设施覆盖率和质量方面的差异仍然显著。根据《可持续发展报告2023》，2020年，低收入国家获得清洁饮用水的人口比例和获得清洁燃料的人口比例分别比高收入国家低37.52个百分点和87.8个百分点，用电人口比例比高收入国家低59.61%，使用互联网的人口比例比高收入国家低69.69%。2018年，高收入国家的物流网指数为3.46，而低收入国家仅为2.08。

在高收入国家，获得基本饮用水服务的人口比例从2000年的98.61%上升到2019年的99.52%和2020年的99.59%；获得清洁燃料和烹饪技术的人口比例在2000~2020年一直维持在100%；获得电力供应的人口比例从2000年的99.51%上升到2019年的99.99%和2020年的100%；使用互联网的人口比例从2000年的22.37%上升到2019年的87.86%和2020年的89.36%；物流网指数在2018年为3.46。

在中高收入国家，获得基本饮用水服务的人口比例从2000年的89.19%上升到2019年的96.05%和2020年的96.2%；获得清洁燃料和烹饪技术的人口比例从2000年的66.83%上升到2019年的83.38%和2020年的83.74%；获得电力供应的人口比例从2000年的89.03%上升到2019年的96.16%和2020年的96.5%；使用互联网的人口比例从2000年的3.21%上升到2019年的69.5%和2020年的73.66%；物流网指数在2018年为2.58。

在中低收入国家，获得基本饮用水服务的人口比例从2000年的70.34%

---

[1]　物流网指数即贸易和运输相关的基础设施的质量指数，取值区间为1~5。

上升到2019年的82.22%和2020年的82.58%；获得清洁燃料和烹饪技术的人口比例从2000年的28.81%上升到2019年的44.13%和2020年的44.9%；获得电力供应的人口比例从2000年的52.36%上升到2019年的79.85%和2020年的81.31%；使用互联网的人口比例从2000年的0.89%上升到2019年的44.35%和2020年的50.07%；物流网指数在2018年为2.36。

在低收入国家，获得基本饮用水服务的人口比例从2000年的47.4%上升到2019年的61.46%和2020年的62.07%；获得清洁燃料和烹饪技术的人口比例从2000年的7.35%上升到2019年的11.93%和2020年的12.2%；获得电力供应的人口比例从2000年的15.91%上升到2019年的38.66%和2020年的40.39%；使用互联网的人口比例从2000年的0.15%上升到2019年的16.48%和2020年的19.67%；物流网指数在2018年仅为2.08。

（二）贫困国家的基础设施仍然落后，阻碍其经济复苏

疫情证明了工业化、科技创新和具备韧性的基础设施在重建更美好的家园和实现可持续发展目标方面的重要性。拥有多元化工业部门和强大的基础设施（如交通运输、互联网连接和公用事业服务）的经济体遭受的损失较小，并且正在快速复苏。贫困国家的基础设施仍然落后，阻碍其经济的复苏。

案例：坦桑尼亚——疫情前后的基础设施建设

疫情对坦桑尼亚的基础设施投资和建设部门产生了重大影响。根据坦桑尼亚国家统计局（NBS）的一份报告，坦桑尼亚建筑业的增长率从2020年第一季度的11.9%下降到2020年第二季度的5.8%，降幅超过50%。该行业面临着供应链中断、劳动力短缺、建筑服务需求减少、融资挑战以及项目延误和取消等诸多挑战。在疫情期间，坦桑尼亚政府实施了几项支持建筑业的措施，包括税收减免、免除基本建筑材料的进口税、快速发放建筑许可证、提供财政援助、促进电子建筑、实施安全协议等。

坦桑尼亚政府加强了对重大基础设施项目的投资，如标准轨距铁路（SGR）、朱利叶斯·尼雷尔水电站和达累斯萨拉姆港口扩建等。坦桑尼亚政府对基础设施项目的投资预计将推动该国未来几年的经济增长和发展，符合其到2025年成为中等收入国家的愿景。

确保坦桑尼亚基础设施部门的持续增长面临的主要挑战之一是融资困难。特别是在疫情之后，这导致贷款人和投资者的风险厌恶情绪加

剧。政府需要与金融机构密切合作，确保为基础设施项目提供资金，包括通过公私伙伴关系和其他创新融资机制。另一个挑战是熟练劳动力短缺。政府需要投资于培训和能力建设项目，以应对这一挑战。

五、自然灾害

（一）自然灾害的发生分布区域广，受灾人数多，经济损失大

根据国际灾难数据库（The International Disaster Database，EM-DAT）的数据，自2000年以来，全球自然灾害主要发生在亚洲，其次是非洲、美洲和欧洲，最后是大洋洲。2000~2022年，亚洲、非洲、美洲、欧洲和大洋洲每年发生自然灾害的平均次数分别为161次、95次、88次、53次和16次（见图2.21）。因面积广袤、气候多样，亚洲遭受的自然灾害种类多，且发生更频繁。非洲的自然灾害与气候条件及变化、医疗卫生水平和土地退化密切相关。美洲受飓风、洪水、地震和火山活动等影响较多。欧洲由于地理和气候条件相对稳定，自然灾害较少。大洋洲虽然因为面积小，遭受自然灾害的较少，但仍受到热带气旋、洪水和海平面上升等的影响。

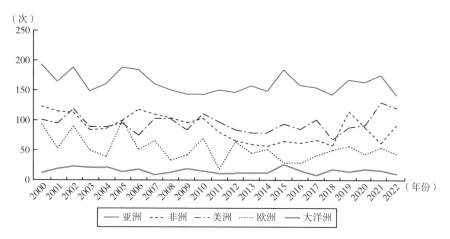

图2.21 2000~2022年五大洲自然灾害发生次数

资料来源：EM-DAT。

从灾害类型来看，水文灾害、气象灾害和生物灾害是全球发生频次排名前三的自然灾害。因为地理环境的差异，各大洲多发的自然灾害类型有所不同。如图2.22所示，亚洲多发水文灾害、气象灾害和地质灾害。亚洲的地质灾害以

地震为主，2000~2022年共计发生419次地震，占全球的66.93%；其中，2022年亚洲发生21次地震，占全球的67.74%。美洲多发水文和气象灾害，此外还受到气候冲击。2000~2022年，美洲发生了120次野火事件和93次干旱；其中，在2022年发生了7次野火事件和3次干旱。由于医疗卫生欠发达、自然环境特殊，非洲饱受生物灾害的侵袭。2000~2022年，非洲共发生虫害22次，遭受传染病冲击586次（其中，细菌性传染病354次、病毒性传染病176次、寄生虫病9次，其他类型47次）；2022年，非洲遭受了6次细菌性传染病的冲击和7次病毒性传染病的冲击。因地理位置、地形和地质条件、气候特点和气候变化影响，大洋洲发生的气象灾害次数较水文灾害次数更多，其中，气象灾害以热带气旋为主，水文灾害以洪水为主。2000~2022年，大洋洲受到了105次热带气旋冲击和97次洪水侵袭；2022年，大洋洲主要发生了1次对流风暴、1次热带气旋和5次洪水灾害。

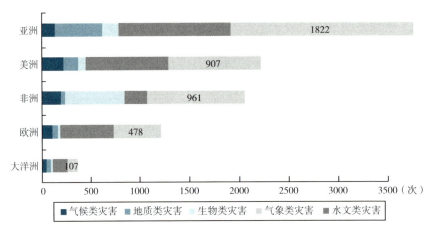

图2.22　2000~2022年五大洲发生的各类型自然灾害次数

资料来源：EM-DAT。

受自然灾害影响的人群主要分布在亚洲和非洲，而水文灾害和气象灾害是影响最大的灾害类型。如图2.23所示，以人数为基准，亚洲是受自然灾害影响最多的大洲，2000~2022年共有约36.22亿人受到影响，占全球受灾人口的81.19%；其次是非洲，有约5.13亿人受到影响，占全球受灾人口的11.5%。从2022年的数据来看，非洲是受自然灾害影响人口最多的大洲，约有1.11亿人受到影响，占总受灾人口的59.49%；亚洲紧随其后，约有0.64亿人受到影响，占该年总受灾人口的34.52%。2000~2022年，在各类自然灾害中，水文灾害影响的人口最多，特别是在亚洲。这一时期，亚洲约有16.29亿人受到水文灾害的影响，占亚洲受灾人口的44.97%。同时，气候类灾害在亚洲和非洲也对大量人口产生了影响。在亚洲，约有11.61亿人受到气候类灾害的影响，占亚洲受灾人口的32.05%。2000~2022年，干旱、野火等气候灾害影响了非洲4.11亿人；其中，在2022年非洲有1.01亿人受气候灾害的影响，有15.93万人受生物灾害的影响。地质灾害（如地震）影响的人口相对较小，但在欧洲和亚洲仍有一定程度的影响。

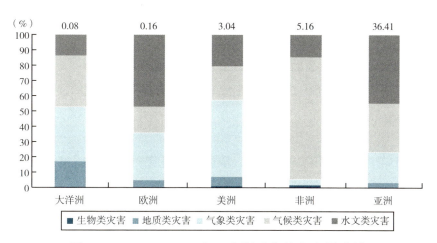

图2.23　2000~2022年五大洲受自然灾害影响的
人数分布及总受灾人数

资料来源：EM-DAT。

如图2.24所示，2000~2022年，受自然灾害影响的总受损金额最高的是美洲，达到了约19384.83亿美元，其次是亚洲（16715.33亿美元）和欧洲（3860.36亿美元），大洋洲（1109.28亿美元）和非洲（409.48亿美元）的受损金额相对较低。2022年，美洲仍然是自然灾害总损失金额最高的大洲，约为1557.91亿美元，其次是亚洲（487.46亿美元）、大洋洲（85.89亿美元）、非洲（85.56亿美元）和欧洲（21.56亿美元）。2000~2022年，气象灾害给美洲造成了14941.21亿美元的损失，其中，2022年为1254.32亿美元。亚洲地区位于环太平洋地震带，2000~2022年，地质灾害使亚洲损失了6386.95亿美元（占亚洲受损金额的38.21%），水文灾害和气象灾害给亚洲分别带来5544.67亿美元和4151.22亿美元的损失；2022年，亚洲多发水文灾害，造成255.27亿美元的损失，而地质灾害给亚洲造成了121.94亿美元的损失。

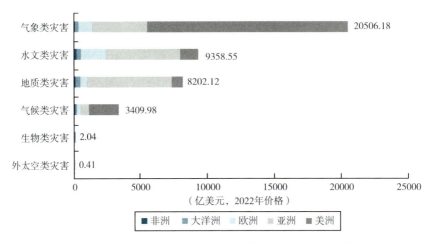

图2.24 2000~2022年五大洲各类型自然灾害造成的损失

资料来源：EM-DAT。

（二）自然灾害影响减贫进程，国际援助是应对灾害和减贫的重要力量

自然灾害对贫困人口产生直接影响的方式多种多样。首先，灾害对人们的生计和财产造成直接破坏。洪水、地震和飓风等灾害可以摧毁人们的家园和农田，使他们失去生计来源。基础设施（如道路、桥梁和供水系统）受损也会削弱人们的生活条件。其次，自然灾害对农田和农业产量造成重大影响。洪涝和干旱等灾害会导致农作物减产甚至歉收，使农民陷入困境。灾害还可能破坏渔业和畜牧业，使捕捞和畜牧业者面临生计压力。此外，灾害引发的人员伤亡和失业问题也加剧了贫困。自然灾害可能造成人员伤亡，使家庭失去主要经济支柱，加剧了贫困。在灾后重建阶段，许多人因失去工作机会而面临失业和收入减少，进一步加深了贫困。

自然灾害还通过间接途径对贫困产生影响。首先，灾害对经济造成冲击，如农业产量下降和基础设施受损。这会导致经济活动的减少，影响就业和收入机会。其次，灾后物价上涨和资源短缺对低收入人群造成压力。灾后需求的激增导致物价上涨，使贫困人口难以承受高昂的生活成本。同时，资源短缺，如水源和粮食短缺，也加剧了贫困问题。最后，灾后恢复和重建阶段对贫困人口具有重要影响。恢复和重建项目的实施可以提供就业机会，帮助贫困人口重建家园和恢复生计。然而，对于贫困人口而言，灾后恢复和重建的机会可能受限，需求的满足程度可能不够，这可能导致贫困的延续。

　　加强灾害管理、提高灾害应对能力和减轻灾害对人们生计的影响有助于减少贫困的发生和持续性。同时，确保贫困人口在灾后恢复和重建中得到充分支持是促进减贫事业的重要一环，包括国家救助、社会组织救助和国际援助等。

　　国际援助是应对灾害和减贫的重要力量。如图2.25所示，亚洲获得了最多的国际援助，达121.28亿美元，其次是美洲（54.79亿美元）和非洲（12.68亿美元）。因为自然灾害较少、经济较为发达等原因，大洋洲（1.26亿美元）和欧洲（0.7亿美元）收到的援助金额相对较少。从自然灾害类型来看，援助资金多流向应对地质灾害（79.44亿美元）和水文灾害（62.9亿美元）。地质灾害发生频次较低，但往往会造成更大的损失；水文灾害造成的损失较低，但是发生的频次较高。在美洲，地质灾害（如地震）获得了相对较高的援助金额（49.39亿美元），这可能与该地区地震风险较高有关。这些援助资金有助于受灾国家和地区应对自然灾害的影响，提供紧急救助和恢复重建。政府和国际组织还通过提供救助和庇护所来帮助受灾人口。这些救助和庇护所可以提供食物、水、医疗和安全等基本需求，并帮助灾民重建他们的生活。这些援助措施可以帮助减轻贫困人口的困境，提高其抵御自然灾害的能力，并为他们的可持续发展提供支持。

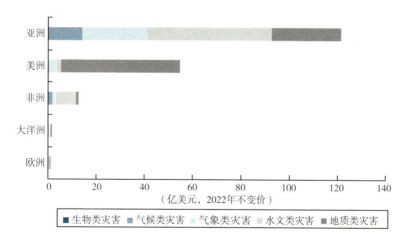

图2.25　2000~2015年五大洲因自然灾害收到的国际援助金额

注：因数据完整性限制，选取2000~2015年的数据。
资料来源：EM-DAT。

　　灾后重建和经济恢复的过程可能对贫困人口产生积极影响。通过恢复基础设施、提供就业机会和重建社区，可以促进贫困人口的生计恢复和经济增长。

各国政府在灾后采取的应对和减轻贫困的政策措施对于受灾地区的恢复至关重要。这可能包括建立早期预警系统、加强灾害风险管理和提供财政援助等措施。国际组织和外部援助机构在灾后重建和减贫方面发挥着重要作用。通过提供资金、技术援助和专业知识，国际组织和外部援助可以帮助受灾国家实施灾后重建和减贫计划。

在灾后重建和减贫过程中，应考虑可持续发展目标的重要性。这包括促进社会、经济和环境的可持续性，以确保受灾地区能够长期应对灾害和贫困问题。为了促进灾后减贫和可持续发展，可以采取一系列策略和建议，包括加强灾害风险管理，改善社会保障体系，提供职业培训和教育机会，以及促进可持续农业和可再生能源等。

> ### 案例：气旋"亚斯"
>
> 气旋"亚斯"是2021年印度洋飓风季的一场强烈气旋，于2021年5月登陆印度东海岸，其持续风速为70~80公里/小时，阵风高达90公里/小时。气旋"亚斯"袭击了印度东部的奥里萨邦和西孟加拉邦，也影响了孟加拉国南部。根据EM-DAT的数据，气旋"亚斯"使印度162.5万人和孟加拉国130万人受到影响，对印度造成约32.4亿美元的损失。孟加拉国的部分农村地区因为遭受气旋"亚斯"侵袭，甚至无法提供干净的饮用水。
>
> 气旋"亚斯"严重冲击了当地经济，使失业率攀升。基础设施被破坏导致生产中断和交通困难，进而影响当地企业的运作和供应链。当地的农业、渔业和旅游业等重要行业受到破坏性影响，导致GDP下降和就业岗位流失。气旋"亚斯"造成房屋破坏，大多数人利用贷款来修复受损的房屋，使贫困人口陷入债务陷阱。气旋"亚斯"造成的农田损失使灾民失去收入来源，被盐水淹没的土壤至少在未来两到三个作物周期内都不适合耕种，所有的淡水池塘也变成了咸水，导致养殖的鱼类死亡。

六、地区冲突

（一）地区冲突的发生和伤亡人员分布比较集中

根据"武装冲突地点和事件数据库项目"（Armed Conflict Location and Event Data Project，ACLED）的数据，2022年地区暴力冲突事件大幅增加，当年全球共发生超过6355起地区冲突事件，亚洲和欧洲的政治动荡事件增加。2022年，亚洲共发生超过2796件地区暴力冲突事件，欧洲发生了1226件，其次则是非洲（1211件）、美洲（1115件）和大洋洲（7件）。如图2.26所示，2022年发生在亚洲的地区冲突包括890次抗议示威活动，503次爆炸事件，424次战役，272次攻击平民事件。欧洲发生了超过1226次地区冲突事件，包括755次爆炸事件和216次战役。2022年地区冲突事件发生较多的国家包括乌克兰（1015件）、叙利亚（446件）、缅甸（435件）、巴西（316件）、墨西哥（299件）、印度（282件）、伊拉克（249件）、巴基斯坦（237件）和也门（231件）等。

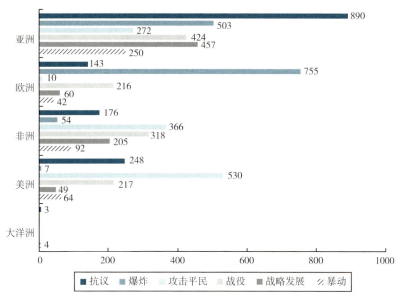

图2.26　2022年五大洲各类型暴力冲突事件

资料来源：ACLED。

　　2022年，欧洲、非洲和亚洲因政治动荡而丧生的人数较多，分别达2724人、1904人和1434人（见图2.27）。在各次区域中，西非和东非是受政治动荡影响最严重的地区，分别有866人和748人丧生。中东和欧洲的死亡人数也相对较多，分别为702人和2724人。这与以上地区发生的政治动荡数量和类型密切相关。2022年，全球因暴力冲突事件而丧生的人数超过7264人，战役、爆炸和针对平民的攻击分别导致2838人、2590人和1218人死亡。

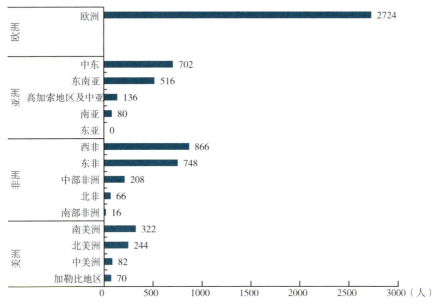

图2.27 2022年五大洲及其次区域暴力冲突事件中的死亡人数

资料来源：ACLED。

（二）地区冲突影响减贫进程，实现区域和平稳定是促进减贫的关键所在

地区冲突对人们的生活和财产造成直接破坏，使人们面临生命安全的威胁。地区冲突损毁了道路、桥梁、电力供应和通信网络等基础设施，限制了交通和物流。地区冲突破坏了农田和农业设施，导致农民无法正常进行种植和养殖活动，进而陷入贫困。此外，地区冲突还导致人员伤亡、强迫流离失所和失业等问题加剧。同时，地区冲突也迫使大量人口离开家园，成为难民或内部流离失所者，失去安全和生计来源。冲突还严重影响工业和商业活动，导致大量人员失去工作机会，增加失业和贫困的风险。

地区冲突间接影响减贫进程。首先，冲突对经济造成冲击，如生产活动中断和投资减少。同时，由于冲突引发的不确定性和风险，投资者对该地区的投资意愿下降，限制了经济增长和就业机会。其次，冲突导致资源短缺和市场萎缩，使贫困人口更加难以获取基本生活资源，限制了贫困人口的收入来源和经济活动，加剧了贫困。最后，冲突还导致教育、医疗和社会服务等基本公共服务中断。战争和冲突导致学校关闭、医疗机构被破坏，并削弱了社会服务的提供能力。这使贫困人口失去了接受良好教育和医疗保健的机会，限制了他们摆脱贫困的可能性。

　　解决地区冲突，实现区域和平稳定是促进减贫事业的关键所在。此外，为受冲突影响的地区提供支持和援助，帮助其重建和恢复，是减轻冲突对贫困影响的重中之重。

第三章

世界主要地区及典型国家推进减贫的政策供给与实施成效

本章要点

众所周知，消除全球极端贫困是联合国千年发展目标（MDGs）和可持续发展目标（SDGs）的首要任务，但到2030年基本消除全球极端贫困（即基于国际贫困线的全球、区域和国家一级的贫困发生率低于3%）依旧是当今世界面临的最大挑战。为此，众多发展中国家和新兴经济体分别制定和实施了一系列减贫战略、政策和措施，联合国、世界银行、国际货币基金组织和诸多发达国家也为其提供了形式多样的援助支持。细致梳理并实时追踪世界主要国家和地区的减贫政策供给，有助于为众多发展中国家政府构建和完善适合自身实际的减贫政策体系提供经验参考，进而为早日实现联合国2030年可持续发展议程，尤其是减贫目标，提供可资借鉴的政策模式。

一、世界主要地区及典型国家推进减贫的政策供给类型

（一）全球推进减贫治理的宏观背景变迁

尽管疫情已得到有效抑制，但各国内部普遍面临增长乏力、开支疲软、货币紧缩、通货膨胀等经济困境，以及分配失衡、贫富差距、粮食匮乏、保障缺失等社会危机；外部又遭遇主要供应链中断、债务不可持续、外来援助规模受限等不确定性挑战，以及地区冲突、生态恶化、环境污染、疾病传播等非传统安全挑战。新局势不仅直接导致粮食、燃料和肥料价格飞涨，而且持续冲击着世界上的脆弱国家和脆弱人群，西方国家居民存款和外国直接投资存在骤降风险，欧洲人道主义危机加剧，非洲粮食储备和卫生系统存在崩溃风险，拉丁美洲资源竞争和极端

暴力事件普遍增加，亚洲居民失业和生计困难状况有所恶化。全球消除极端贫困的进展缓慢，2030年基本消除全球极端贫困的预定目标或将难以实现。

（二）不同国家推进减贫治理的政策层级与供给内涵

众所周知，贫困问题是结构经济和文化行为等一系列复杂因素共同作用的结果，因此减贫政策的供给也应针对致贫的不同诱因和不同群体进行综合考虑。本报告认为，一国在减贫领域的主要政策供给包括以下类型：一是宏观层面的战略导向型政策供给，主要指国家主导构建的减贫战略框架、行动纲领、目标规划、法制法规、专项机构等；二是中观层面的需求导向型政策供给，主要指农业农村、人力资源、社会保障、区域开发、医疗卫生、教育科技、劳动就业等相关部门制定和实施的专项减贫政策措施，以及中央和地方政府专项减贫机构的建立健全；三是微观层面的工具导向型政策供给，主要指中央和地方政府、企业和社会等参与主体在推进减贫过程中运用的财政转移、减税降费、开发融资、保障救济等政策组合。

二、世界主要地区及典型国家推进减贫的政策供给实践

本部分将参照联合国经济和社会事务部关于世界地理区域的分类方法，将全球划分为非洲、亚洲、拉丁美洲和加勒比地区、北美洲、大洋洲、欧洲六大区域①，分别聚焦各区域和典型国家的社会经济概况、贫困形势演变和减贫政策供给，以期为了解全球的贫困现状和减贫进展提供信息支持。

（一）亚洲

根据联合国地理区域划分标准，亚洲共有48个国家：阿富汗、阿联酋、阿曼、阿塞拜疆、巴基斯坦、巴勒斯坦、巴林、不丹、朝鲜、东帝汶、菲律宾、格鲁吉亚、哈萨克斯坦、韩国、吉尔吉斯斯坦、柬埔寨、卡塔尔、科威特、老挝、黎巴嫩、马尔代夫、马来西亚、蒙古国、孟加拉国、缅甸、尼泊尔、日本、塞浦路斯、沙特阿拉伯、斯里兰卡、塔吉克斯坦、泰国、土耳其、土库曼斯坦、文莱、乌兹别克斯坦、新加坡、叙利亚、亚美尼亚、也门、伊拉克、伊朗、以色列、印度、印度尼西亚、约旦、越南、中国。

1.亚洲地区的贫困特征与演化趋势

（1）亚洲地区的主要贫困特征

第一，亚洲地区公共服务水平较为落后，部分国家经济基础薄弱，外汇不

---

① 联合国经济和社会事务部基于大洲范畴，将全球划分为亚洲、非洲、拉丁美洲和加勒比地区、北美洲、大洋洲六个地区（http://unstats.un.org/unsd/methodology/m49/）。此外，本报告所有国家的中文名称均来自中华人民共和国外交部。

足且依赖进口。

例如，自2022年以来，斯里兰卡因外汇不足而出现粮食、燃料和药品短缺。粮食短缺迅速引发粮食和食品价格飙升；燃料短缺不仅导致普通民众的摩托车、汽车等交通工具加油困难，更引发全国范围的严重停电，影响工业生产和居民生活；药品和医疗设备短缺则严重影响普通民众的就医诉求，一些危重病人甚至因此面临生命危险。尽管斯里兰卡政府采取了诸如改组政府、向国际货币基金组织寻求援助、通过双边渠道寻求支持等措施，但未能扭转经济危机恶化势头，斯里兰卡总理维克拉马辛哈在讲话中也表示，"国家已经破产，粮食、能源和药品短缺的经济危机将持续到2023年底"①。除此之外，不丹因经济严重依赖进口，长期处于严重失衡状态，加之2020年以来受疫情影响，不丹国内外汇储备急剧萎缩，从2021年4月的14.6亿美元缩减至2022年8月的8.45亿美元。

第二，亚洲国家人口增长率高，社会贫富差距较大，极端贫困问题严峻。

目前，亚洲地区贫困人口仍旧集中于南亚。全球知名数据统计库Statista的数据显示，2022年，印度生活在极端贫困线下的男性约3800万人，女性约4500万人，合计约8300万人。2022年世界银行重新修正标准，按照2017年购买力平价（PPP）计算，新的极端贫困线由每天生活费1.9美元上调至2.15美元。按照原标准，印度极端贫困发生率为10.4%，而按最新标准则为13.6%，极端贫困人口不降反增。预计2026年，印度人口将达到15亿人，但经济增长速度并不足以满足这些新增人口每年至少2000万个工作岗位的就业需求。从经济角度看，印度国内生产总值（GDP）中，农业产值约占16%，但从业人口占全国的65%~70%。由于缺少大规模工业化，以及服务业多集中于金融、制药和IT等高端领域，导致印度人口无法在三产间实现转换，尤其是大规模农村人口无法转化为产业工人，造成农村和城市出现大批流民和贫困人口。

（2）亚洲地区的贫困演化趋势

良好的社会经济状况能够促进减贫工作的顺利开展，而居民生活水平提高和贫困人口减少又对社会经济条件产生影响。本部分主要从联合国2023年《世界经济形势与展望报告》、人类发展指数，以及世界银行等发布的数据出发，分析亚洲目前的贫困演化趋势。

联合国2023年《世界经济形势与展望报告》显示，亚洲各地区由于受到疫情等影响而面临金融条件趋紧等压力。其中，2023年东亚国家GDP的增速估

---

① 参见："斯里兰卡多重危机破局艰难"，光明网，https://m.gmw.cn/baijia/2022-07/14/1303044117.html。

计为4.4%，但经济复苏态势仍然脆弱；南亚国家GDP的平均增速从2022年的5.6%放缓至2023年的4.8%（见图3.1）；西亚国家已经逐渐摆脱经济低迷状态，但非石油生产国的复苏仍然乏力，估计GDP的平均增速从2022年的6.4%降至2023年的3.5%（见图3.2）。

图3.1　部分南亚国家的GDP增长

资料来源：联合国经济和社会事务部，根据世界经济预测模型的评估。

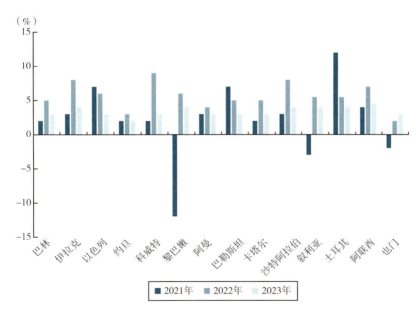

图3.2　部分西亚国家的经济增长预测

资料来源：联合国经济和社会事务部，根据世界经济预测模型的评估。

2.亚洲国家推进减贫的主要政策供给

（1）积极优化贫困识别，提供专项减贫帮扶

根据《2022年全球多维贫困指数》报告，亚洲存在基础设施薄弱、产业结构转型困难的贫困特征。针对这一领域的贫困问题，亚洲各国可进行更具针对性的贫困识别与评估，从而有效加强基础设施建设、推动产业转型与升级，由此逐渐改善亚洲的区域贫困问题。

具体针对升级贫困识别、推动产业转型问题，亚洲各国在该领域聚焦分析近年来导致贫困的各类因素，对目标区域及人口进行准确定位，持续投入，实施区域针对性的基础减贫。例如，在改善贫困识别方面，可参考巴基斯坦贝纳齐尔收入支持计划（BISP），瞄准贫困和弱势人群，消除贫困，提升边缘化和弱势阶层的社会地位。借鉴其确定贫困人群的方式，采用世界银行设计的贫困记分卡工具对国内的家庭经济情况展开调查，使用代理平均数测试（PMT），以0~100分来评定家庭贫困水平，并对分数在16.7及以下的贫困家庭提供BISP的资助。在产业转型方面，则可参考泰国黎敦山区开发计划，即通过改善基础设施、发展旅游业等组合措施来根除极端贫困，推动当地经济开发。该计划可视为山地减贫的模范经验，供亚洲存在相似情况的国家借鉴，使亚洲各国能因地制宜实施不同区域规模的扶贫开发项目，从而达到疫后复苏经济、减贫的作用。

（2）实施公共服务项目，提升基础设施水平

公共服务与公共工程的实施一直是推进减贫的重要内在动力，而公共服务水平落后是亚洲地区贫困的一个突出特征，在2022年主要体现在公共卫生与安全等方面。对此，参考《2022年全球多维贫困指数》的减贫衡量指标，亚洲减贫的公共项目的针对性可进一步延伸细化至公共卫生领域，包括饮用水、卫生设施及基础教育等，从基础公共服务方面改善亚洲贫困现状。

例如，在饮用水方面，尼泊尔在2022年实施的清洁用水项目取得了良好的减贫作用。在该因地制宜的减贫项目中，尼泊尔通过加大对卫生设备的投资，提高了饮用水的获取度，改善了儿童营养，并通过减少腹泻降低了儿童死亡率。其中，巴章地区的变化是尼泊尔政府减贫工作取得成效的生动见证。联合国开发计划署2022年10月发布的《2022年全球多维贫困指数》报告显示，2011~2019年，尼泊尔的多维贫困指数从0.185大幅降至0.075，贫困发生率从39.1%降至17.7%。联合国开发计划署认为，尼泊尔的公共卫生设施得到显著改善，卫生事业取得积极进展。尼泊尔政府制订了多期营养计划，由该国健康、教育、卫生、农业等领域的多个机构合作实施，旨在进一步改善粮食安

全、卫生设施状况。例如，为改善尼泊尔公共卫生情况，政府花费近10年时间，使每个家庭都用上了新型卫生厕所。政府还实施清洁用水项目，保障民众用水安全，大大降低儿童死亡率。尼泊尔加大与国际组织的合作力度，引入成功经验及先进技术。尼泊尔政府与联合国开发计划署共同启动发展小微企业试点项目，增加就业机会，改善民生，减少贫困。尼泊尔政府还在此基础上推出了"发展小微企业以减少贫困"项目，目前已覆盖尼泊尔全国各地。国际竹藤组织在尼泊尔实施竹林修复和管理项目，推广实践经验和现代技术，帮助当地农民提高竹笋产量，扩大销售市场，目前尼泊尔约有300万户家庭参与竹业相关的活动。

在教育方面，马来西亚政府2022年向教育部拨款526亿令吉，实施高教基金贷款计划（公共教育），占联邦发展支出总额的16%，教育部也成为获得拨款最多的部门。具体包括：发放7亿4600万令吉用于修葺东马年久失修的学校（其中，112个项目在沙巴，165个在砂拉越）；考虑到教师在居家教学期间的付出，首次提供特别教材奖励，为超过40万名隶属教育部的教职人员发放每人100令吉的一次性奖励；提高开学援助金补助，从2021年的每人100令吉增至2022年的150令吉，总额高达4亿5000万令吉，可惠及300万名学生。

（3）尝试收紧货币政策，努力加速经济复苏

全球大宗商品价格上涨、全球需求增速放缓、全球投资者转向避险市场等因素导致发展中经济体风险溢价。例如，面对由全球燃料及粮食等价格上涨导致的消费通货膨胀加速问题，印度储备银行和孟加拉国中央银行早在2019年第二季度便收紧货币政策，巴基斯坦和斯里兰卡也于2022年底开启了货币紧缩的政策周期。

（4）优化自营职业制度，实施现金转移支付

建立自营职业制度并进行有条件的现金转移支付对一个国家的长远发展具有关键作用，该类制度的建立与服务的提供隶属社会福利的范畴。近年来，众多亚洲国家在减贫行动中采取类似的政策措施，以实现国民福祉与减贫目标。

孟加拉国的社会安全网络项目体现了这方面的减贫作用。在减贫工作中，孟加拉国政府一直在持续推进社会安全网络项目，希望通过改善极端贫困人口的经济社会状况来减缓贫困。政府运用社会安全网络生命周期法，通过预算规划，从政策层面帮扶最贫困人口。修订后的2020~2021年政府预算针对贫困问题共拨款9568.3亿塔卡，约占总预算的五分之一（17.75%）。这一拨款金额占该财政年度GDP的3.1%，可见政府决心进行扶贫干预。社会安全网络项目由多种干预措施组成，这些干预措施又分属于不同的子计划和子项目，如一户一

农场、住所、房屋、重返家园。这些政策措施注重为贫困人口的生活带来积极变化，建设更美好、更宜居的社会。社会学专家指出，社会安全网络项目能够有效推动可持续发展。这些项目针对性强，旨在惠及社会特定人群，如丧偶人群、被丈夫遗弃的贫困妇女、老年人、残疾人等。以现金或实物形式帮扶贫困人口的项目应通过正规渠道，这样才能让目标人群真正受惠。相关机制涉及政府银行、农村储蓄银行、不同运营商运营的移动银行业务，以及地方行政部门积极参与。

（5）关注极端贫困人口，完善社会保障制度

关注极端贫困人口生存现状，实施专项贷款计划，完善社会保障制度对于极端贫困人口生存现状的关注是减贫计划实施的重要抓手。亚洲国家积极实施专项贷款计划，完善社会保障制度，助力经济复苏，提升减贫成效。

例如，2022年极端气候条件及自然灾害导致南亚国家通货膨胀飙升，贫困人口持续增加，巴基斯坦政府为应对粮价高涨推出了针对性补贴，并努力增加社会保护；孟加拉国政府降低大米进口关税，增加肥料补贴和农业部门的预算拨款。尼泊尔则公布了一项货币政策：其央行行长阿迪卡里在2021年7月13日宣布2021~2022财年（自2021年7月中旬起）货币政策时公布了纾困措施，包括延长贷款偿还期限、减少分期付款数额、重组和重新安排贷款还款计划、以更优惠利率提供信贷等。其中，餐饮、公共交通、教育机构和娱乐业可将贷款还款期延期一年并可至少分四期偿还，旅游业和电影业可重组和重新安排还贷计划。孟加拉国政府则采取措施帮助那些极端贫困但有劳动能力的农村人口就业，于2020~2021年将拨款金额增加到165亿塔卡。日本政府从2020年3月开始向生活困难家庭紧急实施一个"特例贷款"，这是无息贷款，且无须保证人即可申请。表3.1列出了近年来亚洲典型国家的减贫政策供给。

表3.1 近年来亚洲典型国家的减贫政策供给

国家	减贫战略	重点领域	减贫目标	目标年份
印度	经济救助计划——扩大PMGKY、直接福利转移、Deen Dayal国家生计项目；Ujjawala计划、职工公积金、"农村青年就业计划""总理/国家技能发展计划""总理/国家贫困福利计划""国家健康保障计划"	食品补给、健康护理、现金救济、女性权益、基础设施、	主要针对农民进行疫情经济救助，预计在4个月内使8690万农民受益，使7000万妇女受益	2020

续表

国家	减贫战略	重点领域	减贫目标	目标年份
巴基斯坦	天课制度、巴基斯坦基金委员会（PBM）、贝纳齐尔收入支持计划（BISP）	财务救济、粮食资助、儿童支持、职业培训、医疗中心支持、女性权益	天课税只针对穆斯林征收，税收收入转移给穆斯林贫困群体，尤其是寡妇、孤儿和残障人士；PBM主要向寡妇、孤儿、残疾人、体弱多病者等贫困人群提供援助；BISP瞄准贫困和弱势人群，消除贫困，提升边缘化和弱势阶层（尤其是女性）的社会地位	至今
孟加拉国	"老年人津贴项目""残疾人津贴""民办孤儿院补助"（按人）"自由战士荣誉津贴项目""负伤自由战士及烈士家庭荣誉津贴和医疗津贴""母亲津贴""哺乳期母亲津贴""赤贫女性财政援助""吉卜赛人专项项目""第三性别项目"等	财务救济、社会赋权、资金拨款、女性权益、灾后重建、就业支持	社会安全网络项目包括一系列子项目，旨在改善贫困人口生计，从而提升其经济社会地位；针对最弱势和最贫困人口的专项扶贫措施	2025
斯里兰卡	税收改革、推动落实IMF的29亿美元救助计划	财务救济	应对经济困境以及粮食不安全问题	2023
尼泊尔	清洁用水措施、多期营养计划、"发展小微企业以减少贫困"项目、国际竹藤组织在尼泊尔实施竹林修复和管理项目、2021~2022财年（自2021年7月中旬起）货币政策纾困措施	卫生基础设施、清洁用水、食品安全、就业支持、增加农业产量、货币政策	改善儿童营养，通过减少腹泻降低了儿童死亡率；面向小微企业开展试点项目，增加就业机会，改善民生，减少贫困；面向当地农民，提高竹笋产量，扩大销售市场；餐饮、公共交通、教育机构和娱乐业延长贷款还款期一年并可至少分四期偿还，旅游业和电影业可重组和重新安排还贷计划	2022

国家	减贫战略	重点领域	减贫目标	目标年份
不丹	"亚太救灾基金""亚太疫苗援助计划"（ACVAX）、"日本繁荣及活力亚太基金"（APFPV）、印度支持不丹"十二五"规划（2019~2023年）、暂停机动车进口以减少外汇流失、解除香烟进口禁令、"2024全民接种免疫计划"	疫苗援助、医疗救助、财务救济、食品救济、粮食资助、进出口贸易改革、职业教育援助、贸易支持	提升不丹医务人员的专业技能和国内应急医疗水平；印度通过贸易支持机制和项目援助方式，向不丹多个项目提供发展援助，通过跨境贸易支持机制提升双边贸易便利化水平；不丹暂停机动车进口以减少外汇流失；解除禁烟令以缓解疫情导致的财政状况持续恶化	2023、2024
马尔代夫	中马友谊大桥	旅游业、交通		2024

资料来源：根据部分亚洲典型国家近年来的减贫政策综合整理。

（二）非洲

根据联合国地理区域划分标准，非洲国家共有54个：阿尔及利亚、埃及、埃塞俄比亚、安哥拉、贝宁、博茨瓦纳、布基纳法索、布隆迪、赤道几内亚、多哥、厄立特里亚、佛得角、冈比亚、刚果（布）、刚果（金）、吉布提、几内亚、几内亚比绍、加纳、加蓬、津巴布韦、喀麦隆、科摩罗、科特迪瓦、肯尼亚、莱索托、利比里亚、利比亚、卢旺达、马达加斯加、马拉维、马里、毛里求斯、毛里塔尼亚、摩洛哥、莫桑比克、纳米比亚、南非、南苏丹、尼日尔、尼日利亚、塞拉利昂、塞内加尔、塞舌尔、圣多美和普林西比、斯威士兰、苏丹、索马里、坦桑尼亚、突尼斯、乌干达、赞比亚、乍得、中非。

1.非洲地区的贫困特征与演化趋势

总体而言，作为当今世界发展中国家（尤其是最不发达国家）分布最为集中的大陆，非洲的贫困人口基数大，减贫能力弱，国际援助不足，导致贫困面广、贫困程度深、贫困发生率高、绝对贫困率高。从减贫挑战的类型来看，非洲国家的贫困主要表现为社会保障体系缺失，基础教育水平低下，气候变化和生态退化加剧，基本粮食安全难以维系，农村地区贫困问题日益突出，城镇人口就业机会匮乏等。据世界银行预测，到2030年，非洲极端贫困人口将占世界极端贫困总人口的86%，非洲仍将是世界极端贫困人口最集中、贫困发生率最高的地区。

近两年来，非洲各国并未实现大幅减贫目标，多数非洲国家的减贫事业进展缓慢。部分国家的极端贫困和返贫发生率显著上升，减贫进程明显滞后于全球其他地区。例如，基于2022年6月PovcalNet的统计数据，南苏丹绝对贫困（即家庭人均生活费每天低于1.9美元）人口占比高达76.4%，CPIA[①]评分为1.6；马拉维绝对贫困人口占比73.5%，CPIA评分为3.1分；布隆迪绝对贫困人口占比72.8%，CPIA评分为2.9分；刚果（金）绝对贫困人口占比77.2%，CPIA评分为3.0分；中非绝对贫困人口占比65.9%，CPIA评分为2.6分；索马里绝对贫困人口占比68.6%，CPIA评分为2.1分；莫桑比克绝对贫困人口占比63.7%，CPIA评分为3.1分；赞比亚绝对贫困人口占比58.8%，CPIA评分为3.1分；利比里亚绝对贫困人口占比44.4%，CPIA评分3分；乍得绝对贫困人口占比38.1%，CPIA评分为2.8分（见图3.3）。

图3.3　2022年部分非洲贫困国家的CPIA评分

资料来源：CPIA database，2022。

2.非洲国家推进减贫的主要政策供给

（1）将减贫治理置于国家发展战略的突出位置

自1999年起，世界银行、国际货币基金组织与非洲国家政府共同制定《减

---

① CPIA评价体系由经济管理指标、结构政策指标、社会包容与公平政策指标、公共部门机构与管理指标四部分构成。

贫战略报告》，多数非洲国家也以此作为本国的减贫计划和行动纲领。例如，卢旺达政府先后出台了一系列中期转型战略，包括2002~2005年的"减贫战略计划"（PRSP1）、2008~2012年和2013/2014~2017/2018年"经济发展和减贫"一期战略（EDPRSⅠ）和二期战略（EDPRSⅡ）、2018/2019~2023/2024年"国家转型战略"（NST-1）。过去20多年间，卢旺达减贫政策成效显著，贫困率从1994年的78%下降至2017年的38%。2020年，即卢旺达"2020愿景"的收官之年，政府颁布了"2050年愿景"，将本国发展目标设定为到2035年成为中高收入国家，到2050年成为以知识型经济为主导的高收入国家，其战略构想和政策框架的根本落脚点在于改善民生。又如，布隆迪政府也制定了《国家发展规划（2018~2027年）》，同时明确了"人人有饭吃、家家有储蓄"和"2040年将布隆迪建成新兴国家"等发展目标，并将2022年确立为"布隆迪农业年"，以期将农业农村发展与摆脱绝对贫困有机结合起来。索马里政府制定了第九份国家发展规划，即《2020~2024年国家发展规划》。再如，科特迪瓦国家统计部门发起了一项针对2011~2021年该国贫困状况的专项调查，以期通过详细和持续的数据跟踪与数据对比来关注贫困和脆弱群体，从而为制定和实施减贫项目规划提供政策依据。此外，为了更好地适应国家经济社会发展形势，毛里塔尼亚政府制定了新的统计发展战略（2020~2030年）和优先行动计划（2021~2025年），该国国家统计机构也由此开始实施重大改革。[1]牙买加统计局与卫生部和其他专家合作领导了一个委员会，将数据需求与危机期间指导政策所需的现有数据相匹配。为了帮助填补可持续发展目标方面的数据缺口，肯尼亚国家统计部门启动了与民间社会组织的伙伴合作关系，并将一套居民产生数据的质量标准纳入其新发布的肯尼亚统计质量保证框架[2]。

（2）推进贫困地区基础设施和公共服务升级

例如，南非政府在10年内（2021~2030年）拨款1000亿兰特的基础设施基金计划正在稳步推进，优先支持能源、道路、水利、电力、通信、公共卫生、福利住房等民生保障领域。具体来看，南非提出扩大农村桥梁建造计划，从2021年每年交付14座桥梁逐步增加到95座，还在2023年之前升级建设了685公里的农村公路。又如，针对近年来本国基础设施增速明显落后于人口增速的不利局面，尼日利亚联邦政府于2022年7月拨付500亿奈拉用于国家传统

---

① World Bank, Office of the Chief Economist for the Africa Region. *Assessing Africa's Policies And Institutions*, OCT. 2022, p.48.

② 参见：联合国，《2022年可持续发展目标报告》。

产业基础与技术升级，如农业部将专项资金用于农村道路建设和太阳能等可再生能源的开发利用。又如，在2019年塞西总统提出的"体面生活"政策倡议之下，埃及政府计划拨款近万亿埃镑，面向20个贫困省份的近5000个村庄和全国52%的人口实施千余个项目，分三个阶段逐步改善医疗、教育、住房、道路、电力、供水等各项基础设施。具体来看，在天然气管道建设方面，截至2022年8月，埃及先后完成了对120个村庄的天然气管道建设，使超过41万户贫困家庭用上了天然气。再如，阿尔及利亚能源和矿产部联合内政部、国土部及地方政府展开调查，确认全国8000多个存在电力和天然气等基础设施短板的所谓"灰区"（这些地区因在国家治理规划图中被标注为灰色而得名），并在2020~2024年专门启动一项计划，帮助超过14万户家庭接入电网，同时帮助7万户家庭接入天然气。2022年9月，阿尔及利亚石油天然气总公司推出了一项新的社会投资计划，为全国21省的"灰区"提供37个发展项目；相关通信企业优先为"灰区"架设互联网和移动通信网络；医疗机构还组织骨干力量到"灰区"巡诊并设立流动诊所。

（3）努力提升减贫财政开支的使用效率

一些非洲国家政府努力提升财政开支，尤其是减贫事业支出的使用效率。例如，南非政府决定灵活拓宽融资渠道，将针对贫困家庭的社会救济金计划延长至2023年3月。2022年7月，尼日利亚联邦政府参照国家减贫和增长战略，批准了4000亿奈拉资金用于特定福利计划，具体包括政府企业和赋权计划、有条件的现金转移、农民资金和市场资金支持等。2022年1月，加纳财政部宣布削减该年度20%的财政支出，以应对财务负担沉重带来的财政危机。为此，其采取了限制退休返聘人员数量、暂停减贫框架计划（IPEP）项目实施等财政开支限制措施。

（4）依托青年就业创业促进社会凝聚包容

鉴于长期以来青年失业率居高不下，2020年南非政府启动的"总统就业刺激计划"正在稳步推进，全国各类学校将雇用超过50万名教学等相关人员，内政部也将逐步招收约1万名失业青年，负责政府机构的无纸化办公和文件的数字化处理等工作，社会就业基金则有望在城市农业、幼儿教育、公共艺术等领域创造5万个工作机会。又如，埃及政府的"体面生活"倡议包含为贫困地区民众提供培训和促进就业的相关政策设计。在2021~2022财年的减贫规划当中，埃及政府继续推出各类项目以支持小型创业和家庭生产，并通过青年职业培训中心为妇女和青年提供新的就业机会。

（三）拉丁美洲和加勒比地区

根据联合国地理区域划分标准，拉丁美洲和加勒比地区有 33 个国家：阿根廷、安提瓜和巴布达、巴哈马、伯利兹、玻利维亚、巴西、巴巴多斯、智利、哥伦比亚、哥斯达黎加、古巴、多米尼加、多米尼克、厄瓜多尔、格林纳达、危地马拉、圭亚那、洪都拉斯、海地、牙买加、圣基茨和尼维斯、圣卢西亚、墨西哥、尼加拉瓜、巴拿马、秘鲁、巴拉圭、萨尔瓦多、苏里南、特立尼达和多巴哥、乌拉圭、圣文森特和格林纳丁斯、委内瑞拉。

1.拉丁美洲和加勒比地区的贫困特征与演化趋势

（1）拉丁美洲和加勒比地区的主要贫困特征

第一，社会贫困和社会分化加剧，低收入群体难以从经济增长中受益。

拉丁美洲和加勒比地区一直是全球贫富差距最大的地区，受疫情影响，这一差距仍在拉大。据联合国拉丁美洲和加勒比经济委员会（拉加经委会）的数据，2020年该地区新增贫困人口约2200万人，贫困率达到33.7%，极端贫困率达12.5%。而据拉加经委会早前发布的《2020年拉丁美洲社会全景报告》，2020年该地区贫困人口总数增加到2.09亿人，其中7800万人处于极端贫困状态，比2019年增加了800万人。疫情导致拉丁美洲和加勒比地区贫困人口和失业人口上升的同时，也使该地区的富人变得更加富有。2020年3~6月，拉丁美洲和加勒比地区73名亿万富翁的财富总额至少增长了482亿美元。据瑞士信贷集团发布的2020年全球财富报告，在巴西，49.6%的资源掌握在全国最富有的1%的人（约210万人）手上，在十个贫富差距最大的国家中排名第二。

疫情期间，因流通封锁等管控措施以及美国经济下行压力，多项经贸活动瘫痪，旅游、交通、贸易等部门首当其冲，而这些领域恰恰集中了大量中美洲移民。收入减少、失业压力导致侨民无力周转资金，流向中美洲的侨汇总量骤减。以萨尔瓦多为例，据该国中央储备银行统计，2019年萨尔瓦多全年侨汇总计超56亿美元，相当于其国内生产总值的16%，但受疫情影响，仅2020年4月，侨汇总额较2019年同期下降了40%，国民经济景况不容乐观。

经济社会发展形势不仅难以在短期内改善，还进一步加剧了拉丁美洲和加勒比地区国家阶层向下流动的态势，使本作为"缓冲"的新中间阶层人口大量流动到下一阶层。该地区严重的贫富分化使多国民众上街示威抗议，社会矛盾大大激化。

第二，部分国家非正规就业占比过高，非正规就业群体极易遭受外部因素

冲击。

　　总体上，拉丁美洲和加勒比地区各国在非正规部门就业的人口占城市经济活动人口的比重很大，且这一比重自21世纪以来变化幅度不大。根据历史经验，非正规就业比率在国家经济转轨以及国内经济遭受外部冲击时会上升。疫情暴发后，拉丁美洲和加勒比地区各国的非正规就业随即受到影响。在统计了危地马拉、秘鲁等15国的就业情况后发现：2019年，有11个国家非农业部门的非正规人口占比达50%以上（见图3.4），超统计国家的2/3，其中，洪都拉斯以76%的非正规就业人口占比高居榜首；智利与圣卢西亚等国的非正规就业人口占比维持在30%上下。值得注意的是，在阿根廷、哥伦比亚等较高收入国家，非正规就业人口占社会就业的比重也很大。

　　由于非正规就业进入门槛低，使各种年龄、性别和技术水平的求职者都能融入劳动力市场，因而能提高整个劳动力市场的劳动参与率，从而扩大就业、增加劳动收入。从这个意义上讲，非正规就业对于减少贫困具有积极作用。但是，如果因经济衰退导致的正规就业人员进入非正规就业部门，则会加剧贫困。非正规就业群体通常最易受到经济下行影响而失业，非正规就业也通常伴随着社会保障系统的缺失，对长期减贫发展不利。

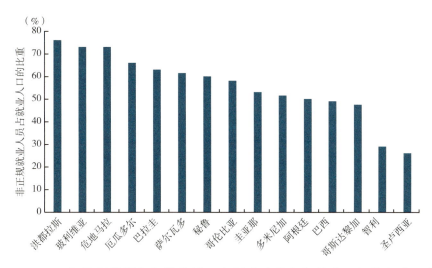

图3.4　2019年拉丁美洲和加勒比地区各国非农业部门的非正规就业人口占比

　　资料来源：Martin Abeles et al. The COVID-19 Crisis and the Structural Problems of Latin America and the Caribbean：Responding to the Emergency with a long-term Perspective. https：//www.cepal.org/en/publications.

第三，多数国家社会保障体系薄弱，社会保障制度构建存在明显的缺口。

一方面，失业保障体系不完善。在拉丁美洲和加勒比地区，只有少数国家的社会保障体系包含失业保险相关内容，如南美地区仅有墨西哥、阿根廷、巴西、智利、哥伦比亚、厄瓜多尔和乌拉圭建立了失业保险计划。其中，墨西哥和厄瓜多尔两国仅为超过工作年龄的老人提供养老金；巴西的援助失业者计划则不属于失业社会保险。在拉丁美洲和加勒比地区，失业不仅通常有持续性、长期性和结构性的特征，而且还存在大量就业不足和非正规就业的现象。另一方面，失业保障覆盖范围不全面。拉丁美洲和加勒比地区国家失业保险的覆盖范围有限，部分劳动者被排除在外，如乌拉圭的农业、家庭服务和银行等部门的劳动者。拉丁美洲和加勒比地区绝大多数国家还不具备为失业保障投入充足资金的能力，导致失业者往往得不到适当救济和补贴，丧失生计来源。因此，拉丁美洲和加勒比地区国家的失业者所受到的冲击和生活压力远高于发达国家的失业者。

第四，极端贫困与多维贫困共存，"增长性贫困"现象偶发。

只有当经济增长达到一定水平时，贫困发生率才会持续下降。而拉丁美洲和加勒比地区贫困面对经济衰退或波动时非常敏感，一旦经济增长出现下滑或波动，贫困发生率会立刻反弹。增长因素和分配因素对贫困发生率均有较大影响，但相对而言，增长因素的作用更大。经济增长可以降低失业率，增加家庭收入，进而降低贫困发生率。只有当经济发展到一定水平时，失业率才可能降低，从而真正实现减贫目标。

拉加经委会对17个拉丁美洲和加勒比地区国家2005年和2012年左右的多维贫困状况进行了测量和观察。研究发现：首先，在这17个国家中，多维贫困现象最严重的国家基本上都是中美洲国家。其中，2012年尼加拉瓜、洪都拉斯、危地马拉均有超过70%的居民处于多维贫困当中。其次，多维贫困发生率最低的国家几乎都是经济发展水平较高的国家，如智利、阿根廷、乌拉圭、巴西和哥斯达黎加，其多维贫困人口分别占各自总人口的10%左右。最后，贫困发生率较高的国家，其多维贫困强度也较高，即多维贫困人口或家庭越多的国家。

（2）拉丁美洲和加勒比地区的贫困演化趋势

拉丁美洲和加勒比地区经济的稳步增长，为全球减贫作出了积极贡献。2021年延续了21世纪头20年的向好发展态势，按世界银行的收入划分标准，拉丁美洲和加勒比地区各国收入水平普遍提高，中低收入国家向中高收入群组跃进。20年间，高收入国家数量从最初的1个增加到2020年的6个，再到2021年的10个；中高收入国家从最初的13个增加到2020年的17个，再到2021年的18个。到2021年，中低收入国家仅剩海地、洪都拉斯、萨尔瓦多、尼加拉瓜、玻利维亚五个国家。另外，拉丁美洲和加勒比地区人均国民收入存在较大差异，人均国民收入最高的国家（巴哈马，27780美元/人）是人均国民收入最低的国家（海地，1250美元/人）的22倍（见图3.5）。

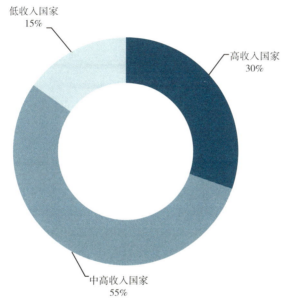

图3.5　拉丁美洲和加勒比地区的收入水平

资料来源：根据世界银行全球发展数据整理。

　　从21世纪初起，该地区大部分中低收入国家的贫困发生率较高，经过20年的努力，这些国家的贫困发生率明显下降，减贫成果显著。但据《可持续发展报告》的估算，世界可持续发展目标指数受疫情暴发与其他多重危机的影响，从0.5继续下降，并停滞不前。从2020年开始，疫情延缓了中低收入国家的减贫进程。经疫情调整后的人类发展指数（HDI）出现广泛但不均衡的下降。其中，拉丁美洲和加勒比地区经疫情调整后的HDI的损失达30.4%，远超世界平均水平（21.7%），是受疫情影响最严重的地区（见图3.6）。

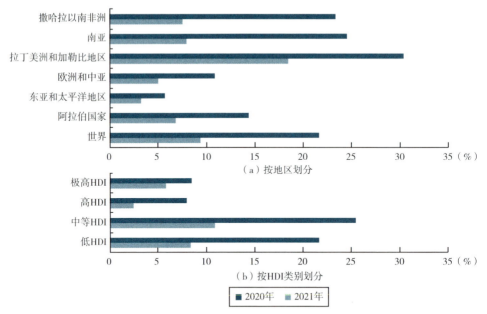

图3.6　2020年和2021年经疫情调整的HDI损失

资料来源:《人类发展报告》办公室。

　　联合国开发计划署提出的可持续发展目标(Sustainable Development Goals, SDGs)包含联合国制定的17个全球发展目标,将社会、经济和环境三个维度的发展相结合,综合衡量各个国家与地区的发展水平。

　　在《2023年可持续发展报告》统计的33个拉丁美洲和加勒比地区国家中,古巴、巴西、阿根廷等八个国家的可持续发展水平超过拉丁美洲和加勒比地区平均水平(70.2),玻利维亚、巴拉圭等15个国家的可持续发展水平超过世界平均水平(66.7),尼加拉瓜、伯利兹、洪都拉斯等八个国家的可持续发展水平处于世界平均水平以下,在194个国家和地区中排名处于后50%。同时,位于拉丁美洲和加勒比地区的海地以52.6的评分在地区位列倒数第一(见表3.2)。

表3.2　　　　　　　2023年拉丁美洲和加勒比地区可持续发展水平

国家	2023年SDG得分	2023年SDG排名
乌拉圭	77.7	32
古巴	74.1	46
巴西	73.7	50
阿根廷	73.7	51

续表

国家	2023年SDG得分	2023年SDG排名
多米尼加	72.1	62
秘鲁	71.7	65
萨尔瓦多	70.7	73
厄瓜多尔	70.4	74
牙买加	69.6	82
巴巴多斯	69.4	84
玻利维亚	68.9	87
巴拉圭	68.8	88
苏里南	68.2	92
圭亚那	67.4	96
巴拿马	67.3	97
尼加拉瓜	64.8	104
伯利兹	64.6	107
特立尼达和多巴哥	63.0	114
洪都拉斯	62.9	116
委内瑞拉	62.9	117
巴哈马	60.9	124
危地马拉	59.4	127
海地	52.6	152

注：联合国可持续发展目标指数对国家的指数指标提出了80%（至少75%）的要求，列举了27个未达到指数指标要求的国家，其中5个位于拉丁美洲和加勒比地区。安提瓜和巴布达、多米尼克、格林纳达、圣基茨和尼维斯、圣卢西亚的数据缺失。

资料来源：《2023年可持续发展报告》。

2.拉丁美洲和加勒比地区国家推进减贫的主要政策供给

（1）依托融资引资促进经济恢复

美洲开发银行在资金融通、专项扶贫方面对拉丁美洲和加勒比地区的经济发展起着巨大的推动作用，是该地区社会经济发展最主要的资金来源。美洲开发银行认为，全球增长放缓、利率上升、货币政策紧缩、财政逐步整顿以及现有的高债务水平是2023年拉丁美洲和加勒比地区经济增长乏力的主要原因，因而呼吁拉丁美洲和加勒比地区国家应对日益增长的社会需求、解决财政资源有限等问题，以应对降低通货膨胀和减轻公共债务负担的挑战，同时建议各成员国利用多边发展银行的长期融资来优化其债务构成。自2023年以来，美洲开发银行已向拉丁美洲和加勒比地区16个国家提供了多笔用于减贫的信贷。

（2）探索发展家庭农业及生态农业

拉丁美洲和加勒比地区国家在发展家庭农业和生态农业方面进行了许多探索。例如，巴西政府出台了"低碳排放农业计划"，通过提供长期低息信贷，鼓励农业生产者采用农作物轮作、免耕直播、生物固氮以及农林牧一体化生产等先进生产方式来减少碳排放。同时，巴西政府还通过实施粮食收购计划来改善农村地区的粮食获取渠道和家庭农业发展现状。

（3）针对脆弱群体持续提供财政支持

拉丁美洲和加勒比地区国家积极实施定向财政支持项目。例如，针对贫困家庭和抗风险能力差的脆弱群体，巴西于2023年重启了"家庭补助金计划"（Programa Bolsa Família, PBF）。该项目将资金以公民收入福利、补充福利、幼儿福利、家庭可变福利四种途径发放，重点关注幼儿、未成年人和孕妇。其中，幼儿福利于2023年3月开始发放，项目的其他福利从2023年6月开始发放。在此之前，巴西援助计划的"一篮子福利"则继续支付，并增加了项目的幼儿福利。在过去，家庭补助金计划已经在教育、健康和粮食领域为极端贫困家庭和贫困家庭提供了巨大的资金援助。截至2022年底，"家庭补助金计划"的受益人口从1400万人增加到1700万人，平均补助金额由189雷亚尔升至400雷亚尔。

又如，针对贫困的失学青少年，哥斯达黎加推出了"超越自我计划"（Avancemos），旨在鼓励12~25岁贫困失学青少年留在学校或重返教育系统接受中等教育。该项目由社会福利联合研究所实施。2014年，该项目的预算接近490亿科朗（约合9000万美元），相当于该国当年GDP的0.2%。2015年8月，该项目帮助了全国来自12.4万个家庭的15.7万名学生，约占该国高中学生的40%。"超越自我计划"使用目标人口信息系统（SIPO）和社会信息工作表（FIS）确定来自贫困、极端贫困或弱势家庭的项目受众。SIPO是一种定位机制，用于根据家庭的社会经济、人口和住房条件来对家庭进行分类。FIS通过与家庭的直接访谈来收集数据，有时还在贫困居民高度集中的社区进行贫困人口普查。在同样的理念下，哥斯达黎加实施了一项名为"发展之桥"（Puente al Desarrollo）的援助战略，重点关注哥斯达黎加最贫困的75个地区。该战略旨在通过被称为共同管理人员的社会工作者识别穷人，为他们提供直接的、有针对性的支持。

（4）积极挖掘特殊就业项目潜力

就业对于减少贫困和缓解不平等至关重要。拉丁美洲和加勒比地区国家已为拉动就业、提振经济出台了多项举措，包括针对个人推出社会福利计划、强化远程培训；对受灾行业扩大基础设施建设、加大贷款发放力度，以及支持中小企业发展。例如，针对失业青年，墨西哥实施了"青年建设未来"计划，为无业青年提供技能培训以增加就业机会，并且还将支付其在培训期间的医疗保险等开支。针对商业、旅游业、运输业和建筑业等，智利政府于2020年出台了一项20亿美元的就业补贴计划，为受疫情影响严重的行业提供工资补贴。智利还投资了340亿美元用于新建公路、港口、机场、文体中心等，努力通过完善城市基础设施来创造就业岗位。

（四）大洋洲

根据联合国地理区域划分标准，大洋洲共有16个国家：澳大利亚、巴布亚新几内亚、斐济、基里巴斯、库克群岛、马绍尔群岛、密克罗尼西亚联邦、瑙鲁、纽埃、帕劳、萨摩亚、所罗门群岛、汤加、图瓦卢、瓦努阿图、新西兰。

按照世界银行的收入划分标准，2023年大洋洲14个国家中（暂无库克群岛和纽埃的数据）有四个高收入国家（澳大利亚、新西兰、瑙鲁、帕劳），四个中高收入国家（斐济、马绍尔群岛、汤加、图瓦卢），六个中低收入国家（巴布亚新几内亚、所罗门群岛、瓦努阿图、密克罗尼西亚联邦、基里巴斯、萨摩亚）。

1.大洋洲的贫困特征与演化趋势

按照世界银行的2.15美元标准，2023年三个大洋洲国家（瓦努阿图、巴布亚新几内亚和所罗门群岛）的贫困发生率高于10%，汤加、斐济和萨摩亚的贫困发生率为1%~2%，澳大利亚则低于1%。这说明，大洋洲贫困状况依然呈现出两极化的态势——澳大利亚、新西兰以及汤加等高收入国家和中高收入国家的贫困发生率较低，瓦努哈图、巴布亚新几内亚和所罗门群岛等中低收入国家的贫困发生率较高。大洋洲未来的减贫进程仍然取决于这三个中低收入国家。

与疫情暴发之前相比，2023年，澳大利亚和新西兰的贫困率比较稳定，保持在较低水平，而其他太平洋岛国则处于恢复中，比2022年和2021年略有下降，但是大部分国家依然没有恢复到疫情之前（2019年）的水平（见表3.3）。这说明太平洋岛国还没有完全从疫情影响中完全恢复过来，或者说目前的经济恢复和减贫态势依然十分脆弱。

表3.3   大洋洲国家的贫困发生率

国家或地区	代码	贫困发生率（%）				
		2019年	2020年	2021年	2022年	2023年
澳大利亚	AUS	0.34	0.34	0.34	0.34	0.34
新西兰	NZL	0.01	0.01	0.01	0.01	—
汤加	TON	1.19	1.29	1.07	1.09	1.06
斐济	FJI	1.65	2.92	3.47	2.44	2.00
萨摩亚	WSM	1.70	1.51	1.20	1.36	1.23
瓦努阿图	VUT	12.39	15.53	16.10	16.09	15.44
巴布亚新几内亚	PNG	27.76	29.61	29.79	29.04	27.89
所罗门群岛	SLB	25.04	33.53	34.83	38.98	38.53

资料来源：https://dashboards.sdgindex.org/profiles；根据《2023年可持续发展报告》的数据整理。新西兰的数据为2022年的数据。

2.大洋洲国家推进减贫的主要政策供给

（1）实施经济复苏计划，扶持中小企业发展

为了支持中小企业的复苏，澳大利亚政府推出了"中小企业复苏贷款计划"（SME Recovery Loan Scheme）。该计划于2021年3月推出，2022年6月30日结束。该贷款计划主要面向受疫情冲击最为严重的中小企业，符合条件的企业可申请最长两年的无息贷款，最高贷款额可达500万澳元，政府将为该贷款提供80%的担保。[①]

新西兰政府在2020年5月出台了"小企业现金流贷款计划"和"中小企业商业融资政府担保计划"。"小企业现金流贷款计划"为雇用50名及以下全职雇员的公司提供高达1万新西兰元的支持，向每位全职员工提供1800新西兰元的额外贷款。2022年2月，政府宣布该项目基础贷款将从1万新西兰元增加到2万新西兰元，贷款还款期为5年（60个月），如果在一年内还清贷款则可享受免息。该项目原计划2020年12月底截止，后来根据疫情情况而延长到2023年

---

① The Treasury. Australian Government. SME Recovery Loan Scheme，https://treasury.gov.au/coronavirus/sme-recovery-loan-scheme.

12月31日。^①根据"中小企业商业融资政府担保计划",年收入为25万新西兰元~8000万新西兰元的新西兰中小企业可以向新西兰政府合作的认证银行申请最高50万新西兰元的贷款,贷款期为三年。该项目计划为新西兰企业提供总计62.5亿新西兰元的贷款,该计划于2021年6月30日结束。^②

（2）推出数字经济战略,依托转型促进减贫

大洋洲岛国在过去几年一直大力扩展其数字基础设施。疫情暴发后,大洋洲岛国更加重视数字经济发展。2021年以来,数字经济也是大洋洲岛国优先考虑的事项之一。^③2021年10月,太平洋岛国论坛贸易部长批准了5500万美元的《太平洋区域电子商务战略和路线图》。

2021年,联合国贸易和发展会议与联合国开发计划署合作启动太平洋数字经济计划。该计划旨在支持太平洋地区包容性数字经济的发展,首先在斐济、汤加、萨摩亚、瓦努阿图和所罗门群岛实施。第一阶段启动时间为两年,已经于2022年12月结束。经过两年的努力,该计划已经初见成效。所罗门群岛在2022年9月正式批准了"国家电子商务战略"（NECS）,与Island Tech的KlikPei平台进行合作,推出了自己的电子商务聚合平台KlikPe。瓦努阿图在2022年9月推出了自己的电子商务平台Maua,帮助中小微企业更容易、低成本和公平地进入市场。汤加在2022年11月也推出了自己的电子商务平台Digicel。斐济在2022年起草了《金融和数字扫盲战略》。未来,该计划还将扩展到巴布亚新几内亚、基里巴斯、密克罗尼西亚联邦和马绍尔群岛。

通过发展包容性数字经济,增强农村社区、妇女、流动工人以及中小微企业的市场参与度,能够促进经济增长,改善民生,减少贫困,为实现可持续发展目标作出贡献。^④

（3）重新启动旅游产业,大力发展蓝色经济

旅游业是诸多南太平洋岛国的支柱产业。疫情缓解后,多国重启了旅游业,吸引游客来南太平洋旅游。斐济在2021年12月开放边境,逐步取消了针对全球游客的所有入境限制要求,其旅游业迅速恢复,2022年的游客人数达

①　Inland Revenue. COVID-19 Small Business Cashflow Scheme（SBCS）, https://www.ird.govt.nz/covid-19/business-and-organisations/small-business-cash-flow-loan.

②　The Treasury. New Zealand Government. Business Finance Guarantee Scheme, https://www.treasury.govt.nz/information-and-services/new-zealand-economy/covid-19-economic-response/measures/bfg.

③　赵少峰,王作成.太平洋岛国发展蓝皮书2022［M］.北京:社会科学文献出版社,2022.

④　UNCDF. Pacific Digital Economy Programme Annual Report 2022, March13, 2023, https://unctad.org/system/files/information-document/PDEP_Annual_Report_2022_13Mar2023_Final.pdf.

到了2019年的71%，估计2022年的GDP增长率为16%。① 巴布亚新几内亚在2021年5月还决定发展博彩旅游业，以吸引游客，增加政府收入。②

对于小岛屿发展中国家，在制定适合本国独特优势的发展战略时，蓝色经济是出路之一。许多小岛屿发展中国家的专属经济区比其陆地面积大至少30倍。很多岛国都在探讨在海底开采稀土矿物、药品和化妆品所用资源的生物勘探、海洋养殖等方面的可能性。库克群岛专属经济区估计含有120亿吨富钴结壳。2022年，该国向三家公司颁发了深海勘探许可证，允许它们在其领海范围内进行勘查，并在未来五年内确定持续开采的可行性，库克群岛或许能成为第一个允许深海采矿的国家。③

（五）北美洲

北美洲位于西半球北部，是全球经济第二发达的大洲，根据联合国地理区域划分标准，北美地区有两个国家（美国、加拿大）和三个地区（百慕大、格陵兰、圣皮埃尔和密克隆）。

1.北美洲的贫困特征与演化趋势

北美洲的两个国家——加拿大和美国都是发达国家。按照世界银行的2.15美元标准，2023年加拿大的贫困发生率为0.2%，自2016年以来基本保持稳定；④ 2023年美国的贫困发生率为0.55%，自2015年以来基本保持稳定（2016年最低，为0.64%；2020年最高，为0.71%）。⑤ 整体而言，美国和加拿大这两个发达国家的贫困发生率低，贫困人口数量少。加拿大和美国的贫困主要表现为相对贫困。

根据加拿大政府2023年5月公布的数据，2021年加拿大的贫困发生率为7.4%，高于2020年的6.4%，比2019年的10.3%略有下降。其中，18岁以下人口的贫困率为6.4%。18~64岁人口的贫困率为8.2%，65岁以上人口的贫困率为5.6%（见表3.4）。⑥

---

① 中国经济快讯.国际货币基金组织：斐济经济因旅游业复苏而强劲反弹，http：//dmc-global.com/news/guonei/6339.html.

② 国家博彩管理理事会着眼于博彩旅游业，http：//www.png-china.com/forum.php?mod=viewthread&tid=13444&highlight=%B2%A9%B2%CA.

③ 太平洋岛国对深海采矿意见不一，http：//ggmd.cgs.gov.cn/DepositsNewsCen.aspx?id=4703.

④ Sustainable Development Report 2023, Canada. https：//dashboards.sdgindex.org/profiles/canada.

⑤ Sustainable. Development Report 2023, United States, https：//dashboards.sdgindex.org/profiles/united-states.

⑥ Statistics Canada. Low income statistics by age, sex and economic family type, May 23, 2023, https：//www150.statcan.gc.ca/t1/tbl1/en/tv.action?pid=1110013501.

表3.4		2015~2021年加拿大贫困率变化情况				（单位：%）	
类别	2015年	2016年	2017年	2018年	2019年	2020年	2021年
所有人群	14.5	12.9	11.9	11.2	10.3	6.4	7.4
18岁以下	16.3	13.9	11.7	10.6	9.4	4.7	6.4
18~64岁	15.7	14.0	13.4	12.8	11.8	7.8	8.2
65岁及以上	7.1	7.1	6.1	6.0	5.7	3.1	5.6

资料来源：Statistics Canada。

根据美国人口普查局2022年9月公布的数据，按照官方贫困衡量标准，2021年美国的总人口为3.282亿人，有3790万人处于贫困状态，总体贫困率为11.6%，与2020年（11.4%）相比，上升了0.2%。而在2020年之前，贫困率从2014年的14.8%连续六年下降。按年龄划分，65岁以上老年人的贫困发生率为10.3%，低于整体水平，18岁以下人口的贫困发生率为15.3%；按种族划分，贫困发生率存在种族差异，黑人的贫困发生率（19.5%）最高，非西班牙裔白人的贫困发生率（8.1%）最低；按婚姻状况划分，已婚夫妇家庭贫困发生率（4.8%）最低，单亲母亲家庭贫困发生率（23%）最高；按教育程度划分，个人的教育水平对贫困有巨大影响，没有高中文凭的成年人贫困发生率为27.2%，而拥有大学学位的成年人贫困发生率仅为4.1%。[①]

根据世界银行的标准，加拿大和美国自2020年以来贫困状况变化不大，而根据加拿大和美国政府公布的数字，两国2021年的贫困率比2020年略有上升。有迹象表明，加拿大2022年的贫困率继续上升，达到9.8%，可能会攀升到2019年的水平，[②]而美国2022年的贫困率也有可能继续上升。[③]美国哥伦比亚大学贫困与社会政策中心指出，由于疫情期间纾困法案中的儿童税收抵免优惠到期，美国儿童贫困率从2021年12月的12.1%上升至2022年5月的16.6%，增加了330万贫困儿童。[④]这些数据显示，两国的贫困率在2020年以后有所恶化。

① John Creamer, Emily A. Shrider, Kalee Burns, Frances Chen. Poverty in the United States: 2021 Current Population Reports, September 13, 2022, https: //www.census.gov/library/publications/2022/demo/p60-277.html.

② Burton Gustajtis, Andrew Heisz. Market Basket Measure poverty thresholds and provisional poverty trends for 2021 and 2022, January 17, 2023, https: //www150.statcan.gc.ca/n1/pub/75f0002m/75f0002m2022008-eng.htm.

③ Santul Nerkar, Michael Tabb. The U.S. Poverty Rate Hit A Record Low – But Don't Expect It To Stay That Way, Dec. 16, 2022, https: //fivethirtyeight.com/videos/the-u-s-poverty-rate-hit-a-record-low-but-dont-expect-it-to-stay-that-way/.

④ 李志伟.美国需要正视儿童贫困的严峻现实, http: //world.people.com.cn/n1/2022/0809/c1002-32497677.html.

之所以会出现这种情况，主要原因是两国政府在疫情期间推出的纾困项目和经济刺激计划已经到期。另外，两国在贫困区域不平衡、贫困人口结构不均衡等减贫顽疾方面没有获得实质性的进展。

2.北美洲国家推进减贫的主要政策供给

（1）积极制定气候和能源转型战略，创造全新就业机会

美国政府高度重视能源和气候问题，拜登政府提出在2050年之前实现100%的清洁能源经济和净零排放总目标。拜登提出美国能源行业要为普通民众提供大量的就业机会，设想通过创造新的就业机会、重建美国基础设施来促进美国能源的转型和升级。

2022年8月16日，美国总统拜登签署《通货膨胀削减法案》，使之具有法律效力。该法案是近年来美国促进绿色环保转型、削减弱势群体医疗负担、优化税制、促进公平以及应对财政赤字最为重要的经济改革计划，预期将产生4330亿美元的财政支出并新增7400亿美元的财政收入。虽然被冠以"通货膨胀削减"的名称，但《通货膨胀削减法案》其实是美国历史上应对气候危机方面采取的最积极的行动，并将在全美范围内创造更多高薪、有保障的工作机会，提供更多的制造业岗位；降低居民医疗负担，兑现拜登竞选时平价处方药的承诺；通过税制改革缩小贫富差距，提高所得税税制的公平性，增加财政收入并为美国政府急需的投资项目筹集资金[1]。

加拿大联邦政府也高度重视实现气候目标，并把实现大规模减排作为向绿色低碳经济过渡的重要抓手。通过一系列政策工具和投资，加拿大进一步鼓励低碳前沿技术创新和增长，支持低碳新兴产业结构和规模不断完善和扩大，从而打造低碳经济新格局。一方面，这有利于提升加拿大减排效率，促进气候目标的实现；另一方面，这能够创造绿色经济新增长点，为加拿大在疫情后实现经济复苏注入动力。

2021年6月2日，加拿大政府启动了"智能可再生能源和电气化改造计划"。该计划由加拿大自然资源部管理，在四年内为智能可再生能源和电网现代化项目提供最高9.64亿加元的支持。通过重点关注清洁能源技术和电力系统运营现代化，支持建设加拿大的低排放能源未来和可再生电气化经济。该计划将支持三个领域的项目，即现有可再生能源、新兴技术和电网现代化，目标是增加加拿大电网的可再生能源能力，并提高其可靠性和弹性，为加拿大人提供

---

① 周静虹，胡怡建.美国通货膨胀削减法案的政策背景、形成过程和应对思路〔J〕.国际税收，2023（3）：39-40.

更清洁、更可靠的电力供应。该计划的目标是到2050年实现净零排放。截至2023年5月1日，该计划已签署88个项目，金额达到9.67亿加元；已批准为73个项目提供资金，这些项目完成后可以增加约2800兆瓦的可再生能源产能，相当于每年减少330万吨二氧化碳排放。其中，38个项目为原住民所有，金额超过7亿加元，每年预计能产生14000个就业岗位。[①]

（2）应对族群间贫困等非均衡挑战，推出差别化的减贫政策

整体来看，美国和加拿大不同族群的贫困率差别很大，这是两国减贫工作中的一个长期存在的结构性问题。美国人口普查局2022年9月公布的数据表明，美国经济显示出从疫情中复苏的迹象，但是贫困的性别、种族和民族差距仍然存在，黑人和西班牙裔的贫困率已经接近几十年来的最低水平，但是白人与黑人和西班牙裔之间差距依然很大（见图3.7）。[②]

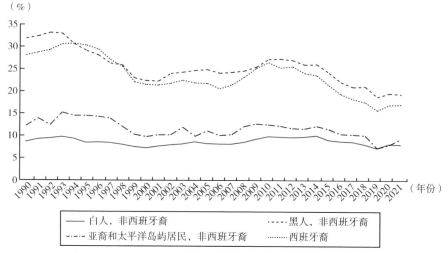

图3.7　1990～2021年美国不同族群的官方贫困率

资料来源：American Progress. The Latest Poverty, Income, and Food Insecurity Data Reveal Continuing Racial Disparities, DEC 21, 2022, https：//www.americanprogress.org/article/the-latest-poverty-income-and-food-insecurity-data-reveal-continuing-racial-disparities/.

① Government of Canada. Smart Renewables and Electrification Pathways Program, May 23, 2023, https：//natural-resources.canada.ca/climate-change/green-infrastructure-programs/sreps/23566.

② John Creamer, Emily A. Shrider, Kalee Burns, Frances Chen. Poverty in the United States：2021 Current Population Reports, September 13, 2022, https：//www.census.gov/library/publications/2022/demo/p60-277.html；American Progress. The Latest Poverty, Income, and Food Insecurity Data Reveal Continuing Racial Disparities. DEC 21, 2022, https：//www.americanprogress.org/article/the-latest-poverty-income-and-food-insecurity-data-reveal-continuing-racial-disparities/.

在加拿大，除菲律宾裔外，少数族裔群体的贫困率均显著高于全国贫困率（8.1%），韩裔的贫困率是全国平均水平的两倍多（19.0%），华裔和非洲裔也不低，分别是 15.3% 和 12.4%。①针对不族群之间的差别，两国政府也推出了公平而有差别的政策，试图降低或缓解族群之间的不平等。在美国，拜登政府为黑人家庭和社区提供经济机会，先后签署了《美国救援方案法》《两党基础设施法案》和《通货膨胀削减法案》，帮助非裔美国人创造新的经济机会，加强对黑人企业和黑人社区的投资。②加拿大政府在 2022 年预算中提出，在未来六年内追加投入 110 亿加元，继续支持原住民儿童及其家庭，并帮助原住民社区持续发展。这些措施主要包括通过"约旦原则"（Jordan's Principle）支持原住民儿童，实施原住民儿童福利立法，解决臭名昭著的寄宿学校遗留问题，改善原住民社区的健康状况，提供心理健康和保健服务，加大对原住民社区的住房投资，支持原住民企业和社区经济发展等。③美国和加拿大政府的这些措施或许会在一定程度上改善族群间的贫困差异，但是"种族不平等问题是一个系统性问题，短期措施在漫长的种族不平等历史面前显得非常苍白"。④

（3）持续采取扩张性财政政策，推出普惠性社会福利项目

疫情期间，美国和加拿大政府启动了多项纾困项目。2021 年 3 月，美国国会通过了高达 1.9 万亿美元的《美国救援方案法》，以对各州和地方政府提供援助，并提供更多的福利保障和实施大规模疫苗接种。加拿大政府也推出了紧急福利补助、复苏补助、康复护理补助、康复疾病补助等项目。为了进一步应对经济社会发展的突出问题，两国政府对抗疫纾困补助措施作出了调整，面向企业和就业者出台新的扶持措施。例如，加拿大政府将康复护理补助、康复疾病补助延长到 2022 年 5 月 7 日，为因地方性的防疫封城措施而无法工作的人提供每周 300 加元的补助。2023 年 3 月，加拿大政府又宣布为 1100 万加拿大人和最需要的家庭提供有针对性的通货膨胀救济。美国为了应对不断攀升的儿童贫困

---

① Statistics Canada. Disaggregated trends in poverty from the 2021 Census of Population, November 9, 2022, https：//www12.statcan.gc.ca/census-recensement/2021/as-sa/98-200-x/2021009/98-200-x2021009-eng. pdf.

② The Whitehouse. Fact Sheet：The Biden-Harris Administration Advances Equity and Opportunity for Black Americans and Communities Across the Country, February 27, 2023, https：//www.whitehouse.gov/ briefing-room/statements-releases/2023/02/27/fact-sheet-the-biden-%E2%81%A0harris-administration-advances-equity-and-opportunity-for-black-americans-and-communities-across-the-country/.

③ Department of Finance Canada. Moving Forward on Reconciliation, April 7, 2022, https：//www. canada.ca/en/department-finance/news/2022/04/moving-forward-on-reconciliation.html.

④ 张春满.政坛老手能否解决老问题？简评拜登政府推动种族平等的措施, https：//fddi.fudan.edu. cn/_t2515/93/05/c21253a430853/page.htm.

率，计划扩大儿童养育税收抵免，将每个六岁以下儿童的税收抵免额度从2000美元上调至3600美元，六岁以上则为3000美元。

（六）欧洲

根据联合国地理区域划分标准，欧洲国家和地区共有45个：阿尔巴尼亚、爱尔兰、爱沙尼亚、安道尔、奥地利、白俄罗斯、保加利亚、比利时、冰岛、波黑、波兰、北马其顿、丹麦、德国、俄罗斯、法国、梵蒂冈、芬兰、荷兰、黑山、捷克、克罗地亚、拉脱维亚、立陶宛、列支敦士登、卢森堡、罗马尼亚、马耳他、摩尔多瓦、摩纳哥、挪威、葡萄牙、瑞典、瑞士、塞尔维亚、圣马力诺、斯洛伐克、斯洛文尼亚、塞浦路斯、乌克兰、西班牙、希腊、匈牙利、意大利、英国。

1.欧洲的贫困特征与演化趋势

欧洲各国的整体经济社会发展条件较好，基础设施相对完善，家庭收入普遍较高，是全球最为发达的区域之一，因此相关国家的减贫治理进程主要针对相对贫困范畴，普遍面临贫困群体结构化、社会排斥风险持续性、贫困区域不平衡发展等一系列挑战。作为全球福利国家的发源地，欧洲各国普遍颁布了社会福利专项法律法规，构建起全方位的社会福利制度体系，为所有国民提供普惠性的保险和救济保障，这成为保护社会贫困群体的首道防线。与此同时，欧洲"福利国家"普遍实行普遍福利与就业促进相结合的减贫战略，主管部门在财政支出和资源配置等方面积极承担减贫责任并实施政策干预，努力克服就业竞争性和保障性之间的政策张力。例如，保加利亚政府专门制定和实施了《2021~2022年行动计划》和《2030年国家减贫和促进社会包容战略》。保加利亚政府计划到2022年使贫困人口占总人口的绝对比例降至31%，到2030年降至25%，同时使贫困人口的相对比例从2020年的23.8%降至2022年的22.5%和2030年的18%。与此同时，罗马尼亚政府也正式批准《2022~2027年国家促进社会包容和减贫战略》和行动计划，决定拨款1.61亿列伊，包含建立100个老年人社会服务中心，目标是到2027年将面临贫困或社会排斥风险的人口减少7%。除此之外，在持续经济增长和政府政策支持等因素的共同作用下，2022年克罗地亚的贫困率已降至1.6%，并有望到2024年进一步降至1.5%[①]。

2.欧洲国家推进减贫的主要政策供给

（1）持续实施创新增长与平衡发展的纾困措施

疫情防控限制的进一步放松以及需求的进一步释放，为欧洲国家政府持续

---

① World Bank/International Bank for Reconstruction and Development. Macro Poverty Outlook，Washington DC，Oct.，2022，p.55.

实施纾困战略和政策奠定了坚实基础。例如，2022年4月，英国政府决定一系列用于建筑物脱碳的绿色技术将免征商业税等，这将在未来五年内使相关企业减少超过2亿英镑的成本；此外，"管理和数字化成长帮扶计划"将为相关中小企业提供价值数千英镑的支持，包括100万英镑的年度投资津贴。葡萄牙国土融合部决定将"内陆就业促进项目"延长至2023年底，该项目旨在创造条件以吸引更多民众尤其是年轻人回到乡村地区，移居乡村一年以上的民众最多可获得4827欧元的安家补贴。西班牙七个自治区的27个村镇于2021年推出"全国远程工作者友好村镇网络项目"，面向对所有常住人口在5000人以下并希望吸引更多居民的村镇，预计未来将有50~100个村镇加入。

（2）积极推进普惠性的社会保障全覆盖

鉴于儿童、妇女、老人、少数民族、残疾人等弱势群体占全世界贫困人口的比重不断攀升，欧盟及欧洲国家积极调动多项政策与资源，尝试通过改善区域整体的发展空间和贫困人口的生计空间来实现协同减贫。例如，德国舒尔茨政府决定以"公民津贴"（Bürgergeld）取代自2002年起实施的哈茨4（Hartz Ⅳ）补助政策，前者较之于后者的补贴标准和免税额度更高，但对申请人的住房面积和家庭资产方面的要求则更低。2022年7月，德国联邦政府专门启动了针对贫困家庭儿童的补贴计划，发放标准为每人每月20欧元，直至引入基本的儿童安全保障，同时决定将国内最低工资标准上调为每小时12欧元。同年9月，德国执政联盟就第三轮救助方案（总金额达650亿欧元）达成一致，以补贴民众与企业因能源价格大幅上涨和高通货膨胀遭受的损失，住房补助领取者在9月至12月将获得一次性的额外供暖补贴。与此同时，社会低保福利领取者的基本保障将从2023年1月1日起由每月449欧元提高至每月500欧元，养老金领取者将从12月1日起获得一次性300欧元的能源补贴，学生和学徒工则将获得一次性200欧元的能源补贴，对于有孩子的家庭来说，每月每个孩子可领取的儿童福利金也将提高18欧元。

2022年，西班牙政府第三轮纾困措施投入超过100亿欧元，以期减轻能源和食品等价格上涨对民众生活的影响。具体来看，政府在2022年底前向年收入低于1.4万欧元的低收入者、自由职业者和失业者发放200欧元一次性补助；将非缴费型养老金上调15%；为农业、渔业、航运业和公路运输业等从业人员提供燃料补贴，对每升燃油提供20分补贴，为发电用天然气价格设定上限以平抑电价；向普通民众提供公共交通折扣和优惠，如2022年9月1日起将国有公共交通月票价格下调50%，各地公共交通月票价格下调30%；在2023年上半年取消对面包、牛奶、鸡蛋、蔬菜等食品征收增值税。

（3）努力完善多样化的就业培训与扶助政策

由于欧洲地区贫困状况更多地表现为相对贫困，且相对贫困的持续多与失业相关联，因此疫情后欧洲国家的减贫政策供给更多聚焦于就业和劳动市场领域。在1000亿欧元本土复苏计划和450亿欧元"下一代欧盟"复苏基金（Next Generation EU Funds）的支撑下，法国政府决心依托"融入经济活动"（IAE）等政策框架，努力通过促进就业来对抗贫困，以期使青年、移民和失业群体能够从中获益。2022年底之前，法国政府已承诺斥资1.5亿欧元，增加27万个工作岗位，同时专项拨款1.2亿欧元用于改善城市优先区域的就业，国家补助的政策比重已由50%增至80%。与此同时，欧盟及其成员国的政策供给更关注贫困背后的精神健康等因素，而非单纯的物质贫困、能力贫困和绝对贫困等议程，这凸显了区域社会支持政策视角下的全方位、多维度、宽领域的整合型减贫理念。例如，鉴于国内未成年人贫困率（UMIC poverty rate）已增至近4%[①]，俄罗斯联邦政府相继推出42项社会支持政策，其中包括200万人次的再就业培训和20万人次的就业招聘。

三、世界主要地区及典型国家推进减贫的政策实施成效

稳健的宏观政策、良好的治理结构和社会的积极参与是减贫战略和政策得以有效制定和实施的基本条件。从国际减贫的传统理论和一般实践来看，一国摆脱贫困的基本路径是在经济起飞阶段依靠政府克服市场失灵，通过调动和配置资源发展现代化大产业，积极重视经济增长的益贫问题。但与此同时，国家经济增长的减贫作用受到社会不平等程度的直接影响，后期只有通过包容性的经济增长模式并关注收入分配益贫问题，才能使贫困人口真正从经济社会发展进程当中受益。

（一）现金转移支付有助于保护弱势群体，但政府赤字和公共债务有升高趋势

世界各国政府努力加大教育、医疗、社会保障、人力资本等领域的政策投入，众多国际组织和非政府组织也积极通过提供资金援助、技术支持和经验交流等方式参与发展中国家减贫治理，这种"赋物"型政策供给模式有助于降低国民的日常生计负担，提升贫困人口的生活水平和质量，并在一定程度上改善

---

① World Bank/International Bank for Reconstruction and Development. Macro Poverty Outlook，Washington DC，Oct.，2022，p.75.

了其生存环境和健康状况。然而，疫情或引发通货膨胀上升，扩张性财政支出或导致财政赤字翻倍、主权债务危机将进一步加重，"福利陷阱"问题在一定程度上削弱了政策供给效果。例如，在经济增速放缓叠加通货膨胀冲击的背景下，荷兰未来几年政府赤字将继续上升，公共财政恶化，政府正逐步取消临时支持措施，预计将有更多的居民面临跌破贫困线的风险。荷兰经济政策分析局（CPB）发布的经济分析报告预测，2024年荷兰贫困人口占荷兰总人口的比重将由4.7%上升至5.8%，达到约995000人，扩大普惠型社会政策的供给空间已经有限，实际成效也未能达到民众预期。联合国《2022年可持续发展目标报告》指出，"尽管几乎所有国家都推出了新的社会保障措施以应对危机，但是很多措施都是短期性的。"[1]此外，一些国家的专项减贫项目由许多子项目和独立方案构成，具体制定和执行政策又由中央和地方政府、企业、非政府组织等众多行为体参与，这无疑加大了不同项目之间的协调和合作难度，增加了政策运行效率、运作成本方面的风险，甚至资源浪费风险。

（二）税费杠杆调节有助于缩小收入差距，但融资创新和金融监管有待强化

疫情等引发的物价上涨和通货膨胀迫使绝大多数国家政府在生产、消费、流通等多个环节出台税费减免、经济补贴和就业保护等紧急救助措施，以在一定程度上缓解劳动者、经营者、消费者和小微企业等市场主体的生产生活压力。众所周知，一国的绝对贫困发生率和贫困人口规模往往会伴随着经济社会发展进程而不断下降，甚至完全消失，但即使一国的经济发展程度达到较高水平，低收入阶层也会始终存在，相对贫困人口也不会完全消失。具体而言，生活在全国收入中位数一半以下人口的比例是衡量一个国家社会排斥、收入分配和相对贫困的一个重要指标，收入分配差距过大将影响经济发展惠及贫困人口的程度。就此而言，通过税收政策杠杆灵活调节收入分配差距、社会两极分化、相对贫困发生等问题，有助于缓解由此引发的社会矛盾。例如，拉丁美洲和加勒比地区等的"有条件现金转移支付计划"对于推进减贫的总体影响是积极的，但在政策制定和实施过程中仍存在一些不足，如覆盖范围不足、相关机制精准度有待提高等。此外，"非洲发展新伙伴计划"尝试通过促进小额信贷机构和项目以及改善营销系统等多种方式来鼓励私营部门投资和促进经济增长，减少非洲大陆的贫困和促进可持续发展，但此类计划大多是以现金援助的

---

① 参见：联合国，《2022年可持续发展目标报告》。

方式实现的，这也容易导致通货膨胀、商品价格上涨以及私人现金被压制等一系列负面影响。在非洲，不断上涨的粮食和能源价格影响着最脆弱的群体，公共债务和通货膨胀从2022年就开始处于数十年来的最高水平，大约一半的国家出现了两位数的通货膨胀[①]。

（三）人力资本投入有助于缓解经济收缩，但亟须扩大教育培训和社区赋能

尽管以上相关政策计划和项目对于减少饥饿和缓解贫困至关重要，但其并未真正解决为弱势群体提供就业机会和提升企业竞争力之间的平衡问题，换句话说，一些国家针对贫困人口"输血式"的政策供给并未产生"造血式"的政策功效。提高人力资本水平是消除贫困的根本策略。例如，欧美等发达国家在"福利到工作"等政策设计和实施方面已经积累的一些经验，但谨防福利性依赖造成的贫困陷阱仍然是未来欧洲国家减贫事业面临的主要挑战之一。根据葡萄牙政府公布的数据，2020年"内陆就业促进项目"实施一年，国土融合部收到了560份申请，超过980人因此受益。其中，年龄小于34岁的申请人占比超过五成，63%的申请者接受过高等教育。但目前葡萄牙人口主要集中于大西洋沿岸地区，内陆乡村地区往往缺少必要的公共基础设施和服务设施，很难吸引大量人口尤其是年轻人长期居住。又如，南非政府在联合国粮农组织的支持下制定了《农业和农村发展部门青年赋权战略》，以解决该国青年失业率高企的问题。该战略旨在确保青年有效和平等地融入农村农业，已于2022年举行了启动会议和一系列项目指导委员会会议，随后举行了多次利益攸关方磋商讲习班，征求主要利益攸关方的意见，但参与式减贫对于贫困人口的行为矫正和社区赋能有待深入，其推动减贫治理的可持续效应亦有待观察。

---

① IMF. Regional Economic Outlook for Sub-Saharan Africa, https：//www.imf.org/en/publications/reo?sortby=Date&series=Sub-Saharan%20Africa.

第四章
中国巩固拓展脱贫攻坚成果同乡村振兴有效衔接政策和实践

本章要点

脱贫攻坚成果是全面推进乡村振兴的底线任务，中国推进巩固拓展脱贫攻坚成果同乡村振兴有效衔接意义重大。巩固和扩展脱贫攻坚成果是实现乡村振兴的基础，建立和完善防止返贫的监测机制，实施有效的帮扶措施，对稳定和增加收入至关重要。高质量发展乡村产业，扩大就业机会，发展壮大新型农村集体经济以及通过技能培训提升脱贫能力，都是推动增强脱贫地区及其居民内生动力的重要举措。为接续推进乡村振兴，需要借鉴和实施一些典型做法，这包括但不限于推动乡村产业的高质量发展，扎实推进宜居宜业和美丽乡村建设，以及健全党组织领导的乡村治理体系。

脱贫攻坚战全面胜利以后，中国面临的首要问题就是防止返贫。对此，中国实施了对脱贫县设立五年过渡期、在西部地区设立乡村振兴重点帮扶县等措施。在过渡期内，对脱贫攻坚阶段的帮扶政策逐项分类优化调整，逐步由集中资源支持脱贫攻坚向全面推进乡村振兴平稳过渡，不仅可以实现对脱贫攻坚成果的全方位巩固拓展，还可以为已脱贫地区理清乡村振兴发展思路，因地制宜制定乡村振兴发展路径，实现脱贫攻坚与乡村振兴的有效衔接。

一、巩固拓展脱贫攻坚成果

巩固拓展脱贫攻坚成果是全面推进乡村振兴的底线任务。《"十四五"推进农业农村现代化规划》强调脱贫攻坚政策体系和工作机制同乡村振兴有效衔接，脱贫人口"两不愁三保障"①成果有效巩固，防止返贫动态监测和帮扶机制健全完善并有效运转，确保不发生规模性返贫。2022年发布的中央一号文件聚焦全面推进乡村振兴，明确了两条底线任务：保障国家粮食安全、不发生规模性返贫。防止返贫监测帮扶是巩固拓展脱贫攻坚成果的关键举措。进入全面实施乡村振兴战略的新发展阶段，中国已经出台实施了30多项过渡期衔接政策，防止返贫动态监测帮扶机制全面建立。经过各方共同努力，脱贫攻坚成果得到进一步巩固拓展，守住了不发生规模性返贫的底线。

（一）建立健全防止返贫监测机制

防止返贫动态监测范围全覆盖。坚持"全域覆盖、动态监测、一户不漏"的原则，开展动态监测，将集中排查、重点筛查、日常排查等多措并举，确保应纳尽纳；以行业部门为依托，发挥专业化监测作用，多部门联合监测，开展常态化调研摸排，将业务工作和防返贫动态监测帮扶工作有机结合，提前介入，防患于未然；拓宽渠道，引导全社会参与监测。发挥好预警响应作用，切实做到早发现、早干预、早帮扶，将返贫致贫风险把控关口前移，及时发现、快速响应、精准帮扶、动态管理、动态清零。

全面提升防返贫动态监测数据质量。提升防返贫动态监测数据质量是巩固拓展脱贫攻坚成果同乡村振兴有效衔接不可或缺的工作。高质量的监测数据是巩固拓展脱贫攻坚成果同乡村振兴有效衔接的基石，是做好精准管理工作的基础前提，是推进乡村振兴的必然要求。一是明确专人负责，压实工作责任。二是强化数据清洗，提高数据质量。三是坚持问题导向，紧抓问题整改。认真梳理省、市、县反馈的疑点数据，认真总结分析，逐条进行梳理，找准问题症结，确保反馈的疑点数据第一时间全部整改到位。

健全机制体系，筑牢监测防线。健全工作领导机制，成立防止返贫监测帮扶集中排查工作专班。健全全员排查机制，各区县、乡镇明确排查工作联系人、负责人，各村将所有农户分区划片，每户农户明确排查走访责任人，包户到人。健全筛查会商机制，加强与行业部门的会商研讨，部门专人对接，对监测重难点问题、政策堵点事项及时会商研判，集体研究解决。健全录入审核机制，排查走访负责人、信息录入员、信息审核第一负责人对其职责范围内信息数据的准确性完全负责。健全培训督导机制，确保排查工作步调一致、内容一致、标准一致。健全责任倒查机制，将防止返贫监测帮扶集中排查工作纳入年

---

① "两不愁"即不愁吃、不愁穿，"三保障"即义务教育、基本医疗和住房安全有保障。

度巩固拓展脱贫攻坚成果同乡村振兴真抓实干考核内容。例如，贵州省铜仁市碧江区在不断探索创新、健全防返贫动态监测与帮扶机制过程中建立起了"553311"机制，在责任、监测、预警、帮扶、巩固等方面持续发力，兜紧筑牢返贫致贫防线。

（二）落实帮扶措施，稳住增收基本盘

优化帮扶举措。一是先行帮扶。对因受灾、意外事故等突发情况导致"三保障"出现严重风险的农户，先行救助帮扶，后履行相关程序，增强帮扶成效。二是开发式帮扶。对有普通或技能劳动力家庭但存在突发性、隐蔽性、过渡性等临时困难的农户，重点落实产业帮扶、就业帮扶等政策，提高自身"造血"能力，实现稳定发展。三是综合帮扶。对整户无劳动力导致收入较低、生活困难的农户，因户施策，重点落实低保、"五保"、残疾人补贴等兜底保障措施。对多种风险叠加的农户和障碍性无劳动力户，就近落实公益岗、帮扶产业带动和兜底保障相结合的综合性保障措施。

细化帮扶管理。结合巩固拓展脱贫攻坚成果和乡村建设信息采集结果、部门数据比对和镇村（社区）定期走访情况，以家庭收入综合考虑"两不愁三保障"等因素对农户进行精准分类，根据分类情况及时调整帮扶责任人，对于重点脱贫户和监测户采取一对一重点帮扶并制定针对性的帮扶措施以达到精准帮扶。以强化驻村帮扶管理为重要抓手，强化组织领导，压实帮扶责任，强化选派管理，优化帮扶力量，严格轮换管理，强化督查指导。

强化帮扶力量。一是深入推进东西部协作，确保财政援助资金和干部人才尽快到位，加快协作项目实施和资金支出进度。例如，京蒙携手推进"两个基地"建设，谱写京蒙协作新篇章；粤桂、粤黔实施"四项工程"，助力脱贫人口稳岗就业；山东省积极实施"东产西移"工程，助力重庆市、甘肃省产业发展，变"资金输血"为"产业造血"。二是加强与中央定点帮扶单位对接，积极争取对定点帮扶县的指导和支持。例如，中国农业银行在定点帮扶贵州省黄平县的实践中创新设立"三个基金"（防返贫基金、乡村振兴产业发展基金、教育培训基金），构筑起短、中、长期防返贫致贫安全网与可持续利益联结机制。三是加大社会力量帮扶力度。充分发挥驻村第一书记"领头雁"作用，把推进精准扶贫与加强阵地建设、加大基础保障、拓展致富门路等工作紧密结合，为推进精准扶贫、精准脱贫工作提供坚强保障。四是加强企业和社会组织帮扶。例如，北京字节跳动科技有限公司基于新媒体产业优势，依托抖音、今日头条等数字平台，实施"山货上头条"、新农人培训项目，开展消费帮扶、乡村旅游开发、人才培训、公益救助等活动，将有特色、高品质的"山货"带出乡村，将乡村风土人情、乡村风貌带出山区，将农民培养成新媒体强人。

二、增强脱贫地区和脱贫群众内生动力

民族要复兴，乡村必振兴。党的二十大报告提出，巩固拓展脱贫攻坚成果，增强脱贫地区和脱贫群众内生发展动力。2023年中央一号文件对2023年乡村全面振兴的重点工作进行了全面部署，对加快建设农业强国提出了总体要求，特别是对如何增强脱贫地区和脱贫群众内生发展动力作出了具体部署。脱贫地区干部群众要坚持系统观念，多措并举，增强脱贫地区和脱贫群众的内生发展动力，促进脱贫县加快发展，增加脱贫群众收入，全面推进乡村振兴，加快建设农业农村现代化。

（一）高质量发展乡村产业

发展乡村产业是增强脱贫地区和脱贫群众内生发展动力的内生增长引擎。首先，推进农业特色产业发展。进一步发掘当地特色资源、生态环境、土地、劳动力、资本等要素禀赋，因地制宜、因村施策，培育和发展产业。贯彻落实中央一号文件精神，抓住"国家乡村振兴重点帮扶县实施一批补短板促振兴重点项目"的契机，带动脱贫群众增加收入。其次，促进产业规模化经营。以规模经营为主导，通过发展新型农村集体经济，整合农业要素形成一定规模，产生规模经济效应。发挥龙头企业带动作用，牵引种养大户、农民专业合作社等全面快速发展，同时"要健全利益联结机制，带动农民增收"。最后，推动产业链延伸以及产业升级。重点补齐技术、设施、营销、人才等支撑发展动力的短板，更好发挥驻村干部、科技特派员产业帮扶作用，加快数字化、智能化转型，打造科技产业、智慧产业等，提高农业信息化和现代化水平。

（二）积极扩大就业

加强脱贫人口就业帮扶是增加脱贫人口收入的有效方式，是巩固脱贫攻坚成果的基本举措，是守住不发生规模性返贫底线的重要保障。一是突出就业优先政策。对吸纳脱贫人口就业的企业，给予创业担保贷款、吸纳就业补贴和社会保险补贴。对提供有组织劳务输出的中介机构，给予就业服务补贴。对脱贫人口个人，在公益性岗位就业的给予岗位补贴，参加培训的给予职业培训补贴、培训期间食宿交通费补贴。二是加大创业支持力度，鼓励返乡入乡创业。充分利用现有园区等资源建设一批返乡入乡创业园等；为脱贫劳动力等创业人

员提供培训、贷款、开业指导等"一站式"创业服务，按规定落实税费减免、创业担保贷款等政策支持；在脱贫村深入开展创业担保贷款信用村建设，免除反担保手续，支持脱贫劳动力创业。三是培育壮大特色劳务品牌，激发带动就业新动力。在劳务品牌建设培育过程中，脱贫人口、农村劳动力有大量机会，通过参加技能培训掌握务工的一技之长，实现高质量稳定就业。四是持续深化劳务协作，稳定劳动力就业。建立常态化的跨区域岗位信息共享和发布机制。充分发挥对口帮扶机制作用，着力提升劳务协作的组织化程度和就业质量，积极拓展省际、省内劳务输入地和输出地的对口协作，完善跨区域、常态化的劳务合作机制，在信息交流、跨区招聘、跟踪服务等方面搭建对接平台，实现信息的有效衔接。

（三）发展壮大新型农村集体经济

发展壮大新型农村集体经济是完善农村基本经营制度的重要内容，是巩固脱贫攻坚成果和推进乡村振兴战略的重要举措。一是要因地制宜。中国幅员辽阔，东中西部农村资源禀赋、市场条件存在较大差异，发展农村集体经济不能依赖一个模式，要努力构建产权关系明晰、治理架构科学、经营方式稳健、收益分配合理的运行机制，增强农村集体经济内生动力和发展活力。在经济发达的地方，发展都市农业、休闲农业，市场前景广阔；在有产业基础但缺乏能人带动的村庄，可以通过各类新型经营主体带动，与农民紧密利益联结，共同做大产业；而对于一些产业基础薄弱的地区，则可以通过联村抱团发展，发挥规模优势。二是要积极盘活集体资产资源。充分发挥农村集体经济组织作为集体资产所有权行使主体在积极盘活集体资产资源、引领集体成员实现共同发展方面的重要作用，灵活运用各种方式，包括资源发包、物业出租、居间服务、资产参股等较为稳健的经营活动，直接经营、入股经营、合作经营、委托经营等灵活多样的经营方式，农业生产、物业服务、休闲旅游、民宿康养等多种产业。三是要切实保障农民受益。一方面，要通过紧密利益联结机制，调动农民参与积极性，鼓励大家拧成一股绳，促进人才、技术等各类要素内外联动，挖掘山水田园间的潜力；另一方面，要健全农村集体资产监管体系，管好"三资"责任田。

（四）大力推进技能培训，提升技能脱贫本领

巩固拓展脱贫攻坚成果助力乡村振兴，需要突出技能提升的精准性和有效性，让脱贫人口有技能、好就业、能致富。技能培训是贫困劳动力就业增收、实现脱贫的重要举措。

一是精准施训促提升。结合贫困劳动力从业领域分布特点，对不同群体分类施训。全面详细掌握贫困劳动力培训意向，根据培训意愿有针对性地开设培训工种。贫困户可根据自身的素质层次、能力水平、就业创业意愿等情况，报名技能培训，依据各自"口味"开展短期技能培训。二是多措并举增实效。大力发展农村实用技术培训，围绕特色优势产业开展种植、养殖、加工和产销对接、农村电商直播带货电子商务师等实用职业技能培训；"流动课堂"进乡村，把教师请下乡，把器材搬进村，把课堂开在家门口，学习劳务两不误；开展以工代训促进稳岗，支持农村合作社、扶贫车间等吸纳贫困劳动力就业，并有序开展岗前培训、以工代训和技能提升培训，用好政策叠加，落实培训补贴资金稳就业、保就业的作用。

三、接续推进乡村振兴的典型做法

（一）推动乡村产业高质量发展

一是注重发展特色产业。加快发展现代乡村服务业，培育乡村新产业新业态。二是加强对农业科技的支持。加快完善国家农业科技创新体系；持续加强农业基础研究；大幅提升企业在农业科技创新中的地位；激发农业科技创新人才创新活力。三是做大做强农产品加工流通业。实施农产品加工业提升行动，支持家庭农场、农民合作社和中小微企业等发展农产品产地初加工，引导大型农业企业发展农产品精深加工。四是培育壮大县域富民产业。完善县乡村产业空间布局，提升县城产业承载和配套服务功能，增强重点镇集聚功能。实施"一县一业"强县富民工程。支持国家级高新区、经开区、农高区托管联办县域产业园区。

（二）扎实推进宜居宜业和美乡村建设

一是加强村庄规划编制。坚持县域统筹，支持有条件有需求的村庄分区分类编制村庄规划，合理确定村庄布局和建设边界；将村庄规划纳入村级议事协商目录；规范优化乡村地区行政区划设置，严禁违背农民意愿撤并村庄、搞大社区。二是扎实推进农村人居环境整治提升。加大村庄公共空间整治力度，持续开展村庄清洁行动；巩固农村户厕问题摸排整改成果，扎实推进户厕改造，切实提高农村改厕质量实效；加强农村卫生公厕建设维护；分区分类推进农村生活污水治理，加强农村黑臭水体治理；健全农村生活垃圾收运处置体系，在有条件的地方推进源头分类减量。三是持续加强乡村基础设施建设。深化"四好农村路"示范创建，加强较大人口规模自然村（组）、具备条件农户通硬化路建设，推动农村公路建设项目更多向进村入户倾斜；推进农村规模化供水工程建设和小型供水工程标准化改造，加快解决农村季节性缺水和因旱临时饮水困难问题，持续巩固饮水安全成果；持续巩固提升农村电力保障水平，开展农村能源革命试点县建设，加快农村地区能源清洁低碳转型，推进数字技术与农村生产生活深度融合，持续开展数字乡村试点。四是提升基本公共服务能力。推动基本公共服务资源下沉，着力加强薄弱环节；推进县域内义务教育优质均衡发展，提升农村学校办学水平；落实乡村教师生活补助政策；推进医疗卫生资源县域统筹，加强乡村两级医疗卫生、医疗保障服务能力建设；统筹解决乡村医生薪酬分配和待遇保障问题，推进乡村医生队伍专业化规范化。

（三）健全党组织领导的乡村治理体系

一是注重基层民主建设，强化农村基层党组织政治功能和组织功能。在乡村治理过程中，要充分发挥村民委员会的作用，加强村民自治，让村民参与决策和管理，提高村民的参与度和满意度。同时，要加强村民代表大会和村民议事会的建设，让村民有更多的话语权和决策权，推动乡村治理的民主化和法治化。二是注重文化传承和创新，加强农村精神文明建设。在乡村治理过程中，要注重传承和弘扬乡土文化，挖掘和发掘乡村文化资源，推动文化创意产业的发展，提高乡村文化的影响力和吸引力。同时，要注重创新，推动乡村治理的现代化和科技化，引入新技术和新模式，提高乡村治理的效率和质量。三是注重生态保护和绿色发展，提升乡村生态环境的质量和可持续性。推进探索实施现代农业农村生态环境治理模式；加强农业农村现代生态环境治理能力建设；推进农业农村实施生态环境系统治理；加强农业农村生态环境治理科技创新与运用。

第五章
全球减贫展望

本章要点

　　当前全球减贫面临多重挑战，经济发展具有不确定性，地区冲突影响政治稳定性，粮食不安全问题日益严重，营养健康危机加剧。我们应多措并举促进全球减贫事业发展，维护区域和平稳定，加大教育投入力度，重视医疗健康发展，加强基础设施建设，共同应对气候变化。以共同发展和合作为核心，积极推进全球化进程，加强国际援助和合作，帮助减少发展中国家的贫困和不平等，深化多边合作，在全球减贫中积极贡献中国力量。

一、全球减贫面临多重挑战

　　疫情过后全球复苏面临多重挑战，经济发展具有不确定性。受地区冲突等多重危机的影响，全球经济发展面临巨大的不确定性。一些国家和地区在疫情控制较好、经济刺激措施积极的情况下，经济出现了较快的复苏。然而，仍有一些国家和地区面临多重挑战，经济复苏步伐缓慢。2022年，全球失业率为5.77%，许多企业破产或者裁员，导致大量失业。虽然随着经济复苏，就业市场逐渐回暖，但仍有许多人面临着就业困难和收入减少问题，给全球减贫带来了巨大的压力和挑战。

　　地区冲突对减贫构成严峻挑战。2022年，全球共发生超过6355起地区冲突事件。一方面，地区冲突破坏了政治稳定，政府无法有效地规划和实施减贫政策。政府资源被重点用于军事行动、安全维护和重建等工作，从而削弱了减贫和社会福利项目，对减贫进程造成严重影响。另一方面，地区冲突严重制约经济发展和就业增长，从而削弱了减贫的效果。冲突导致基础设施受损、生产力减弱，投资和经济活动受到限制，而这种经济困境导致失业率上升和贫困加剧。此外，地区冲突还导致人口流离失所和移民，加剧了全球的减贫挑战。大量民众被迫离开家园，不仅危及人们的生命安全和生计，还给接纳地带来压力，造成社会和经济不稳定。这对全球减贫目标的实现构成了额外的挑战。

粮食不安全问题日益严重，营养健康危机加剧。疫情期间的限制措施导致农业劳动力短缺，影响了农业生产和粮食供应。此外，由于受贸易限制、地区冲突和运输等的影响，粮食价格上涨，使贫困人口面临更大的粮食不安全风险，贫困人口营养摄入不足。与此同时，疫情造成的经济衰退使许多人失去了收入来源，不少家庭不得不削减食物支出，选择较为廉价且营养价值较低的食品，如高糖、高盐和高脂肪的加工食品。这种不平衡的饮食习惯导致慢性病增加，如肥胖、糖尿病和心血管疾病等，使贫困人口的营养健康危机进一步加剧。

二、多措并举促进全球减贫事业发展

维护和平稳定，解决粮食危机。减少地区冲突、应对粮食危机是解决全球贫困问题的重中之重。首先，政府应加强冲突预防和解决机制，通过外交手段促进地区间的和平对话，避免冲突的发生。其次，各国应加大对冲突地区的援助力度，帮助其重建基础设施，提升居民的生活水平。为解决粮食危机，需要进一步加强农业生产能力，通过提高农民收入等方式鼓励农业生产。政府应该制定并实施粮食安全战略，有效增加粮食种植面积，并面向农民提供技术指导和金融支持。再次，推动农业科技创新，引入新的耐旱、抗病虫害的农作物品种，提高农作物产量，保障粮食供应。最后，在营养健康方面，我们应加强对贫困地区的营养健康服务。政府应制定并实施普惠的健康政策，提供免费或低价的营养补助品，并开展营养饮食指导，以提供全面的营养支持。同时，推广以本地农产品为主的健康饮食文化，提倡均衡膳食，努力解决贫困地区的营养不良问题。

加大教育投入力度。教育能够提升个体的能力和素质，增强其适应社会发展的能力，从而增加就业机会和收入来源。为了推动全球减贫，各国应加大对基础教育的投入，尤其应更加关注贫困地区和弱势群体的教育资源配置，提供良好的教育条件和机会，打破贫困的代际传递。政府应当提高教育预算，增加教育财政支出，确保更多的资源用于教育。建立和扩大普遍义务教育制度，保障所有儿童接受优质的基础教育。为贫困家庭提供教育补助金或奖学金，支付子女的学费、教材费和其他相关费用，减轻贫困家庭经济负担，推动儿童接受教育。此外，应加大对教师的培训力度，提高教师的专业素质和教学能力。同时，提高教师的待遇和福利，吸引更多优秀的人才从事教育工作。改善贫困地区的教育资源和设施，包括建设学校、图书馆，以及更新教学设备等，确保贫困地区的孩子也能享受良好的教育条件。加大国际援助力度，向贫困地区提供教育基础设施，提供相关的技术和培训支持，帮助其改善教育水平和教育质量。

重视医疗健康发展。贫困与健康密切相关，缺乏基本的医疗保障将使人们更易陷入疾病和贫困的恶性循环中。为了推动全球减贫，各国应加大对医疗卫生事业的投入，提供普惠的医疗服务和基本医疗保障，特别是在贫困地区和偏远地区，让每个人都能享受到基本的医疗服务，减少因病致贫、因病返贫的情况发生。首先，积极开展医疗服务普及和社区卫生设施建设，确保贫困人口能够获得基本的医疗保健服务，包括健康检查、疫苗接种、基本药物等。积极开展医院、诊所、实验室等医疗基础设施建设，提高医疗服务的可及性和质量。特别是在贫困地区，需要提升医疗设施的数量和质量。其次，建立全面的医疗保险和社会保障制度，确保贫困人口和弱势群体能够获得合理的医疗服务，并提供医疗费用的补贴和保障。提高医疗人员的数量和质量，提高医疗人员的技能水平，加强医学教育和培训，吸引更多的医疗人才到贫困地区提供服务。再次，加强疾病预防、控制和监测，包括提供充足的疫苗接种服务、提高卫生条件、加强疾病监测和防控措施等，以有效减少疾病传播，提高整体健康水平。最后，国际社会应加强合作，提供援助和资金支持，特别是帮助贫困国家建立和发展医疗保健系统，提供技术支持和培训，共同推动医疗健康发展，有效助推全球减贫进程。

加强基础设施建设。良好的基础设施能够创造就业机会并促进经济增长，提高贫困地区的生产力和竞争力，从而带动贫困人口脱贫。各国应投入更多的资源，改善交通、通信、供水、电力条件，提升贫困地区的基础设施水平，为贫困人口提供更好的发展机会。首先，通过增加政府预算、吸引外国直接投资、使用国际银行贷款等方式加强基础设施投资建设。其次，各国政府和国际组织应加强基础设施建设合作，实现资源共享、技术转移、经验分享等，提高基础设施建设的效率和质量。再次，基础设施建设应注重公平性，确保贫困地区和弱势群体能够共享发展成果。最后，应注重可持续性，采用环保和资源节约型建设方式，避免对环境的破坏，确保长期可持续发展。通过引入新技术和创新模式，提高基础设施的效率和质量。例如，利用智能技术优化交通运输系统，采用可再生能源建设清洁能源基础设施等。

共同应对气候变化。 气候变化影响着全球贫困格局，尤其是对农村贫困人口和依赖自然资源的群体的影响更为显著。为了推动全球减贫，各国应加强国际合作，共同应对气候变化，减少温室气体排放，推动可持续发展，适应气候变化的影响，提高发展韧性，降低贫困人口生计受损的风险。第一，减少化石燃料的使用，增加可再生能源的比例，如使用太阳能、风能等清洁能源。第二，保护和恢复生态系统，特别是森林、湿地和海洋，以帮助吸收二氧化碳和其他温室气体。第三，采用低碳排放的农业技术，减少农药和化肥使用，提高农作物的产量和农民的收入。提高能源效率，减少能源浪费。第四，改善城市规划和管理，鼓励可持续交通、能源效率和废物管理等。第五，国际社会应加强合作，确保资源和技术的共享，特别是为发展中国家提供资金和技术援助，共同应对气候变化。

三、推进全球发展倡议，携手构建人类命运共同体

以共同发展和合作为核心，积极推进全球化进程。 中国国家主席习近平在第七十六届联合国大会上提出全球发展倡议，以构建全球发展共同体为目标，秉持发展优先、以人民为中心等理念，重点推进减贫、粮食安全、抗疫和疫苗、气候变化和绿色发展等领域合作。全球发展倡议与减少贫困、提升民生福祉紧密相关，有助于实现联合国2030年可持续发展议程，也为各国制定可持续发展政策提供了思路和启示。当前全球面临着经济社会发展领域的严峻形势，国际社会通力合作、积极践行全球发展倡议将是推动疫后经济恢复、推进减贫工作不断向前的必由之路。全球发展倡议切中世界大变局、疫情的形势之要害，聚焦各国人民对和平发展、公平正义、合作共赢的期盼追求，高度契合各方需要。中国将与全球各国共同携手抗击疫情，继续深化国际减贫合作，积极构建全球减贫合作联盟，为各国在减贫问题上提供国际合作平台。充分发挥中国—联合国和平与发展基金作用，加快实现疫后更好复苏，有力推进全球减贫事业。积极应对气候变化挑战，在卫生健康、数字化、绿色经济等领域为全球减贫事业发挥更大作用。

加强国际援助和合作，帮助减少发展中国家的贫困和不平等。 加强国际援助和合作是帮助发展中国家摆脱贫困的有效途径之一。通过向贫困地区提供经济援助、技术支持和人力资源培训等，可以有效地推动当地社会经济的发展。这不仅可以为当地创造就业机会，提高民众的收入水平，还能够改善当地基础设施，提升社会福利水平，从而有效减少贫困。同时，国际援助和合作也可以

帮助减少发展中国家之间的不平等。在全球化的背景下，发展中国家之间的经济差距日益扩大，这也导致了诸如社会福利、教育水平等方面的不平等。通过加强国际合作机制，如国际金融组织、多边开发银行等，可以为发展中国家提供平等和公正的发展机会，推动各国的经济发展，使资源配置更加平衡。此外，加强国际援助和合作对于应对全球性挑战也至关重要。气候变化、传染病、贸易保护主义等问题已经不再局限于某个国家或地区，而是需要全球合作加以应对。通过加强国际合作，可以共同制定全球性的应对措施，分享技术和经验，共同应对这些挑战，从根本上减少发展中国家所面临的贫困和不平等。

深化多边合作，在全球减贫中积极贡献中国力量。中国的减贫成就为推动全球减贫提供了中国样本和中国方案。习近平主席提出的全球发展倡议也将减贫摆在重点合作领域。为此，中国将持续推动国际交流合作，凝聚国际减贫合力，努力建立以合作共赢为核心的新型国际减贫治理体系。同时，根据自身发展实际，关注世界各国尤其是发展中国家面临的急迫挑战，在特定重点领域积极对接各国需求。在当前情况下，尤其要加强全球南方国家之间的团结与合作，继续支持和帮助广大发展中国家特别是最不发达国家消除贫困，加强与东南亚国家在数字乡村、跨境电商、生态旅游等领域的合作，推进减贫合作提质升级，完善与太平洋岛国的减贫合作，协助其完成数字经济转型。

综上所述，推进全球减贫事业发展是一个团结合作的过程，只有各国共同努力，创造一个和谐、稳定和可持续的世界，才能实现全球共同繁荣和可持续发展的目标。作为国际社会的一员，各个国家应坚持长远眼光和战略视野，将全球可持续发展目标的内涵融入经济社会发展框架中，通过各类多边、双边交流机制和平台，围绕减贫与乡村发展、粮食安全、教育发展等议题，加强交流分享和合作，共同落实2030年可持续发展议程，构建平等均衡的全球发展伙伴关系，携手推进全球减贫进程，携手构建没有贫困、共同发展的人类命运共同体。

参考文献

［1］陈茜.防止规模性返贫的监测预警机制创新——基于湖南省隆回县的案例研究［J］.农村经济与科技,2023,34(2):167–172.

［2］兴产业 促就业 助振兴——芮城县财政局驻村帮扶典型案例［J］.山西财税,2022(4):18–19.

［3］董占峰.建设美丽中国,推动农业和农村地区现代生态环境治理［EB/OL］.http://f.china.com.cn/2022–02/28/content_78076006.htm.

［4］何硕.防止贫困回潮,打好"持久战"更要打好"主动战"——新余市防止贫困返穷监测帮扶工作的主要做法［J］.旧区建设,2020(23):23–24.

［5］湖南怀化:提高技能打赢脱贫攻坚辅导好"收官战"［EB/OL］.https://www.toutiao.com/article/6913845753635013128/? &source=m_redirect.

［6］刘美君.国家乡村振兴局印发文件24条措施巩固扩大脱贫攻坚成果［EB/OL］.https://finance.qianlong.com/2022/0602/7260687.shtml.

［7］刘瑞平.山西显康:预防贫困四机制［J］.中国乡村振兴,2021(12):2.

［8］太平洋岛国围绕深海开采产生分歧［EB/OL］.http://ggmd.cgs.gov.cn/Deposits NewsCen.aspx?id=4703.

［9］乔金亮.新型农村集体经济新形势［EB/OL］.https://m.gmw.cn/baijia/2022–12/06/36210827.html.

［10］谭姿.省级引入新政策协助企业稳定扩大就业［J］.工人,2020.

［11］王世满.多管齐下使扶贫成果更加巩固和促进农村发展［EB/OL］.https://sichuan.scol.com.cn/ggxw/202212/58775924.html.

［12］魏健.新型农村集体经济促进乡村共同富裕［EB/OL］.https://theory.gmw.cn/2022–09/23/content_36044211.htm.

［13］魏敏.巩固脱贫攻坚成果 河北多举措助力贫困人口稳定就业［EB/

OL］. http://district.ce.cn/newarea/roll/202301/06/t20230106_38329902.shtml.

［14］中央政府为何反复强调"在扶贫领域设立五年过渡期？"［EB/OL］.
https://www.toutiao.com/article/6945449823893979662/? &source=m_redirect.

［15］兴默，何晔.农村振兴背景下防止返贫长效机制分析［J］.山西农业
经济，2022（15）: 28–30.

［16］杨光.黑龙江阿城区首批村村书记精准扶贫［EB/OL］. https://www.
nrra.gov.cn/art/2016/6/20/art_5_50681.html.

［17］杨世云.发展壮大新型农村集体经济促进农民和农村共同富裕［J］.
群众，2022（10）: 3.

［18］赵少峰，王佐成.2022太平洋岛国发展蓝皮书［M］.北京:社会科学
文献出版社，2022.

［19］周建生.打攻坚战弥补短板 活化乡村生态环境［J］.江苏农村经济，
2021（6）: 3.

［20］周静宏，胡奕坚.美国通胀减少法案的政策背景、形成过程与应对思
路［J］.国际税收，2023（3）: 39–40.

［21］Asian Development Bank. Asian Development Outlook 2023［R］. 2023.

［22］Burton Gustajtis, Andrew Heisz. Market Basket Measure Poverty Thresholds
and Provisional Poverty Trends for 2021 and 2022［EB/OL］. https: //www150.statcan.
gc.ca/n1/pub/75f0002m/75f0002m2022008-eng.htm.

［23］C.W. Lee. U.S. Needs to Face Up to the Stark Reality of Child Poverty［EB/
OL］. http: //world.people.com.cn/n1/2022/0809/c1002-32497677.html.

［24］IMF: Fiji's Economy Rebounds Strongly On Tourism Recovery［EB/OL］.
http: //dmc-global.com/news/guonei/6339.html.

［25］Deininger Klaus, Ali Daniel Ayalew, Fang Ming. Impact of the Russian
Invasion on Ukrainian Farmers' Productivity, Rural Welfare, and Food Security
［EB/OL］. Policy Research Working Papers, 2023, 10464. http: //hdl.handle.
net/10986/39911 License: CC BY 3.0 IGO.

［26］Global Assessment Report on Disaster Risk Reduction 2022: Our World at
Risk: Transforming Governance for a Resilient Future［R］. United Nations Office for
Disaster Risk Reduction（UNDRR）.

［27］Global Humanitarian Assistance Report 2022［R］. 2022.

［28］Government of Canada: Smart Renewable and Electrification Pathways

Program［EB/OL］. https: //natural-resources.canada.ca/climate-change/green-infrastructure-programs/sreps/23566.

［29］Hart Tom, Lauren Blaxter.Ceasefire Divisions: Violations of the Truce with Gaza Lead to Rising Political Pressures in Israel［EB/OL］. Armed Conflict Location & Event Data Project（ACLED）. https: //www.acleddata.com/2018/11/23/ceasefire-divisions-violations-of-the-truce-with-gaza-lead-to-rising-political-pressures-in-israel/.

［30］John Creamer, Emily A. Shrider, Kalee Burns, Frances Chen. Poverty in the United States: 2021 Current Population Reports［R］. https: //www.census.gov/library/publications/2022/demo/p60-277.html.

［31］Liu Meijun. National Rural Revitalization Bureau Issued A Document 24 Measures to Consolidate and Expand the Results of Poverty Alleviation［EB/OL］. https: //finance.qianlong.com/2022/0602/7260687.shtml.

［32］Statistics Canada: Disaggregated Trends in Poverty From the 2021 Census of Population［EB/OL］. https: //www12.statcan.gc.ca/census-recensement/2021/as-sa/98-200-x/2021009/98-200-x2021009-eng.pdf.

［33］Statistics Canada: Low Income Statistics by Age, Sex and Economic Family Type［EB/OL］. https: //www150.statcan.gc.ca/t1/tbl1/en/tv.action?pid=1110013501.

［34］The United Nations Development Programme Human Development Report Office. Global Multidimensional Poverty Index 2019［R］. 2019.

［35］The United Nations Development Programme Human Development Report Office. Global Multidimensional Poverty Index 2023［R］. 2023.

［36］The United Nations Development Programme Human Development Report Office. Global Multidimensional Poverty Index 2022［R］. 2022.

［37］The White House: FACT SHEET: CHIPS and Science Act Will Lower Costs, Create Jobs, Strengthen Supply Chains, and Counter China［EB/OL］. https: //www.whitehouse.gov/briefing-room/statements-releases/2022/08/09/fact-sheet-chips-and-science-act-will-lower-costs-create-jobs-strengthen-supply-chains-and-counter-china/.

［38］World Bank, OECD, UNICEF, UNESCO Institute For Statistics. Learning Recovery to Education Transformation Insights and Reflections From the 4th Survey on National Education Responses to COVID-19 School Closures［R］.2022.

［39］World Bank, UNESCO. Education Finance Watch［R］. 2022.

［40］UNESCAP. Asia-Pacific Disaster Report 2021［R］. 2023.

［41］UNICEF, Tanzania. COVID-19 Response: Nutrition［R］. 2020.

［42］United Nations. 2030 Agenda For Sustainable Development［R］. 2016.

［43］United Nations. World Economic Situation and Prospects 2023［R］. 2023.

［44］World Bank, Office of the Chief Economist for the Africa Region. Assessing Africa's Policies And Institutions［R］. 2022.

［45］World Bank. East Asia and the Pacific Economic Update［R］. 2023.

［46］World Bank. Global Economic Prospects 2023［R］. 2023.

［47］World Bank. Macro Poverty Outlook 2023［R］. 2023.

［48］World Bank. Poverty and Shared Prosperity 2022［R］. 2022.

［49］World Bank. The Destiny of Turbulence: The Long Term Impact of Rising Prices and Food Security on the Middle East and North Africa［R］. 2023.

全球减贫与发展经验分享系列
The Sharing Series on Global Poverty
Reduction and Development Experience

2024 Annual Report of International Poverty Reduction

Edited by International Poverty Reduction Center in China

2024 Annual Report of International Poverty Reduction

Research Group

International Poverty Reduction Center in China

Li Xin, Xu Liping, He Shengnian, Liu Huanhuan, Yao Yuan, Wu Liming

Central University of Finance and Economics

Gao Boyang, Dai Juncheng, Ou Bianling, Wang Yourong, Zhang Peng, Jiang Tao

Other Editors and Writers

Meng Yue, Jiang Yiyao, Li Zhenzhen, Zhao Kanghua, Han Xiangting, Zheng Meixin, Feng Yuerong, Zhou Wenjing, Pi Fuling, Chen Qi

Preface

The eradication of poverty has always been a wish to be fulfilled. The history of humankind is the history of relentless struggle against poverty. As the world's largest developing country with a population of 1.4 billion, China had long been plagued by poverty because of its weak foundations and uneven development. Ending poverty, improving people's well-being and realizing common prosperity are the essential requirements of socialism and important missions of the Communist Party of China (CPC). In order to fulfill this solemn political commitment, over the past century, the CPC has united and led the Chinese people to wage a long and arduous struggle against poverty with unwavering faith and will. After the launch of reform and opening up, China has carried out well-conceived and well-organized initiatives for development-driven poverty alleviation on a massive scale, and devoted its focus to releasing and developing productive forces and to ensuring and improving public wellbeing, securing great and unprecedented achievements in the process. Since the 18th CPC National Congress, the CPC Central Committee with Xi Jinping at its core has prioritized poverty elimination in its governance. President Xi Jinping has assumed leadership, made plans and directed in person in order to implement the basic policy of a targeted strategy in poverty alleviation and mobilize the whole Party, the entire nation and all sectors of society, thus scoring the largest battle against poverty and benefiting the largest number of people in human history.

The complete victory in the battle against poverty is inseparable from the organic combination of a capable government and an effective market. Over the eight years since the 18th CPC National Congress, the CPC Central Committee with Xi Jinping at its core has centrally and uniformly led the fight against poverty, leveraged the political advantages of the country's socialist system with Chinese characteristics which can bring together the resources necessary to accomplish great tasks, and placed poverty reduction in a prominent position in national governance, providing strong political and organizational guarantees for the fight against poverty. The active participation of market and social forces has been widely mobilized, with the implementation of actions such as the "Ten Thousand Enterprises Helping Ten Thousand Villages" campaign, to encourage private enterprises, social organizations and individual citizens to participate in the fight against poverty, and facilitate the agglomeration of factors such as capital, talent and technology in poverty-stricken areas. By the end of 2020, all of the 98.99 million rural residents, 832 counties, and 128,000 villages that fell below the current poverty line had been lifted out of poverty. Regional poverty had been eliminated on the whole, and the arduous task of eradicating absolute poverty had been completed. China has built the largest education, social security, and healthcare system in the world, and achieved rapid development in step with large-scale poverty reduction, and economic transformation in step with the elimination of extreme poverty.

China has always been an active advocate, strong promoter, and important contributor to the international cause of poverty reduction. According to the World Bank's international poverty line, since reform and opening up in 1978, the number of people lifted out of poverty in China accounted for more than 70 percent of the global total and 80 percent of that in East Asia and the Pacific over the same period. China is home to nearly one fifth of the world's population. Its complete eradication of extreme poverty – the first target of the United Nations 2030 Agenda for Sustainable Development – 10 years ahead of schedule, is a milestone in the history of the Chinese nation and the history of humankind, making an important contribution to the global poverty alleviation.

On the basis of the national conditions and the understanding of the patterns underlying poverty alleviation, China has pioneered a Chinese path to poverty alleviation, given shape to Chinese theory on fighting poverty, and created a "China example" of poverty reduction. Adherence to the people-centered development philosophy, and unswervingly following the path of common prosperity are the fundamental driving force behind China's poverty reduction.

Highlighting poverty alleviation in the governance of China, all CPC members, from top leaders to the grassroots officials work together towards the same goal. China has strengthened top-level design and strategic planning, mobilized forces from all quarters to participate in poverty alleviation, improved the institutional system for poverty eradication, and maintained the consistency and stability of policies. Eradicating poverty through development, China's experience with poverty alleviation has proven that development is essential to solving many of its problems, including poverty and is the most reliable path towards a more prosperous life. Pressing ahead with poverty alleviation based on reality, China has constantly adjusted and reformed its strategies and policies as circumstances and local conditions change. The strategy of targeted poverty alleviation has been the magic weapon for winning the battle against poverty, while the development-driven approach has emerged as the distinctive feature of China's path to poverty reduction. Letting the poor residents play the principal role, China has committed to mobilizing the enthusiasm, initiative, and creativity of impoverished people and inspiring them with the motivation to fight poverty, so that they can benefit from success in the undertaking of poverty alleviation and at the same time contribute to development in China.

Following the decisive victory in the fight against poverty, the Chinese Government has set out a five-year transition period for counties lifted out of poverty for consolidating and expanding these achievements, and comprehensively promoting rural revitalization. In accordance with the deployment of the 20th CPC National Congress, on the new journey of comprehensively promoting the rejuvenation of the Chinese nation on all fronts through a Chinese path to modernization, China is advancing rural revitalization across the board, building a beautiful and harmonious countryside that is desirable to live and work in, and moving towards the higher goal of realizing the all-round human development and common prosperity for all. China's exploration and practice of consolidating and expanding the achievements in poverty alleviation and rural revitalization will continue to provide new Chinese experience and wisdom for human poverty reduction and rural development, and contribute to the promotion of building a community with a shared future for mankind free of poverty.

In the face of new trends and features in the international situation, President Xi Jinping has put forward the Belt and Road Initiative, the Global Development Initiative and other common global actions, with poverty reduction as a key area of cooperation, and has endeavored to promote the building of a community with a shared future for mankind free of poverty and with common development. It has become a global consensus to strengthen the sharing of international experience in poverty reduction and rural development and to contribute to the global poverty reduction and development process.

To this end, since 2019, the International Poverty Reduction Center in China (IPRCC) and the Bill & Melinda Gates Foundation have jointly implemented international cooperation projects. With persistence in carefully planning the project topics from a policy-based and future-oriented perspective, we are committed to leading the frontier hot spots and research trends of poverty reduction and rural development at home and abroad. We have always insisted on bringing China's poverty reduction and rural development experience into line with international standards, explaining China's poverty reduction and rural revitalization path through the international discourse system, and promoting the international dissemination of China's poverty reduction and rural development experience. So far, more than 30 research projects have been implemented, and a number of research results in various forms and with wide influence have been formed, some of which have been released in relevant international exchange activities.

In order to implement the Global Development Initiatives and further promote global exchanges and cooperation on poverty reduction and rural development, IPRCC has carefully sorted out the research results and launched four series of books, including the Sharing Series on Global Poverty Reduction and Development Experience, the Sharing Series on China's Poverty Reduction and Development Experience, the Sharing Series on International Rural Development Experience, and the Sharing Series on China's Rural Revitalization Experience.

The Sharing Series on Global Poverty Reduction and Development

Experience aims to track the progress of global poverty reduction, analyze the trends of global poverty reduction and development, summarize and share the experiences of countries in poverty reduction, and provide knowledge products for promoting the United Nations 2030 Agenda for Sustainable Development and participating in global poverty governance. This series mainly includes global poverty reduction knowledge products, such as *Annual Report on International Poverty Reduction and Theory and Frontier Issues in International Poverty Reduction,* as well as regional poverty reduction knowledge products covering Africa, ASEAN, South Asia, Latin America and the Caribbean.

The Sharing Series on China's Poverty Reduction and Development Experience aims to tell the story of China's poverty reduction, share China's poverty reduction experience with the international community, and provide practical experience for the majority of developing countries to achieve poverty reduction and development. This series focuses on China's experience and practices in targeted poverty alleviation, poverty eradication as well as consolidation and expansion of poverty eradication achievements, and forms knowledge products for sharing China's poverty reduction experience based on international perspectives.

The Sharing Series on International Rural Development Experience focuses on the history, policies and practices of international rural development, compares the experiences and practices of rural development between China and other countries, and provides knowledge products for exchange and mutual understanding for the cause of global rural development. This series mainly includes *Annual Report on International Rural Revitalization, Comparative Analysis Report on International Experience in Rural Governance, Urban-Rural Integrated Development and Rural Revitalization in Counties,* and other research results.

The Sharing Series on China's Rural Revitalization Experience focuses on telling the story of China's rural revitalization, summarizing the experiences, practices and typical cases of rural revitalization in time, and providing references for domestic and foreign policy makers and researchers. This series mainly focuses on rural development, rural planning, common prosperity and other topics, summarizes relevant policies, experiences and practices, and develops and compiles typical cases based on international perspectives.

Finally, I would like to extend my heartfelt appreciation to all the relevant project teams, publishers and editors who have worked diligently for the publication of the series, as well as the government agencies, universities and research institutes, social organizations and friends from all walks of life who have shown their concern and support for IPRCC. All these series have been generously funded by the Bill & Melinda Gates Foundation and have received careful guidance and assistance by the China Office of the Gates Foundation, for which we would like to express our heartfelt thanks.

Global poverty reduction and rural development are dynamic and ever-changing. The book is far from exhaustive, so we look forward to receiving comments from the readers of the books.

Liu Junwen

Director General of the International Poverty Reduction Center in China

January, 2024

Introduction

In the past two decades, noteworthy strides have been made in human development. These achievements include a substantial reduction in global absolute poverty, marked advancements in human health, increased access to education, and an overall improvement in people's quality of life. Nevertheless, poverty alleviation remains a vital and pressing concern for the global community. The COVID-19 pandemic has reversed two decades of progress in poverty reduction, pushing tens of millions of individuals back into absolute poverty and presenting unprecedented challenges to global poverty alleviation efforts.

In the pursuit of global development objectives and the advancement of a world characterized by poverty eradication and shared prosperity, the International Poverty Reduction Center in China (IPRCC) and the Central University of Finance and Economics (CUFE) are proud to continue the tradition of publishing 2024 *Annual Report of International Poverty Reduction*. Building upon the foundation of the previous editions released in 2021 and 2022, this year's report aims to comprehensively assess the global poverty alleviation progress in the aftermath of the COVID-19 crisis and maintain an ongoing commitment to monitoring the state of poverty alleviation efforts worldwide. Through this publication, we seek to foster international dialogues and collaborations that further the poverty reduction.

The report reveals the following key findings:

1. Global poverty alleviation progress. The global poverty alleviation process has rebounded to pre-pandemic levels. Under the US$2.15 standard, the global poverty rate in 2022 has declined from 9.3% in 2020 to 8.4%, with the number of people living in poverty decreasing from 719 million in 2020 to 667 million in 2022. The score of the primary Sustainable Development Goal "No poverty" (SDG1) has improved to 79.8, reinstating pre-pandemic status. The number of individuals living in multidimensional poverty and the global multidimensional poverty rate in 2023 are 1.1 billion and 18.3%, down from 1.3 billion and 23.1% in 2019, prior to the pandemic. Notably, nearly one-third of countries have halved their multidimensional poverty indices over the past 15 years.

2. **Implementation of key poverty alleviation indicators**. The global economy has recovered, but disparities in per capita GDP have widened. Global GDP reached US$101 trillion in 2022, marking an increase of 3.08% from 2021. The unemployment rate has reverted to pre-pandemic levels, standing at 5.77%. However, the disparity in per capita GDP between high-income and low-income countries remains substantial, with a ratio as high as 66.68 times. Educational development has made gradual progress, but issues of inequality persist. Over 60% of countries have initiated community mobilization efforts to reopen schools, with nearly half of the countries providing financial support for economically disadvantaged students to go back to school. The rate of basic education coverage in high-income countries remains high, and stagnates in countries of other income levels. Nutritional health has made significant strides, with the neonatal mortality rate decreasing from 23.01 per 1,000 live births in 2000 to 12.14 per 1,000 live births in 2021. However, neonatal mortality rate in low-income countries remains eight times higher than in high-income countries, and epidemics and food insecurity are hindering progress in child malnutrition. Global infrastructure continues to improve, although there is room for enhancement in impoverished countries. The proportion of people with access to clean drinking water has risen from 75.50% in 2000 to 88.32% in 2020, and the percentage of people using the Internet increased to 69.44% in 2021. Nonetheless, some African countries still face challenges, including infrastructure shortages and financing difficulties. Natural disasters are widespread, affecting a substantial population and resulting in significant economic losses. Asia has witnessed a higher frequency and variety of natural disasters from 2000 to 2022, while Africa, closely tied to climatic

changes, healthcare levels, and land degradation, has experienced the highest total damages at US $1,938,483 million, impeding progress in poverty alleviation.

3. National policy formulation and implementation's role in poverty alleviation. The formulation and implementation of national policies have played a pivotal role in the global efforts to alleviate poverty. Eradicating extreme poverty by 2030 remains the greatest global challenge. In response, many developing countries and emerging economies have meticulously designed and implemented a range of strategies, policies, and measures to combat poverty. Asia, for instance, has taken measures to tighten monetary policy, streamline poverty identification, and bolster poverty alleviation governance through the implementation of public service projects. Africa is focusing on upgrading infrastructure and public services in underserved areas while striving to enhance the efficiency of fiscal expenditures for poverty alleviation. It also promotes social cohesion and inclusiveness through youth employment and entrepreneurship. In Latin America and the Caribbean, economic recovery is being pursued through the strategic attraction of financing and capital, with a proactive exploration of special employment projects. Simultaneously, it is developing family farming and eco-agriculture, and extending sustained financial support to vulnerable groups. Oceania has unveiled a digital economy strategy aimed at reducing poverty through economic transformation, breathes new life into the tourism industry and actively develops the blue economy. In North America, a comprehensive strategy for climate and energy transformation is creating innovative employment opportunities, complemented by differentiated poverty alleviation policies and a commitment to expansionary fiscal policies. Europe is diligently promoting universal social security coverage and striving for the continual improvement of diversified employment training and support mechanisms. Moreover, international organizations such as the United Nations, the World Bank, the International Monetary Fund, and numerous developed countries have provided diverse forms of assistance to help reduce poverty on a global scale.

4. China's poverty reduction and rural revitalization. In China, after securing the complete victory in the fight against poverty, significant progress has been made in consolidating and extending the achievements in poverty alleviation as parts of efforts to promote rural revitalization. Continuous monitoring and assistance mechanisms have been enhanced to prevent populations that have been lifted out of poverty from falling back into it again. Ongoing endeavors in diverse domains, such as rural industrial development, the expansion of employment opportunities, and the cultivation of new rural collective economies, have been steadfastly pursued. All of these efforts are aimed at continually enhance the capacity of regions and individuals which have been lifted out of poverty for sustaining self-development. The results of the poverty alleviation campaign have been further consolidated and expanded, with meticulous attention devoted to the prevention of large-scale reemergence of poverty. Tangible outcomes have been achieved in the comprehensive rural revitalization, marked by substantial progress in rural development, rural infrastructure, and the enhancement of rural governance. These successes have created a domino effect, progressively advancing rural revitalization and promoting the consolidation and expansion of poverty alleviation outcomes.

5. International cooperation on poverty reduction has become a crucial global consensus. Strengthening poverty reduction cooperation and exchanges among countries will contribute to the reduction of poor populations and the enhancement of people's living standards. It is conducive to achieving global poverty reduction goals, and can facilitate the sharing of resources and technologies, thereby, jointly promoting economic development and social progress. Over the years, international organizations and institutions such as the United Nations and the World Bank have effectively promoted the poverty reduction process in underdeveloped countries by providing supports in terms of funding, technology, and human resources. Countries have actively engaged in bilateral and multilateral cooperation, sharing poverty reduction policies and measures, and jointly advancing the process of achieving the Sustainable Development Goals by 2030. On September 21, 2021, Chinese President Xi Jinping proposed the Global Development Initiative at the 76th session of the United Nations General Assembly. He pointed out that, China pledged to "join hands to address global threats and challenges, promote the building of a community with a shared future for mankind, and jointly build a better world".

In April 2022, President Xi reiterated at the Boao Forum for Asia that "humanity shares a common future", and that "all countries should follow the trend of peace, development, cooperation, and mutual benefit. They should work together towards the correct direction of building a community with a shared future for mankind, joining hands to meet challenges and cooperate in creating the future."Currently, amidst the impact of multiple factors such as the COVID-19 pandemic and slow economic recovery, strengthening international cooperation on poverty reduction and jointly promoting the realization of poverty reduction goals has become an important consensus of the international community.

The report is divided into five chapters: Chapter 1, Progress in Global Poverty Alleviation; Chapter 2, Implementation Status of Main Poverty Alleviation Issues; Chapter 3, Policy Provision and Implementation Effectiveness of Major Regions and Typical Countries in the World in Promoting Poverty Reduction; Chapter 4, China Consolidates and Expands the Achievements of Poverty Alleviation and Effectively Connects Policies and Practices with Rural Revitalization; and Chapter 5, Global Outlook for Poverty Reduction.

The primary data sources used in the report include: *Sustainable Development Report 2022*, *Sustainable Development Report 2023*; *Global Multidimensional Poverty Index 2019*, *Global Multidimensional Poverty Index 2023*; the World Bank's Poverty and Inequality Platform, *Poverty and Shared Prosperity 2022*; UNESCO-UNICEF-World Bank Survey on National Education Response to COVID-19 School Closures and UN DESA database, etc.

Chapter 1 Progress in Global Poverty Alleviation

Overview

The COVID-19 has pushed tens of millions of people back into extreme poverty, presenting an unprecedented challenge to global poverty alleviation. The international community has taken a series of proactive measures, such as economic stimulus, social investment, health security, and universal education, to respond to the impact of the pandemic and restart the poverty alleviation process. In 2022, there was significant progress in both absolute poverty and multidimensional poverty worldwide, with the global situation of multidimensional poverty is beyond pre-pandemic levels. However, there are regional disparities in the global poverty alleviation process, and some countries have not yet returned to their pre-pandemic levels of absolute poverty. There is also a variation in the structure of the multidimensional poverty population among countries of different income groups. Looking ahead, the post-pandemic global poverty alleviation process still faces multiple challenges due to economic slowdown, geopolitical conflicts, and climate risks; the multidimensional poverty process is impacted by multiple crises, but some countries have made good progress in addressing multidimensional poverty.

1.1 Poverty alleviation overview

Over the past two decades, remarkable progress has been made in human development: absolute poverty has been reduced, health has improved, access to education has increased, and lives of people have become easier. However, getting rid of poverty is still an important issue that the whole human society faces and needs to solve urgently. The outbreak of the COVID-19 has reversed 20 years of global poverty alleviation and pushed tens of millions of people back into extreme poverty, posing an unprecedented challenge to global poverty alleviation. In response to the impact of the COVID-19, the international community has taken a series of positive measures, including economic stimulus, social investment, health protection and universal education, to restart the process of poverty alleviation. It is worth noting that through unremitting efforts, the impact of the COVID-19 has gradually diminished by 2022, and the global poverty rate has returned to pre-pandemic levels.

The global poverty rate has returned to pre-pandemic levels by 2022. According to *Poverty and Shared Prosperity 2022*, the global poverty rate at the US$2.15 poverty line has fallen from 9.3% in 2020 to 8.4% in 2022, and the number of poor people has fallen from 719 million in 2020 to 667 million in 2022, which is already lower than the pre-pandemic level in 2019. "No poverty" is the first goal of the 2030 Agenda for Sustainable Development (SDG1). According to the *Sustainable Development Report 2023*, SDG1[1] score increased from 74.7 to 78.5 between 2015 and 2019. Progress has been made in the global poverty alleviation process. Affected by the COVID-19 pandemic, the SDG1 score dropped to 77.1 in 2020 and rose to 79.8 in 2022, with progress in poverty alleviation exceeding pre-pandemic levels in 2019.

Affected by multiple shocks, the global economic recovery will slow down in 2023, posing serious challenges to poverty alleviation. According to the UN's *World Economic Situation and Prospects 2024*, the world economy has been hit hard by a series of shocks, such as COVID-19, the food and energy crisis, soaring inflation, tightening debt and the climate emergency, thus the global economic growth of 2023 was 2.7%, and is expected to continue to decelerate to 2.4%, which is below the pre-pandemic growth rate of 3%. The

---

1 In September 2015, world leaders attending the United Nations Summit adopted the *2030 Agenda for Sustainable Development*, which proposed 17 Sustainable Development Goals (SDGs),and called on all countries, whether poor, rich or middle-income, to take action to promote economic prosperity while protecting the planet. The new goals state that poverty eradication must go hand in hand with a range of strategies, including promoting economic growth, addressing social needs for education, health, social protection and employment opportunities, combating climate change and protecting the environment. Among them, SDG1 is "No poverty".The overall SDG Index score is the average of the 17 SDG scores – the score calculation method is detailed in the *Sustainable Development Report 2023* – the higher the score, the better the poverty alleviation effect.

world economy will face the risk of long-term low growth, which will pose challenges to the global poverty alleviation process.

1.2 Poverty alleviation process

In order to monitor the global changes in absolute poverty and multidimensional poverty, the report has conducted a comprehensive analysis using data from multiple sources, include the United Nations' *Sustainable Development Report(2019-2023)*, *Global Sustainable Development Report 2019*, *Global Multidimensional Poverty Index(2019-2023)*, and *World Economic Situation and Prospects 2023*, as well as the World Bank's *Poverty and Shared Prosperity 2022*, *Global Economic Prospects 2023* and *Global Poverty Outlook 2023*.

1.2.1 Absolute poverty

(1) By 2022, global poverty alleviation has returned to its pre-pandemic status as governments have taken proactive measures

Since 2021, there has been a consistent decrease in the global poverty rate and the number of poor people. The COVID-19 has led to a reversal in the global poverty alleviation process, with the poverty rate and the number of poor people in 2020 marking the largest increase in over three decades. However, governments have adopted proactive fiscal and monetary policies to reduce the impact of the COVID-19 on the poor and promote the poverty alleviation, then the global poverty alleviation process has returned to the normal path by 2022 (see Figure 1.1). According to the World Bank's Poverty and Inequality Platform[1], the global poverty rate at the US$2.15 poverty line decreased from 37.89% in 1990 to 8.51% in 2019, and the number of poor people dropped from 2.06 billion to 659 million, showing an overall continuous downward trend. Influenced by factors such as the Asian financial crisis, the global poverty rate at the US$2.15 poverty line increased by 0.21% in 1998. However, in 2020, the global poverty rate at the US$2.15 poverty line increased by 0.79% compared to

---

1   See: https://pip.worldbank.org/home.

2019, an increase of approximately 3.7 times that of 1998. According to *Poverty and Shared Prosperity 2022*, the global poverty rate at the US$2.15 poverty line for the year of 2020, 2021 and 2022 were 9.3%, 8.8%, and 8.4%, respectively, with the numbers of poor people being 719 million, 690 million, and 667 million, respectively, [1] indicating that the poverty levels has returned to pre-pandemic level.

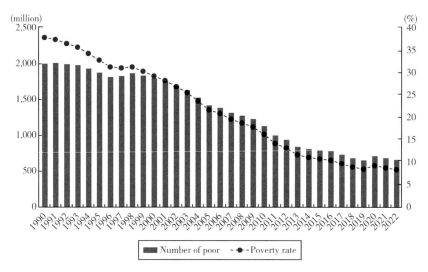

Figure 1.1 Number of people living in poverty and the poverty rate, US$2.15, 1981-2022

Source: Data from the World Bank's Poverty and Inequality Platform (2023) for 1990-2019, and data from *Poverty and Shared Prosperity 2022* for 2020-2022.

The process of eradicating poverty has been restarted, and the global poverty alleviation process is continually advancing. According to the United Nations' *Sustainable Development Report 2023*, between 2015 and 2019, the annual growth rate of SDG1 score was 1.25%. Impacted by the COVID-19, SDG1 score dropped from 78.5 in 2019 to 77.1 in 2020, a decrease of 1.78%, but recovered to 79.8 in 2022, with an annual growth rate of 1.74% from 2020 to 2022, exceeding the pre-pandemic level of 2019 (see Figure 1.2). However, the global

---

1 This data represents the latest estimate as of July 2023, which is slightly higher than the estimates in *Poverty and Shared Prosperity 2022*. According to *Poverty and Shared Prosperity 2022*, the global poverty rate in 2019 was 8.4%, with 648 million people living in poverty.

economic recovery is still influenced by various factors including inflation, policy uncertainty, and challenges in the labor market. The World Bank's *Poverty and Shared Prosperity 2022* indicates that, by the end of 2022, there were still 685 million people living in absolute poverty worldwide. It is projected that by 2030, approximately 6.8% of the global population (about 574 million people) will still be living in absolute poverty, far below the target of reducing the global absolute poverty rate to 3% by 2030. Therefore, the goal of globally eradicating absolute poverty by 2030 may not be achieved, and the global poverty alleviation process needs to be accelerated.

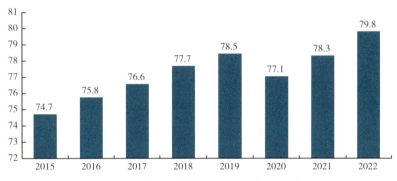

Figure 1.2   SDG1 score, 2015-2022

Source: Data from the *Sustainable Development Report 2023* for 2015-2022.

(2) Progress in poverty alleviation varies across regions. Some countries have yet to return to pre-pandemic levels

The post-pandemic poverty alleviation process not only varies across regions, but also across countries within the same region. Compared to the pre-pandemic period in 2019, in 2022, some countries within regions demonstrated a strong recovery in poverty alleviation process, while others experienced obstructions, stagnation, or even decline in their poverty alleviation process. According to the *Sustainable Development Report 2023*, the poverty rate in 2020 has increased in more than 70% of countries due to the COVID-19, and only a few countries have been less affected by the COVID-19. For example, countries such as Guyana, Brazil, Ethiopia, Djibouti and Sierra Leone have reduced the poverty rate at the US$2.15 poverty line by more than 1% compared to 2019. Among the 159 countries with available data in 2020, 114 experienced an increase in poverty rate, with 41 of these countries seeing an increase of more than 1%. By 2022, 63.64% of countries in Eastern Europe and Central Asia, and 51.06% in Sub-Saharan Africa had a lower poverty rate at the US$2.15 poverty line than post-COVID-19. In Oceania, Latin America and the Caribbean, 66.67% and 55% of countries have not returned to pre-pandemic levels, respectively (see Figure 1.3). Additionally, in Eastern Europe and Central Asia, over 90% of countries either reduced or maintained their poverty rate, swiftly overcoming the impact of the COVID-19 and continuously advancing in their poverty alleviation process. Approximately 20% of OECD countries saw an increase in their poverty rate. Except for Colombia (3.59%), Costa Rica (0.89%), and Mexico (0.76%), the increase in other countries did not exceed 0.02%.

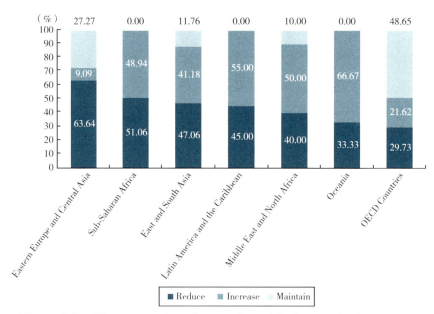

Figure 1.3　The proportion of countries with changes in the poverty rate in major regions, US$2.15, 2019-2022

Source: Calculated according to the United Nations' *Sustainable Development Report 2023*. The regional classification criteria refer to the *Sustainable Development Report 2023*.

The recovery of poverty alleviation process varies in countries of different income groups, and the recovery of poverty alleviation process in low-income

countries is relatively weak. According to the *Sustainable Development Report 2023*, in 80% of high-income countries, the poverty rate has already below or equal to levels in 2019, while in 60% of low-income countries, it has not recovered from the impact of the COVID-19 (see Figure 1.4). The higher the income level, the easier it is to rapidly recover the poverty alleviation process after shocks such as the COVID-19. Conversely, the lower the income level, the weaker the resilience in poverty levels.

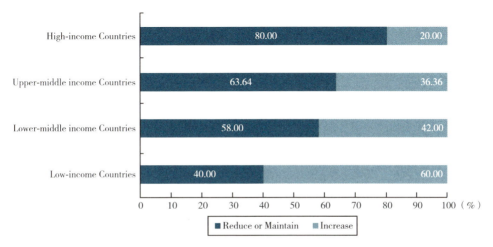

Figure 1.4   The proportion of countries with changes in the poverty rate, by income groups, US$2.15, 2019-2022

Source: Calculated according to the United Nations'*Sustainable Development Report 2023*. The income group is divided according to the World Bank's income group for fiscal year 2022.

(3) The global poverty line adjustment has little impact on the global poverty rate, and the impact varies across regions

The adjustment of the global poverty line has little impact on the absolute poverty rate and the number of poor people in the world. At the new post-pandemic poverty line, the global poverty rate and the number of poor people is slightly higher than that of the US$1.90 poverty line (see Figure 1.5). Regardless of whether it is the US$1.90 or US$2.15 poverty line, the trends in the global poverty rate and number of poor people from 1990 to 2022 are similar. The correlation coefficient for the global poverty rate between the US$1.90 and

US$2.15 poverty line is 0.9998, and for the global number of poor people, it is 0.9997, indicating nearly identical poverty characteristics at both standards. In 2020, there was a significant reversal in global poverty progress at both the US$1.90 and US$2.15 poverty line, with a larger increase in the global poverty rate at the US$2.15 poverty line. The global poverty level continued to decrease in 2021 and 2022.

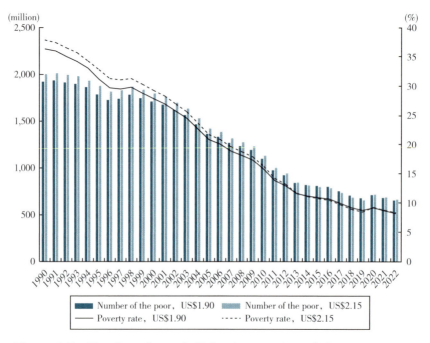

Figure 1.5   Number of people living in poverty and the poverty rate,
US$1.9 and US$2.15, 1990-2022

Source: Data of the number of people living in poverty and the poverty rate at US$1.90 and US$2.15 for 1990-2019 are from the latest estimates of the World Bank's Poverty and Inequality Platform in July 2023. The number of people living in poverty and the poverty rate at US$1.90 for 2020-2022 are calculated according to the United Nations'*Sustainable Development Report 2022*, and the number of people living in poverty and the poverty rate at US$2.15 for 2020-2022 are calculated according to the World Bank's *Poverty and Shared Prosperity 2022*.

The adjustment of the global poverty line has different effects on the poverty rate in different regions. According to the World Bank's Poverty and Inequality Platform, the poverty rate and the number of people living on less than

US$1.90 a day in 2019 decreased compared to the number based on the US$2.15 poverty line in West and Central Africa (AFW), Sub-Saharan Africa (SSA), East Asia and the Pacific (EAP), and Europe and Central Asia (ECA). The poverty rate and the number of people living in poverty increased significantly in Latin America and the Caribbean (LAC), while there was little difference in poverty in South Asia (SAS) (see Figure 1.6).

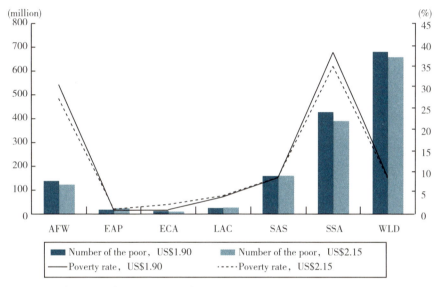

**Figure 1.6   Number of poor people and the poverty rate,
US$1.9 and US$2.15, 2019**

Source: Data of the number of poor people and the poverty rate are from the latest calculations as of July 2023 from the World Bank's Poverty and Inequality Platform.

1.2.2   Multidimensional poverty

(1) The global improvement in multidimensional poverty is better than the situation before the COVID-19, but there are regional differences

According to the *Global Multidimensional Poverty Index 2019* and the *Global Multidimensional Poverty Index 2023*, the number of people in multidimensional poverty and the poverty rate in 2023 are 1.1 billion and 18.3%, down from 1.3 billion and 23.1% before the COVID-19. The Multidimensional

Poverty Index (MPI)[1] fell the most in Sub-Saharan Africa between 2019-2023, followed by South Asia, and Latin America and the Caribbean, while the MPI increased in Europe and Central Asia. The largest decline in the poverty rate of multidimensional poverty occurred in South Asia, followed by Sub-Saharan Africa, Latin America and the Caribbean (see Figure 1.7). Overall, Sub-Saharan Africa and South Asia are making good progress in reducing multidimensional poverty.

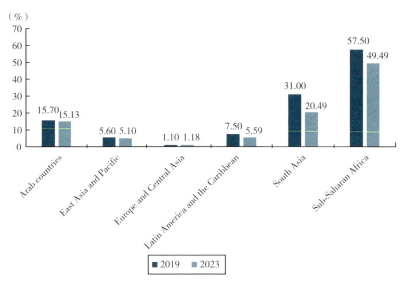

Figure 1.7   Multidimensional poverty rate by region, 2019 and 2023

Source: Calculated based on the *Global Multidimensional Poverty Index 2019* and *Global Multidimensional Poverty Index 2023*.

---

1   The Multidimensional Poverty Index (MPI) is an indicator that goes beyond income and includes access to safe drinking water, education, electricity, food and six other indicators.It was developed by the United Nations Development Programme and the Oxford Poverty and Human Development Initiative.The MPI reflects both the multidimensional poverty (H) and the intensity of multidimensional poverty (A), as well as the amount of deprivation experienced across multiple dimensions of poverty by an individual or household. Where MPI=H*A.

(2) The demographic structure of multidimensional poverty varies among countries with different income groups, and child poverty still needs continuous attention

According to the *Global Multidimensional Poverty Index 2019* and *Global Multidimensional Poverty Index 2023*, the share of poor people in lower-middle income countries decreased from 59.73% to 57.26% between 2019 and 2023, while the share of poor people in low- and upper-middle income countries increased. The *Global Multidimensional Poverty Index 2023* report shows that, the multidimensional poverty rate in the world still exceeds 50% of the total poor population. In addition, the decline rate of Multidimensional Poverty Index and multidimensional poverty rate among children is significantly lower than that of adults. The average annual decline rate of multidimensional poverty rate among children is 4.85% from 2019 to 2023, which is much lower than the average annual decline rate of 6.46% for adults. According to the *Global Multidimensional Poverty Index 2023*, 566 million children globally are in multidimensional poverty, a decline of 97 million from 2019. It is important to note that, child poverty is not only an immediate problem, but will also have long-lasting effects. Reducing child poverty levels deserves continued attention.

(3) The multidimensional poverty index has been halved in nearly a third of countries

According to the *Global Multidimensional Poverty Index 2023*, 25 out of 81 countries with long-term comparable data have managed to halve the multidimensional poverty Index over the past 15 years, and 20 countries have reduced the Multidimensional Poverty Index by more than 10% annually. The annual rate of decline in the multidimensional poverty rate in China and Kyrgyzstan was 18.46% and 15.77%, respectively (see Figure 1.8).

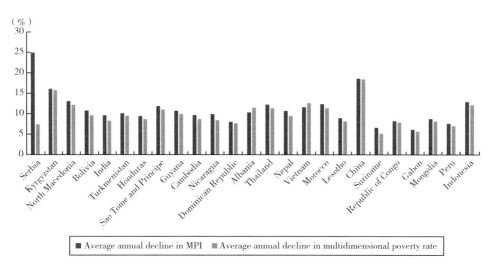

Figure 1.8　Annual rate of decline of Multidimensional Poverty Index and multidimensional poverty rate, 2000-2022

Source: Calculated based on the *Global Multidimensional Poverty Index 2019* and *Global Multidimensional Poverty Index 2023*.

1.3　Poverty alleviation outlook

1.3.1　Global poverty alleviation outlook

The global poverty alleviation process in the aftermath of the COVID-19 pandemic continues to face multiple challenges due to slowing economic growth, geopolitical conflicts and climate risks. The United Nations'*World Economic Situation and Prospects 2023* shows that, the world economy is at risk of a prolonged period of low growth, with many countries at risk of recession in 2023. According to *World Economic Situation and Prospects 2024,* global economic growth is projected to slow from an estimated 2.7% in 2023 to 2.4% in 2024. According to the *Sustainable Development Report 2023*, the process of poverty alleviation has continued to advance since the significant increase in the global poverty rate (US$2.15 per day) in 2020, and the global poverty rate fell to 7.5% in 2023, down from 8.4% in 2022. Meanwhile, SDG1 score rose to 80 in 2023, an increase of 0.25% from 2022, a slower rate of growth.

Multiple crises affect the multidimensional poverty process, but some

countries are making good progress in multidimensional poverty. Prior to the COVID-19 pandemic, 72 of the 81 countries covered by the 2019 Global Multidimensional Poverty Index saw statistically significant declines in MPI values. However, the COVID-19 pandemic has dealt a severe blow to global multidimensional poverty. According to the *Global Multidimensional Poverty Index 2022*, about 1.2 billion people live in multidimensional poverty (about 19.1%). The United Nations Development Programme estimates that, the impact of the COVID-19 pandemic on health, education and incomes will be equivalent to a six-year setback in the Human Development Index and a nine-year setback in poverty alleviation, pushing an additional 490 million people in 70 countries into multidimensional poverty. Overall, however, some countries still show better poverty alleviation. According to the *Global Multidimensional Poverty Index 2023*, out of 81 countries with comparable data, 25 countries, including Cambodia, China, Republic of Congo, Honduras, India, Indonesia, Morocco, Serbia and Viet Nam, have succeeded in halving their MPIs within a period of 4 to 12 years.

1.3.2   Regional poverty alleviation outlook

With reference to the regional classification criteria of the *Sustainable Development Report 2023*, this section divides the 193 economies into seven regions: Sub-Saharan Africa, Oceania, Eastern Europe and Central Asia, Middle East and North Africa, Latin America and the Caribbean, East and South Asia, and OECD countries.

(1) Sub-Saharan Africa

Economic growth slows in Sub-Saharan Africa. The World Bank's *Global Economic Outlook 2023* projects economic growth in Sub-Saharan Africa at 3.2% in 2023, rising to 3.9% in 2024. Sustained economic growth is one of the key drivers of poverty alleviation. According to the *Sustainable Development Report 2023*, Sub-Saharan Africa, with a poverty rate (US$2.15 per day) of 32.1%, remains the region with the highest poverty rate and the largest number of poor people in the world. The World Bank's *Macro Poverty Outlook 2023* estimates that, 8 of the 10 countries with the largest increases in global poverty since the outbreak of COVID-19 are in Sub-Saharan Africa.

The process of poverty alleviation in Sub-Saharan Africa continues to advance. According to the *Sustainable Development Report 2023*, the number of countries in the Sub-Saharan Africa that have returned to pre-prevalence levels of the poverty rate in 2020-2023 is increasing, from 11 to 34 (see Figure 1.9). Among the countries with a reduction of more than 3% in the poverty rate (US$2.15 per day) in Sub-Saharan Africa in 2023 compared to 2019 are Sierra Leone, Ethiopia, Benin, Nigeria, Djibouti, Democratic Republic of Congo, Togo, Burkina Faso and so on. In the face of challenges such as the COVID-19 pandemic, the poverty rate in some Sub-Saharan African countries has still not returned to pre-epidemic levels, with five countries – Somalia, Chad, Central African Republic, Malawi and the Sudan – experiencing an increase in poverty rate of more than 1% in 2023 compared to 2019.

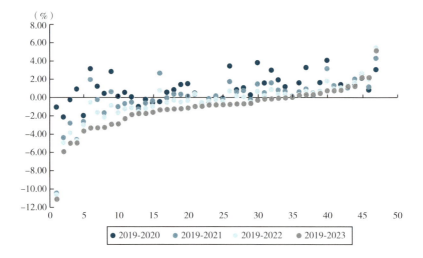

Figure 1.9   Change in the poverty rate in countries of Sub-Saharan Africa, 2020-2023, compared to 2019

Source: Calculated based on the United Nations' *Sustainable Development Report 2023.*

Sub-Saharan Africa is making good progress on the SDGs, especially SDG1. The Sustainable Development Goals (SDGs), introduced by the United Nations in 2015, aim to thoroughly address the three dimensions of development – social, economic and environmental – in an integrated manner from 2015 to

2030, with the SDG Index score reflecting a country's progress on the path to sustainable development. According to the *Sustainable Development Report 2023* and *SDG Report 2023*, Sub-Saharan Africa has been making continuous progress on the SDGs for 2015-2023, with temporary stagnation of the SDGs for 2022 and 2023 due to the impact of the COVID-19 pandemic. Poverty eradication, the overarching goal of the SDGs, progressed well for 2015-2019, with scores dropping to 2017 levels in 2020 and then beginning to rise again as the COVID-19 pandemic receded from 2021 onwards (see Figure 1.10). Progress on poverty eradication, the primary objective of the Sustainable Development Goals, has been faster than the overall Sustainable Development Goals.

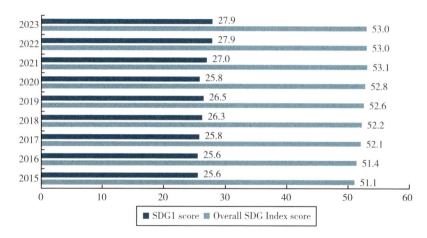

Figure 1.10　Overall SDG Index scores and SDG1 score for Sub-Saharan Africa, 2015-2023

Source: UN, *Sustainable Development Report 2023*.

(2) Eastern Europe and Central Asia

Affected by the COVID-19 pandemic, economic growth in Eastern Europe and Central Asia slows but picks up. According to the latest data from *Global Economic Prospects 2023*, economic growth in the Europe and Central Asia region fell to 1.2% in 2022, with output falling by 20.2% in Eastern Europe. The economic growth forecast for Europe and Central Asia increased from 0.1% to 1.4%, and economic growth is expected to return to 2.7% in 2024-2025.

Poverty levels vary widely within Eastern Europe and Central

Asia. According to the *Sustainable Development Report 2023*, the poverty rate(US$2.15)in 2023 is 7.06% in Eastern Europe and Central Asia. In 20 of the 22 countries for which data are available, their poverty rates are less than 3%, with the exception of Georgia and Afghanistan. In 2023, the poverty rate has fallen below 2019 levels in 21 countries (except Afghanistan). Tajikistan's sustained and rapid economic growth in recent years has driven down the poverty rate, falling to 2.51% in 2023, roughly halving compared to 2019.

Progress on the Sustainable Development Goals in the Eastern Europe and Central Asia region has been slow. Before the pandemic, Eastern Europe and Central Asia has seen a steady increase in overall SDG Index score and SDG1 scores (see Figure 1.11), with the SDG1 score growing at an average annual rate of 0.75% compared to 2015, which is much higher than the average annual rate of growth of the overall SDG Index score (0.44%). Affected by the pandemic and other factors, compared to 2019, SDG1 score in 2023 slightly increased by 0.42%. However, the overall SDG Index score decreased by 5.3%.

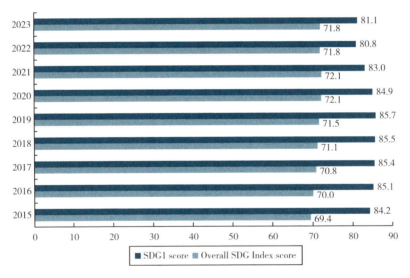

Figure 1.11   Overall SDG Index score and SDG1 score for Eastern Europe and Central Asia, 2015-2023

Source: UN, *Sustainable Development Report 2023*.

Overall, the COVID-19 pandemic has slowed down economic growth and reversed poverty alleviation in Eastern Europe and Central Asia. The recovery in this region is still affected by a combination of rising inflation, supply chain disruptions, policy uncertainty and labour market challenges. The poverty alleviation in the region has yet to return to its pre-pandemic level.

(3) Middle East and North Africa

Economic growth in the Middle East and North Africa has fallen short of expectations, inflation remaining high, and food security risks having increased. According to *Regional Economic Outlook: the Middle East and Central Asia*, published by International Monetary Fund (IMF) in May 2023, despite global shocks in 2022, due to the strong domestic demand and a rebound in oil production in the Middle East and North Africa countries, the economy of the Middle East and North Africa grow higher than expected, with real GDP growth of 5.3%. According to *Conflict and Debt in the Middle East and North Africa* released by the World Bank in April 2024, the economic growth rate of the Middle East and North Africa was 1.9% in 2023, and it is projected to grow by 2.7% in 2024. The region has returned to the low growth levels of the decade preceding the pandemic due to the weak growth, rising debts, and increasing uncertainty caused by the conflict in the Middle East. According to the *Altered Destinies: The Long-Term Effects of Rising Prices and Food Insecurity in the Middle East and North Africa* released by the World Bank in 2023, the inflation in the region is expected to remain high at 14.8% in 2023, falling slightly in 2024. The high inflation is expected to increase food security risks in the region by 24% to 33%, leaving about one-fifth of the population potentially at risk of food security.

Progress in poverty alleviation in the Middle East and North Africa has returned to pre-pandemic levels, but progress has been slow. According to the United Nations' *Sustainable Development Report 2023*, the poverty rate in Egypt, Iran, Jordan and Algeria is lower in 2023 compared to the period before the COVID-19 pandemic. However, the poverty rate in some countries of the Middle East is still higher than the pre-pandemic level in 2019 due to high prices, tightening macro policies, and regional conflicts. According to the World Bank, Middle East and North Africa continues to see a small increase in absolute poverty between 2019 and 2022, rising from 33 million people in 2019 to 36.9 million in 2022, an additional 3.3 million people in absolute poverty. In terms of SDG progress, on the one hand, the SDG index continued to improve between 2015 and 2023, with the first decrease in 2020 due to the impact of the COVID-19 pandemic; since then, the SDG process has been recovering, but slowly. On the other hand, the process of eradicating poverty(SDG1) has not recovered. The overall SDG Index score and SDG1 score in 2023 increased by 1.1% and 0.3%, respectively (see Figure 1.12).

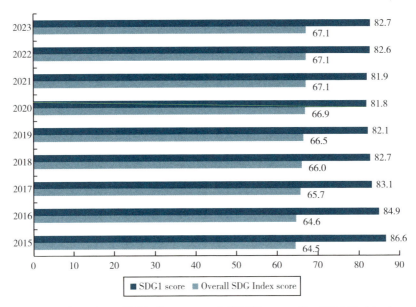

Figure 1.12 Overall SDG score and SDG1 score for Middle East and North Africa, 2015-2023

Source: UN, *Sustainable Development Report 2023*.

(4) Latin America and the Caribbean

Economic growth in Latin America and the Caribbean has slowed. According to the *World Economic Outlook* issued by the International Monetary Fund (IMF) in April 2024, the economy of Latin America and the Caribbean grew by 2.3% in 2023, and it is projected that the economic growth rates of this region will be 2% in 2024 and 2.5% in 2025.

Poverty levels in Latin America and the Caribbean have continued to decline. The poverty rate in Latin America and the Caribbean has declined steadily since 1990. According to the World Bank's Poverty and Inequality Platform, the poverty rate in Latin America and the Caribbean follow similar trends, with the poverty rate at US$2.15 slightly higher than that at US$1.90, and the poverty rate (US$2.15) in 2021 is 0.37% higher than in 2019 (see Figure 1.13). According to the *Sustainable Development Report 2023*, the poverty rate (US$ 2.15) was 6.1% in Latin America and the Caribbean in 2023.

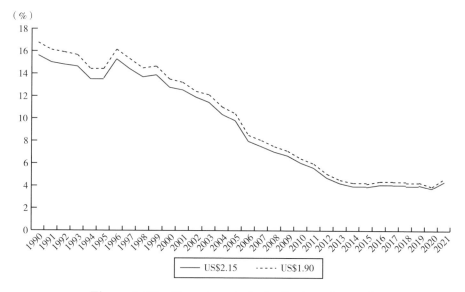

Figure 1.13   Poverty rate in Latin America and the Caribbean, 1990-2021

Source: World Bank, Poverty and Inequality Platform.

There are differences in the recovery of poverty alleviation among countries within the Latin American and Caribbean. According to *Sustainable Development Report 2023*, in Guyana, Brazil, Nicaragua, and Honduras, the poverty rate (US$2.15) fall by more than 1% in 2023 compared to 2019, with 6.56%, 3.98%, 1.89%, and 1.59%, respectively. However, in Ecuador, Haiti, and Venezuela, the process of poverty reduction has not yet recovered to 2019 levels in 2023 due to regional conflicts and the COVID-19 pandemic.

Progress on the Sustainable Development Goals, especially the overarching objectives in Latin America and the Caribbean has been slow but consistently favorable. According to the *Sustainable Development Report 2023*, the overall SDG Index score increased from 69.4 in 2019 to 70.2 in 2023, while the SDG1 score increased from 80.8 to 84 in 2019, indicating that the progress of SDG1 in Latin America and the Caribbean is faster than the progress of overall goals of Sustainable Development Goals(see Figure 1.14).

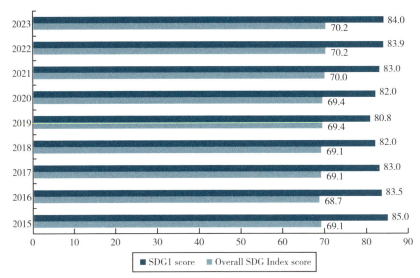

Figure 1.14 Overall SDG Index score and SDG1 score for Latin America and the Caribbean, 2015-2023

Source: UN, *Sustainable Development Report 2023.*

(5) East and South Asia

Accelerated economic growth and rapid recovery of the poverty alleviation process in East and South Asia. According to the World Bank's *Reviving Growth: East Asia and the Pacific Economic Update, April,2023*, economic activity in most developing countries in region has recovered from the shock of the COVID-19 pandemic. According to *Asian Development Outlook 2024,* released by the Asian Development Bank in April 2024, the outlook for the Asia and Pacific region remains robust following the post-pandemic recovery. The growth rate is projected to be 4.9% in 2024 and 2025. Specifically, in East Asia, the GDP growth rate rebounded from 2.9% in 2022 to 4.7% in 2023, and it is anticipated to be 4.3% in 2024. Meanwhile, in South Asia, the GDP growth rate was 5.4% in 2023, and it is expected to rise to 5.8% in 2024.

South Asia was one of the regions hit the most by the COVID-19 pandemic, but poverty levels in most South Asian countries are already lower compared to the levels before the COVID-19 pandemic. The region is one of the most densely populated in the world in terms of total population and poverty density. The extremely high population density and poverty alleviation have increased the pressure for economic recovery and poverty alleviation in South Asia. The United Nations' *Sustainable Development Report 2023* projects poverty rate(US$2.15) of 2.41% in South Asia in 2023, with the vast majority of South Asian countries seeing their poverty rate fall below the level of 2019. According to the *Sustainable Development Report 2023*, poverty rate in Bangladesh, Indonesia, Nepal, and Pakistan in 2023 are projected to decrease by 5.56%, 1.595%, 1.06%, and 1%, respectively, compared to 2019. However, poverty rates of Sri Lanka, Timor-Leste, and Myanmar were still higher in 2023 than in 2019.

Progress on the Sustainable Development Goals (SDGs) in the East and South Asia continues to be favorable, with a sustained increase in SDG1 score, and the overall SDG Index score. According to the *Sustainable Development Report 2023*, the East and South Asia continued to improve its SDG score between 2015 and 2023, increasing from 63 to 67.2. As a result of the COVID-19 pandemic, the score for SDG1 targets of eradicating poverty has decreased to 2018 levels and increased to 89.7 in 2023, a slight increase from 2022. On a country-by-country basis, the vast majority of East and South Asian countries are already at a better level of poverty alleviation than in 2019, however, poverty alleviation gains in Laos, Sri Lanka, Myanmar, and Mongolia need to be further consolidated (see Figure 1.15).

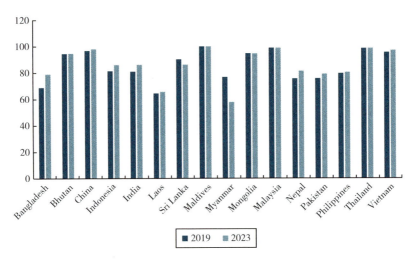

Figure 1.15   SDG1 score for countries in East and South Asia, 2019 and 2023

Source: UN, *Sustainable Development Report 2023*.

(6) OECD countries

Countries of the Organization for Economic Co-operation and Development (OECD) are on a better economic footing, but the recovery from the COVID-19 pandemic remains fragile. According to the OECD *Economic Outlook*, June 2023, GDP growth in OECD countries is projected to be 1.4% in 2024, with inflation declining from 9.4% in 2022 to 6.6% in 2023 and to 4.3% in 2024 as a result of tightening of monetary policy, lower energy and food prices, and reduced supply bottlenecks.

OECD countries as a whole have very low levels of absolute poverty. According to the latest World Bank income grouping criteria, 34 of the 38 OECD member countries belong to the high-income group, with only Costa Rica, Türkiye, Colombia and Mexico belonging to the upper-middle income countries, which has a higher overall level of economic development. According to the United Nations'*Sustainable Development Report 2023*, the poverty rate for OECD countries were 1.3% (US$2.15 per day) and 2.2% (US$3.65 per day), respectively , both of which were below 3%. In terms of Sustainable Development Goals, the SDG1 score of OECD countries is the highest across regions, and is well ahead of the other SDGs, with the overall SDG Index score increasing to

77.8 in 2023. The SDG1 score of OECD countries was already as high as 97.3 in 2019 before the COVID-19 pandemic, dropping to 96.5 in 2020 and recovering to 97 in 2023. Between 2015 and 2023, OECD countries continued to improve in terms of SDGs, but progress was slowed due to the impact of the COVID-19 pandemic in 2021 and 2022 (see Figure 1.16).

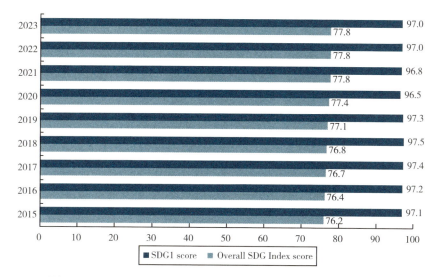

Figure 1.16　Overall SDG Index score and SDG1 score for OECD countries, 2015-2023

Source: UN, *Sustainable Development Report 2023*.

There are differences in absolute poverty levels among OECD countries. According to the UN's *Sustainable Development Report 2023*, the poverty rate(US$2.15) in the high-income OECD countries ranges between 0.01% and 1.13%, and the poverty rate (US$3.65) ranges between 0.01% and 3.75%, However, in the upper-middle income OECD countries, the poverty rate ranged from 0.76% to 9.725% (US$2.15) and from 1.39% to 16.06% (US$3.65), respectively (see Table 1.1). SDG1 score of OECD countries is high. In 2023, in terms of SDG1 score, Chile was the lowest (96.4) among high-income OECD countries, and 25 high-income OECD countries were higher than 99. In 2023, among middle- and high-income OECD countries, the SDG1 scores in Colombia, Mexico, Costa Rica and Türkiye are 77.7, 86.3, 93.8 and 98.1, respectively.

Table 1.1   **Poverty levels of OECD countries, 2023**

Country Code	Country	Income Group	Poverty Rate (US$2.15,%)	Poverty Rate (US$3.65,%)	SDG1 Score
AUS	Australia	High income	0.34	0.43	99.30
AUT	Austria	High income	0.29	0.36	99.50
BEL	Belgium	High income	0.23	0.4	99.50
CAN	Canada	High income	0.20	0.27	99.60
CHE	Switzerland	High income	0.23	0.39	99.50
CHL	Chile	High income	0.01	3.75	96.40
CZE	Czech Republic	High income	0.05	0.07	99.90
DEU	Germany	High income	0.26	0.32	99.50
DNK	Denmark	High income	0.35	0.56	99.20
ESP	Spain	High income	0.59	0.88	98.70
EST	Estonia	High income	0.01	0.01	100.00
FIN	Finland	High income	0.18	0.31	99.60
FRA	France	High income	0.14	0.18	99.70
GBR	United Kingdom	High income	0.50	0.72	99.00
GRC	Greece	High income	0.27	0.60	99.20
HUN	Hungary	High income	0.47	0.77	98.90
IRL	Ireland	High income	0.02	0.04	99.90
ISL	Iceland	High income	0.07	0.09	99.90
ISR	Israel	High income	0.67	0.94	98.60
ITA	Italy	High income	1.13	1.77	97.50
JPN	Japan	High income	0.36	0.47	99.30
KOR	Republic of Korea	High income	0.25	0.36	99.50
LTU	Lithuania	High income	0.01	0.01	100.00
LUX	Luxembourg	High income	0.01	0.02	100.00
LVA	Latvia	High income	0.01	0.01	100.00
NLD	Netherlands	High income	0.32	0.53	99.30
NOR	Norway	High income	0.34	0.56	99.20
NZL	New Zealand	High income	–	–	–
POL	Poland	High income	0.42	0.69	99.00
PRT	Portugal	High income	0.02	0.05	99.90
SVK	Slovak Republic	High income	0.37	0.61	99.20
SVN	Slovenia	High income	0.25	0.44	99.40
SWE	Sweden	High income	0.50	0.79	98.90
USA	United States	High income	0.55	0.78	98.90

Continued

Country Code	Country	Income Group	Poverty Rate (US$2.15,%)	Poverty Rate (US$3.65,%)	SDG1 Score
COL	Colombia	Upper-middle income	9.72	16.06	77.70
CRI	Costa Rica	Upper-middle income	2.19	4.86	93.80
MEX	Mexico	Upper-middle income	5.76	10.06	86.30
TUR	Türkiye	Upper-middle income	0.76	1.39	98.10

Source: Data are from the *Sustainable Development Report 2023*. Income group criteria modelled on the World Bank's FY2022 income subgroups. "−" indicates missing data.

There are differences in relative poverty levels among OECD countries. Unlike middle-income and low-income countries, poverty in high-income countries is mainly manifested as relative poverty. According to the UN's *Sustainable Development Report 2023*, the relative poverty rate (adjusted by tax and transfer payments) varies among OECD countries (see Figure 1.17). In the high-income group, the relative poverty rate in 2023 was lowest in Iceland (4.9%), and highest in Latvia (17.3%), with a median of 10.25% among the 34 high-income countries. In 2023, among the upper-middle income countries, the relative poverty rate of Türkiye, Mexico and Costa Rica were 15%, 16.6% and 20.3%, respectively.

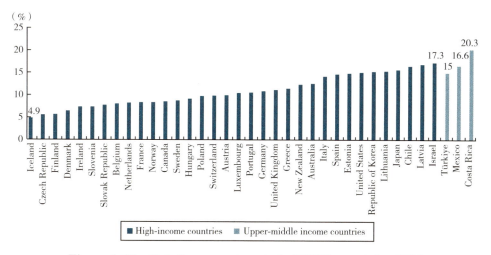

Figure 1.17　Relative poverty rate in OECD countries, 2023

(7) Oceania

The countries in Oceania are polarized in terms of poverty, with large differences among countries, concentrations of poverty, and varying rates of progress in poverty alleviation. Absolute poverty in Oceania countries is concentrated in the Melanesian region, which accounts for more than 90% of the poor. According to the UN's *Sustainable Development Report 2023*, there was more room for improvement of SDGs in Oceania than other regions, with the SDG1 score accounting for less than 70% of the overall SDG Index score. Before and after the COVID-19 pandemic, SDG1 score improved amidst fluctuations, with SDG1 score decreasing by 13.6% in 2020 compared to 2019, from 37.8 to 32.6, as a result of the COVID-19 pandemic, and with a continued decrease in SDG1 score to 32 in 2021, and a recovery to 35.6 in 2023 (see Figure 1.18).

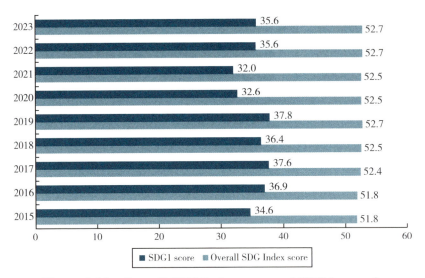

Figure 1.18   Overall SDG Index score and SDG1 score for Oceania, 2015-2023

Source: UN, *Sustainable Development Report 2023*.

Absolute poverty rate are lower in high- and middle-income countries in Oceania, and higher in low- and middle-income Oceanian countries, although there are exceptions. According to the UN's *Sustainable Development Report 2023*, in 2023, the poverty rate (US$2.15) of two upper-middle income countries in Oceania – Tonga and Fiji – were 1.02% and 2%, respectively, which were both less than 3%; although Samoa is a lower-middle income country, its poverty rate (US$2.15), which was 1.23% in 2023, was well below 3% (see Figure 1.19).

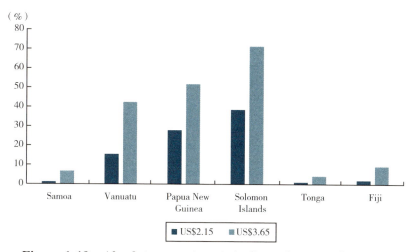

Figure 1.19   Absolute poverty rate in Oceania countries, 2023

Source: UN, *Sustainable Development Report 2023.*

Overall, poverty levels are lower in OECD countries, East Asia and South Asia between 2015 and 2023. The progress of poverty alleviation is the greatest in East Asia and South Asia; although poverty levels were higher in Sub-Saharan Africa and Oceania, but the progress of poverty alleviation in Sub-Saharan Africa is the second highest. Five regions–Eastern Europe and Central Asia, the Middle East and North Africa, Latin America and the Caribbean, East and South Asia, and OECD countries–are making better progress on SDG1 than on the overall Sustainable Development Goals, although SDG1 needs to be focused on in Sub-Saharan Africa and Oceania. According to the UN's *Sustainable Development Report 2023*, SDG1 score in the East and South Asia has risen from 78.5 in 2015 to 89.7 in 2023, a rise of 14.32%, with a level of poverty second only to that of the OECD countries. However, the SDG1 score Sub-Saharan Africa increases by 9.07% from 25.6 in 2015 to 27.9 in 2023, but there is still a lot of room for poverty alleviation (see Figure 1.20).

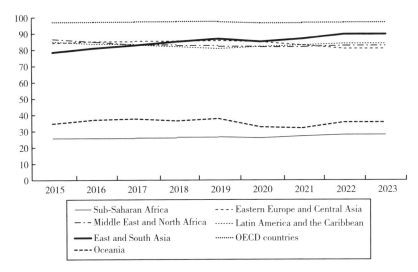

Figure 1.20   Trends of poverty alleviation in key regions, 2015-2023

Source: UN, *Sustainable Development Report 2023*.

Chapter 2　Implementation Status of Main Poverty Reduction Issues

Overview

Continuing to track the implementation of main poverty reduction issues on the basis of the 2021 and 2022 *Annual Reports of International Poverty Reduction*, this chapter discusses the progress in the five topics including education development, nutrition and health, infrastructure, natural disasters and regional conflicts in the context of the slow economic recovery from the impact of the COVID-19. These topics are intertwined and interactive with poverty. A review of their progress will help to understand the global poverty alleviation process and provide inspiration for promoting the work of poverty alleviation.

After the COVID-19, countries around the world have taken active measures to promote the recovery of teaching activities and quality. But educational inequality has deteriorated. The impact of the COVID-19 and the growing food insecurity have exacerbated the nutritional and health crisis of the poor. The restoration and improvement of infrastructure showed regional differences too, which is important for coping with the impact of the pandemic and rebuilding a better environment for mankind. Natural disasters occur in many regions, with a large number of people affected and the serious economic losses, increasing the vulnerability of the poor. International assistance is an important force in disaster response and poverty alleviation. The concentrated distribution of the regional conflicts and casualties has stymied the poverty alleviation process. Maintaining the regional peace and stability is the key to promoting poverty alleviation.

2.1 Economic recovery

2.1.1 Global GDP growth and unemployment rate have returned to pre-pandemic levels, but there is still uncertainty about the economic outlook

In 2022, the global GDP reached US$101 trillion, an increase of 3.08% compared to 2021, and the global economy has recovered from the huge impact of the pandemic. The global GDP growth rate in 2020 was –3.07%, showing a significant negative impact of the COVID-19. In 2021, the world economy achieved a recovery rebound, with the GDP growth rate reaching 6.02%. The average growth rate from 2020 to 2022 was 2.01%, and the GDP growth rate has gradually returned to the pre-pandemic level (see Figure 2.1). However, due to the multiple crises, there is still significant uncertainty in the economic outlook.

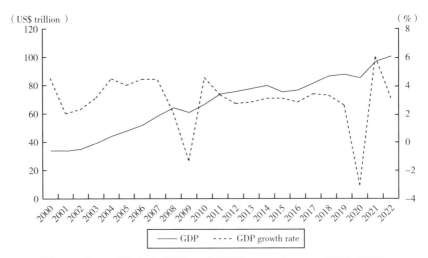

Figure 2.1　Global GDP and GDP growth rate, 2000-2022

Source: World Bank, *WDI.*

The global unemployment rate in 2022 was 5.77%, although slightly higher than 5.54% in 2019 before the pandemic, it significantly decreased from 6.9% in 2020 and 6.2% in 2021(see Figure 2.2). Regional tensions, worsening climate change, crisis of business closure and reduced investment have led to the insufficient potential for job growth. In addition, the development of automation and artificial intelligence technology will also bring new challenges to the global labor market.

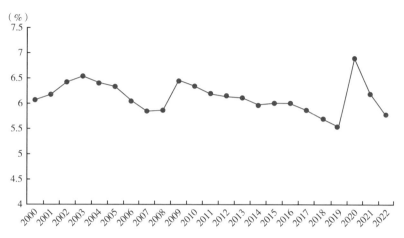

Figure 2.2　Global unemployment rate, 2000-2022

Source: World Bank, *WDI.*

　　The differences in the unemployment rates between the countries and regions are significant. There are differences in unemployment rates between high-income countries, upper-middle income countries, lower-middle income countries and low-income countries. The average unemployment rate of high-income countries is the highest and varies greatly, followed by lower-middle income countries. And the average unemployment rate of low-income countries is the lowest, which may be related to the poor quality of the statistics in these countries. Unemployment rose during the 2008 financial crisis in all income levels except low-income countries, with high-income countries rising the most, from 5.87% in 2008 to 7.95% in 2009. After 2010, the unemployment rate decreased significantly in high-income countries, while other countries remained relatively stable. Similar to the impact of the financial crisis in 2008, unemployment in the countries of different income levels rose significantly after the outbreak of the COVID-19. The unemployment rate in low-income countries rose from 5.14% in 2019 to 5.9% in 2020, then slowly fell to 5.6% in 2021 and 5.52% in 2022, respectively. The unemployment rate in lower-middle income countries rose from 5.73% in 2019 to 7.78% in 2020, and then fell to 6.79%

in 2021 and 6.46% in 2022. The unemployment rate in upper-middle income countries rose from 5.81% in 2019 to 6.52% in 2020, then fell to 6.09% in 2021 and 5.83% in 2022. The unemployment rate in high-income countries rose rapidly from 4.77% in 2019 to 6.51% in 2020, and then fell to 5.61% in 2021 and 4.51% in 2022. See Figure 2.3.

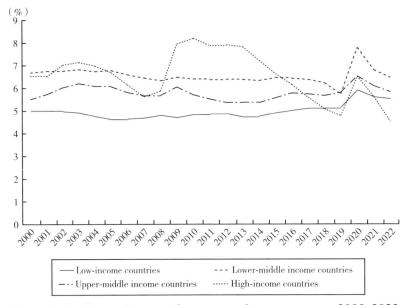

Figure 2.3　Unemployment by country income groups, 2000-2022

Source: World Bank, *WDI.*

The regional difference of unemployment rate reflects the regional imbalance of economic development and the regional difference in the labor market. The unemployment rate in Middle East and North Africa is the highest, but showing a downward trend. The unemployment rate declined from 11.92% in 2000 to 9.33% in 2019, then improved to 10.03% in 2020, affected by the pandemic, and subsequently fell to 9.63% by 2022. In Eastern Europe and Central Asia, and Latin America and the Caribbean, the unemployment rate is the second highest, which fell from 9.79% and 9.33% in 2000 to 6.64% and 7.98% in 2019, respectively. Affected by the outbreak of COVID-19, however, it improved to 7.08% and 10.2% in 2020, respectively, then subsequently decreased to 6.27% and 7.02% in 2022. The unemployment rate of Oceania was the lowest and relatively flat. It decreased from 3.67% in 2000 to 3.02% in 2019, then rose to 3.29% in 2020, 3.38% in 2021 and 3.39% in 2022, respectively. See Figure 2.4.

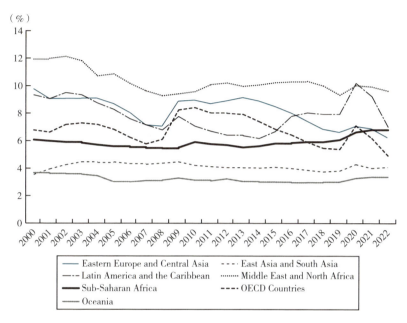

Figure 2.4   Unemployment by regions, 2000-2022

Source: World Bank, *WDI.*

2.1.2 Regional differences in GDP per capita further widened

The regional inequality in terms of economic development is constantly intensifying. In 2010, the GDP per capita of high-income countries was 33.47 times that of low-income countries. The difference in GDP per capita between high income and low-income countries in 2021 and 2022 was as high as 70.81 and 66.68 times, respectively. The GDP per capita as well as its growth rate are relatively high in the high-income countries. In 2000, the GDP per capita in the OECD countries was US$23,026.18, reaching US$39,531.43 in 2019. Due to the impact of the pandemic, it slightly decreased to US$38,341.32 in 2020 and rapidly increased to US$43,260.7 in 2022, with an annual average growth rate of 9.63% in the past three years. As for the low-income countries, the GDP per capita in Sub-Saharan Africa is the lowest and the growth rate is relatively low. It was US$632.35 in 2000, increased to US$1,625.76 in 2019, decreased to US$1,488.8 in 2020 due to the impact of the pandemic, and then increased to US$1,690.39 in 2022, with an annual average growth rate of 4.77% in the past three years, 5 percentage points lower than that of the OECD countries.

The differences in GDP per capita between high-income, upper-middle income, lower-middle income, and low-income countries were significant, and further widened. At the beginning of this century, the GDP per capita of high-income countries was about 50 times that of low-income countries. In the first decade of this century, the difference in the GDP per capita between countries gradually narrowed. In 2010, the GDP per capita of high-income countries was 33.47 times that of low-income countries. However, since 2010, the GDP per capita difference between countries has widened significantly. Especially since the outbreak of the COVID-19, the difference in the GDP per capita between high-income countries and low-income countries reached 70.81 times in 2021, and decreased to 66.68 times in 2022.

The GDP per capita in low-income countries showed a recovery trend after the pandemic, while the growth is still slow. Under the impact of the COVID-19, the GDP per capita in low-income countries fell from US$681.75 in 2019 to US$653.67 in 2020, and then slowly increased, with US$682.78 in 2021 and US$741.24 in 2022. The GDP per capita in lower-middle income countries fell from US$2,411.33 in 2019 to US$2,285.71 in 2020, then recovered to US$2,581.86 in 2021 and to US$2,542.2 in 2022. The GDP per capita in upper-middle income countries fell from US$9,548.2 in 2019 to US$9,166.46 in 2020, but quickly recovered to US$10,835.52 in 2021 and further increased t US$10,953.19 in 2022. The GDP per capita in high-income countries decreased from US$44,744.78 in 2019 to US$43,282.42 in 2020, recovered rapidly to US$47,886.78 in 2021 and further to US$49,430.33 in 2022. See Figure 2.5.

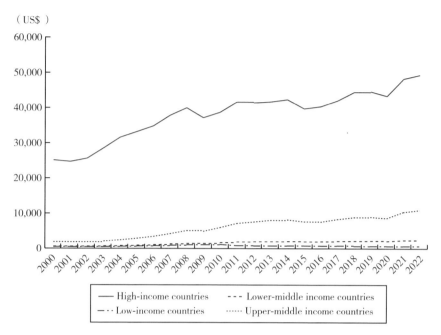

Figure 2.5   GDP per capita by country income groups, 2000-2022

Source: World Bank, *WDI.*

The regional differences in GDP per capita also show a trend of gradual expansion, reflecting the aggravation of the regional imbalance in economic development. As shown in Figure 2.6, the GDP per capita in OECD countries is not only the highest but also showed the fastest growth, reflecting the rapid economic development. Their GDP per capita rose rapidly from US$23,026.18 in 2000 to US$39,531.43 in 2019. Affected by the pandemic, it decreased slightly to US$38,341.32 in 2020, and then gradually increased to US$43,260.7 in 2022. The region with the second highest GDP per capita is Eastern Europe and Central Asia, whose GDP per capita rose rapidly from US$11,667.34 in 2000 to US$24,870.58 in 2019. However, due to the impact of the pandemic, it decreased slightly to US$23,995.15 in 2020, and then gradually increased to US$27,363.87 in 2022. In Sub-Saharan Africa, GDP per capita was the lowest and increased significantly slowly, from US$632.35 in 2000 to US$1,625.76 in 2019, then fell to US$1,488.8 in 2020, and subsequently increased to US$1,690.39 in 2022.

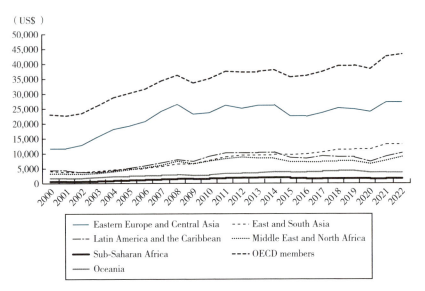

Figure 2.6   Global regional GDP per capita, 2000-2022

Source: World Bank, *WDI.*

2.2   Development of education

2.2.1   Global basic education remains stable, higher education continues to improve

In the past two decades, the global education situation has been gradually improving, the prevalence of education, especially basic education, has increased to a higher level, and higher education continues to develop. However, the penetration of basic education has declined in recent years. Data from the *Sustainable Development Report 2023* shows that, global net primary school enrollment rate decreased from 94.76% in 2019 and 95.54% in 2020 to 92.54% in 2021. The secondary education completion rate showed the same trend, decreasing from 84.44% in 2019 and 87.17% in 2020 to 77.33% in 2021. The higher education completion rate continued to improve globally, increasing from 41.61% in 2019 and 42.65% in 2020 to 45.06% in 2021.

Educational development are more unequal across countries and regions. According to the data from *Sustainable Development Report 2023,* the prevalence of basic education in high-income countries remained at a high level and the higher education level continued to improve, while both basic and higher education in the countries at other income levels stagnated. The net primary school enrollment rate in high-income countries remained around 98%, falling to 96.57% in 2021. The completion rate of secondary education increased from 98.66% in 2018 to 98.78% in 2021, and higher education completion rate increased from 46.98% in 2019 to 48.91% in 2021. In upper-middle income countries, the net primary school enrollment rate decreased from 96.2% in 2019 to 93.34% in 2021. The secondary education completion rate increased from 86.03% in 2018 to 86.92% in 2021. And the higher education completion rate decreased from 29.87% in 2019 to 28.29% in 2021. In lower-middle income countries, net primary school enrollment was almost unchanged, from 92.75% in 2019 to 92.75% in 2021. The completion rate of secondary education increased from 67.45% in 2020 to 72.26% in 2021. In low-income countries, the net primary school enrollment rate decreased from 98.78% in 2020 to 84.91% in 2021, and the completion rate in secondary education decreased from 41.04% in 2019 to 40.35% in 2021.

2.2.2   Various actions including active mobilization and cash subsidies effectively promote teaching recovery

(1) During the pandemic, most countries have taken measures to close schools, and there are regional differences in the planning and measures for the education recovery and transformation after the COVID-19

The COVID-19 has dealt a severe blow to global education. The suspension of education and national and regional differences in attitudes and measures to innovate education methods and reopen schools have further widened the global inequality in educational development. The World Bank and other institutions have launched four waves of education response surveys on school closures, investigating the views and practices of the ministries of education in various countries in response to the closure of schools during the COVID-19 pandemic, the recovery of education and innovative education methods after the pandemic.

The first three waves of the Survey on National Education Responses to COVID-19 School Closures were conducted during May to June in 2020, July in 2020, and February to June in 2021, respectively. The questionnaires included similar questions. The first wave covered three main aspects of the early education in response in 118 countries as education strategies, education participants, and their impact on learning outcomes. Specifically, eight topics were covered in this survey: school reopening plan, school calendar adjustment, distance education system, online distance learning methods, status of teachers, status of students, attitudes of parents and guardians, learning progress and quality, and the implementation of examinations or teaching assessments. On the basis of the first wave, the second wave of the survey covered 149 countries and added some financial measures of various countries, such as the education budget for the coming year, financing support for family education during the pandemic, and financial support for teachers' salaries. The third wave of the questionnaire, where 143 countries participated in the survey, was designed to prepare for the reopening of schools around the world. On the basis of the core modules of the first two waves, the questionnaire added questions on the health conditions of students in various countries, the education recovery plan in 2021, and the flow of international students. The fourth wave of the survey lasted nearly a year and ended data collection in July 2022. Compared with the results from the first three waves of the survey, nearly all schools around the world have reopened. As policy makers in various countries begin to plan how to improve education levels, the scope of the questionnaire was significantly adjusted to focus on reducing future inequalities in the global education system and achieving the Sustainable Development Goals of education. The survey involved six issues in the core module: school absence, health status of students, assessment of the impact of the COVID-19, recovery strategies of education level, education financing, and transformation of digital education. Later, the OECD added related issues on the recovery and development of higher education.

According to the survey, although most countries have taken measures to close schools during the pandemic, there were differences across regions (see

Figure 2.7). Now, as schools reopen after the COVID-19, plans and measures for education recovery and transformation also vary from country to country.

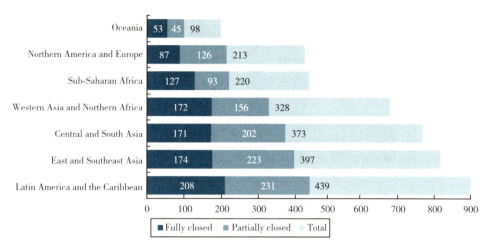

Figure 2.7　Distribution of average days of school closures in all regions during the COVID-19 pandemic

Note: Statistical period: February 16, 2020 to April 30, 2022.
Source: Survey on National Education Responses to COVID-19 School Closures.

(2) Countries encourage students to return to school through mobilization, cash subsidies, and health improvements

Most countries around the world experienced persistent school closures during the pandemic, leading to a sharp rise in student absenteeism after the recovery of education. According to Figure 2.8, at each education stage, more than 80% of upper-middle income countries have seen an increase in student absenteeism, indicating that students in these countries were more vulnerable to school closures during the pandemic and then droppe out or were unable to return to school. In contrast, low income, lower-middle income countries, and high-income countries were less affected, with student absenteeism rising in about half of the countries each.

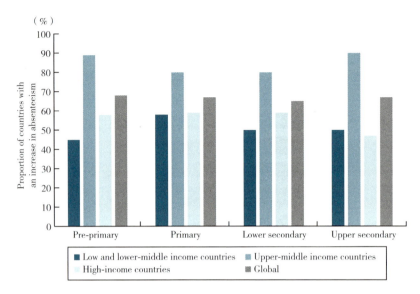

Figure 2.8   Increase of student absenteeism by country income groups

Source: Survey on National Education Responses to COVID-19 School Closures.

In order to promote students to return to school, countries actively adopt community mobilization and financial subsidies. In Figure 2.9, back-to-school community mobilization is an incentive for a large number of low income and lower-middle income countries. In 2022, about 61% of the surveyed countries adopted community mobilization among children at the pre-school level. 68% of countries also implemented this measure in the education of primary to middle school students. In contrast, high-income countries use such incentives less often. Figure 2.10 shows the situation that the government provides cash support for students from poor families to go back to school. Nearly half of low income, lower-middle income and upper-middle income countries provide financial support for students from poor families. In addition, Chile, Romania and other countries reported that they had established early warning measures for students to return to school after the outbreak of pandemic, identifying the barriers to returning to school at different stages, so as to adopt incentives for groups with high probability of absenteeism.

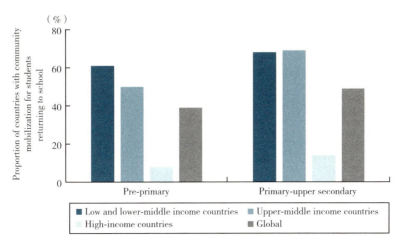

Figure 2.9   Community mobilization to ensure students return to school by country income groups

Source: Survey on National Education Responses to COVID-19 School Closures.

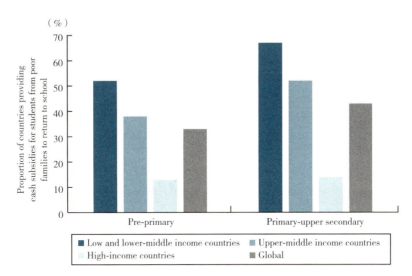

Figure 2.10   Cash subsidies to ensure students return to school by country income groups

Source: Survey on National Education Responses to COVID-19 School Closures.

It is not just the financial difficulties that prevent students to return to school, many parents worry about the health problems of their children going back to school. More than 80% of parents in France, Kuwait and Colombia have expressed concern about sending their children to school, according to UNESCO. Therefore, certain health arrangements and preventive measures should be adopted to promote the return of children and adolescents to normal educational life as soon as possible and reduce the dropout rate. In Figure 2.11, the most widely adopted hygiene measures in the world include promoting frequent hand washing and disinfection on school, as well as forcing teachers to use masks while teaching. Upper-middle income and high-income countries are more encouraging the adjustment of on-campus health infrastructure (e. g., strengthening of ventilation, improved air quality and more flexible teaching space), with more than 81% of upper-middle income countries making these adjustments. Lower income countries prefer mandatory vaccination, with about 72% of low income and lower-middle income countries making mandatory vaccination for teachers and about half of low-income countries requiring vaccination for students returning to school.

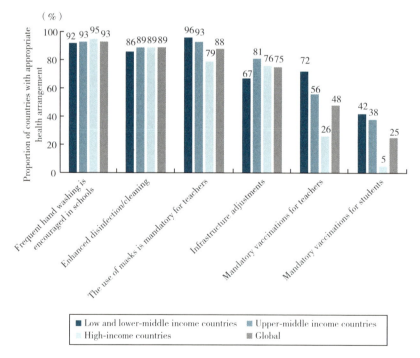

Figure 2.11   Health arrangements adopted by country income groups

Source: Survey on National Education Responses to COVID-19 School Closures.

2.2.3   Restore the teaching quality by adjusting the teaching content and teaching methods

(1) Adjust the learning content and intensity to restore the teaching quality

During the pandemic, the lack of learning time in schools and the poor quality of distance education in various countries have resulted in a large number of students worldwide having lower knowledge levels than required. Such negative effects not only happened in terms of basic skills such as reading and mathematics, but also in terms of social skills, psychological and emotional health. Many countries have actively promoted the recovery of teaching quality by adjusting the teaching content and intensity, improving teachers' teaching ability, and providing psychological counseling.

Formal examinations and teaching assessments have played an important role in measuring the quality of education. Most high-income countries stated that they will reinstate standardized tests for students in large scale to better monitor students' learning progress and quality. Low-income and lower-middle income countries are not proactive in reinstating tests. At the same time, countries are constantly adjusting their teaching content and curriculum design. According to data from the third and fourth waves of the Survey on Educational Responses to COVID-19 School Closures, nearly half of countries stated that they had made adjustments to the curriculum of at least one education stage or grade in the 2021-2022 academic year, and over one-third of countries stated that they would continue to adjust their teaching content in the 2022-2023 academic year.

The recovery of standardized tests is more common in high-income countries, with 93%, 89%, 88% and 85% of high-income countries reporting that they would reinstate standardized tests in preschool, primary, secondary and high schools, respectively, to better monitor students' learning progress and quality. Low-income and lower-middle income countries show a negative attitude in reinstating tests. Taking primary education as an example, only 37% of the surveyed low-income and lower-middle income countries reported that they would immediately reinstate tests (see Figure 2.12).

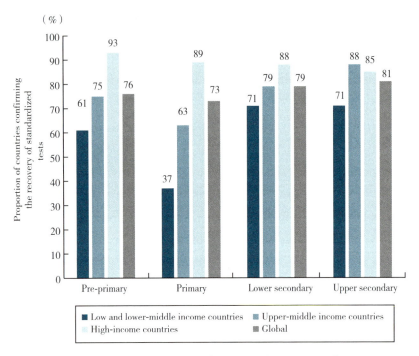

Figure 2.12   Recovery of standardized tests by country income groups

Source: Survey on National Education Responses to COVID-19 School Closures.

The lack of time in school and the poor quality of distance education make the skill levels of a large number of students in reading, mathematics and other basic subjects, social skills, psychological and emotional aspects are lower than the actual education requirements, thus increasing the curriculum load after the recovery. Curriculum overload can lead to lower quality of learning and failure to keep up with teachers. Experts point out that, there is a need to adjust the teaching content and curriculum schedule of each subject and redesign the teaching school calendar. In fact, in the third wave of the survey in 2021, about two-fifths of the countries in the world proposed to implement curriculum adjustment, as shown in Figure 2.13, which mainly included reducing teaching subjects or deleting the content of each subject.

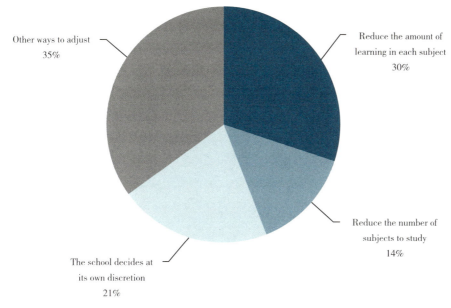

Figure 2.13   Different ways of adjusting the teaching content

Source: Survey on National Education Responses to COVID-19 School Closures (third wave).

Many countries in the fourth wave of the survey are implementing curriculum adjustments. In Figure 2.14, nearly half of the countries reported that they had adjusted the curriculum of at least one subject or grade in the 2021-2022 academic year, and more than a third reported that they would continuously adjust the teaching content in the 2022-2023 academic year. The implementation of curriculum adjustment measures varies with the educational stage and the national income level. High-income countries do not tend to adjust their teaching content, with only 8% of countries adjusting for pre-school content in the 2022 school year and 19% of countries adjusting for primary to high school levels. In contrast, more than half of low-income, lower-middle income and upper-middle income countries have adjusted their teaching contents. The proportion of countries that plan to continuously adjust the teaching content in the 2023 academic year declined, especially in primary to high school education, indicating that the teaching content of education at this stage would not be continuously and substantially adjusted.

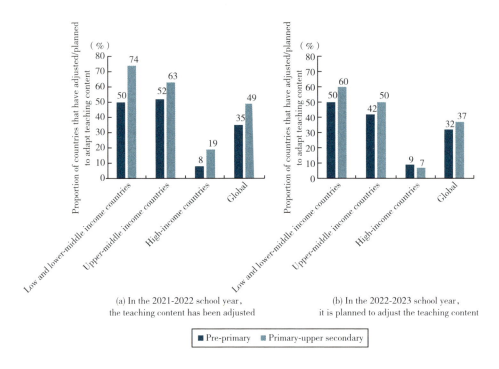

(a) In the 2021-2022 school year, the teaching content has been adjusted

(b) In the 2022-2023 school year, it is planned to adjust the teaching content

■ Pre-primary ■ Primary-upper secondary

Figure 2.14   Adjustment of the teaching content

Source: Survey on National Education Responses to COVID-19 School Closures (fourth wave).

(2) Improve teaching ability and quality

Improving teachers' teaching ability is also an important way to improve the quality of education. Providing teachers with teaching guidance, structured teaching plan and curriculum training can improve teachers' ability, thus improve their teaching quality. Among them, providing structured teaching plans for teachers is one of the most effective measures to improve the quality of teaching in the short term, especially in low-income and high-income countries. According to Figure 2.15, 73% and 64% of the surveyed countries reported that they had implemented the policy of providing structured education programs for preschool education and primary to high school teachers, respectively, in the 2021-2022 school year. In particular, 88% of upper-middle income countries have required primary to high school teachers to conduct structured teaching. However, there was no significant change in the implementation plan of structured teaching over the next few years, meaning that at least a quarter of the surveyed countries will not provide support and train teachers in teaching plans.

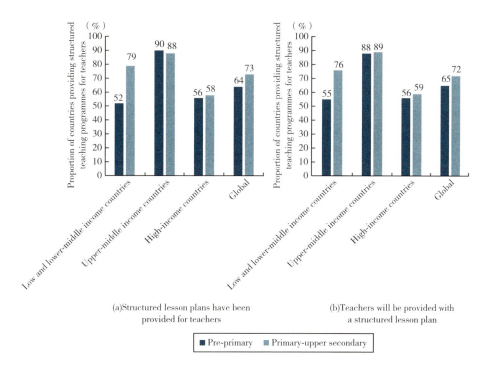

(a)Structured lesson plans have been
provided for teachers

(b)Teachers will be provided with
a structured lesson plan

■ Pre-primary ■ Primary-upper secondary

**Figure 2.15   Status of structured teaching programs for teachers
by country income groups**

Source: Survey on National Education Responses to COVID-19 School Closures.

During the pandemic, forms of teaching in most countries have changed to online teaching, posing new challenges to teachers to apply telecommunication technology. Strengthening teachers' on-the-job or pre-employment digital technology training is conducive to improving education stability and teaching quality in the future. As shown in Figure 2.16, more than half of the countries around the world have trained teachers at different teaching stages in digital technology skills. All countries attach great importance to the ability of high school teachers to use telecommunication technology. 82% of the countries have conducted on-the-job training for high school teachers, and 69% of the countries have also implemented pre-employment training. In contrast, only 57% and 70% of the countries provide pre-employment training and on-the-job training for preschool teachers. There differences may be related to the teaching content and methods at different stages.

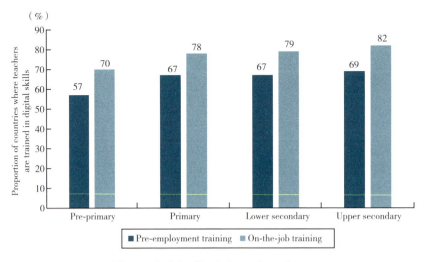

Figure 2.16　Training of teachers

Source: Survey on National Education Responses to COVID-19 School Closures.

Teacher shortages have been a major problem in education globally, with about half of the countries surveyed reporting an increase in teacher absenteeism during the pandemic. To address the problem of teacher shortages, countries adopted diversified strategies, such as recruitment of temporary teachers, assigning students from those absent teachers to other classes, supervising non-professionals to teach at the school, etc. Figure 2.17 shows that, the measures to deal with the shortage of teachers vary in different periods of the development of the pandemic. Before the first closure of schools in 2020, 45%, 15%, 4% and 9% of surveyed countries indicated that they would respond to teacher absences by using spare teacher resources, assigning students who are lacking teachers to other classes, teaching by non-professionals, and discontinuing some classes, respectively. During the pandemic, 24% of the countries around the world chose to hire temporary teachers to teach, and measures to monitor the delivery of lessons by non-professionals are also more common internationally. According to the current survey, after the COVID-19, 44% of countries have spare teacher resources to replace absent teachers, 18% of countries plan to find temporary teachers, 13% of countries will redistribute students, and 4% and 6% of countries will employ non-professional teachers or temporarily suspend some courses, respectively. In order to maintain effective teaching work for a long time, countries must also attach importance to the communication and support with education providers (including teachers' unions and associations). Teachers are at the forefront of education policy implementation, and ensuring that their concerns are included is essential to developing policies.

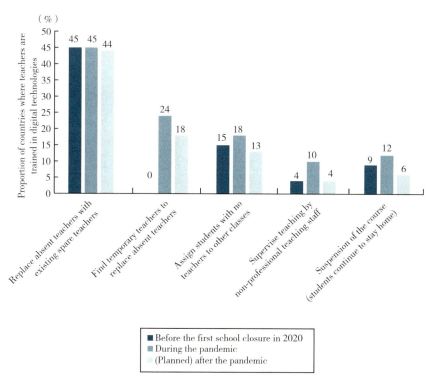

Figure 2.17   Measures taken in response to teacher absenteeism

Source: Survey on National Education Responses to COVID-19 School Closures.

(3) Improve the students' psychological health by providing psychological counseling

Psychological health, like nutrition, water, environmental hygiene and personal hygiene, is crucial to supporting students' normal attendance and study efficiency. As shown in Figure 2.18, to ensure that students can get comprehensive support and services in school, about 62% and 41% of countries respectively indicated that they had provided psychological health support such as counselling to students at the primary to high schools and preschools. 35% and 29% of countries recruited psychologists and counsellors to provide mental health well-being to students at the primary to high schools and pre-primary schools, respectively. More than half of the countries also provide psychological support to teachers to help them better provide mental health support to their students. Low- and lower-middle income countries were significantly less likely to provide such support than upper-middle and high-income countries.

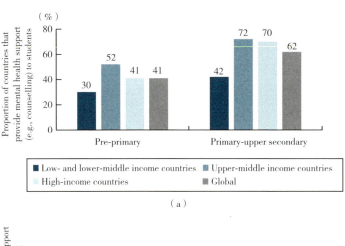

(a)

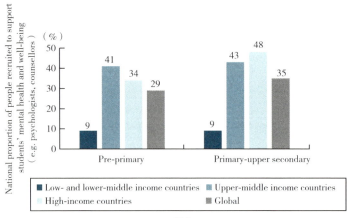

(b)

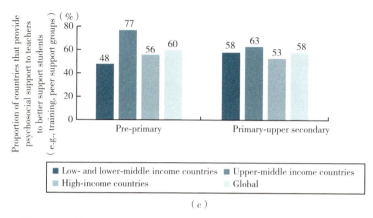

(c)

Figure 2.18   Specific forms and distribution of psychological assistance and support provided to students by country income groups

Source: Survey on National Education Responses to COVID-19 School Closures.

2.2.4 Education inequality has further deteriorated globally

The differences in both educational response measures during the COVID-19 and educational recovery measures after pandemic across countries are significant. The pandemic has been threatening global education, so it is necessary to expand educational investment to ensure that global students return to learning as more as possible. However, there are significant differences in the financial investment in education among different countries. Thus, the issue of inequality in education will continue and further worsen[1].

In 2020, after the outbreak of the COVID-19, many countries reduced government expenditure on education. 40% of low-income and lower-middle income countries have reduced actual education expenditure, with an average decrease of 13.5% in 2020 compared to 2019[2]. Between 2020 and 2021, most countries maintained or increased their fiscal expenditures on education, but there were significant differences among different countries. Globally, as shown in

---

1   UNESCO Institute for Statistics, UNICEF, The World Bank and OECD. Learning Recovery to Education Transformation: Insights and Reflections from the 4th Survey on National Education Responses to COVID-19 School Closures, 2022.

2   World Bank,GEM,UIS. *Education finance watch 2022*.

Figure 2.19, in terms of primary to high school, more than 70% of the surveyed countries increased their government budgets in 2021, only 7% of countries reduced their budgets, and only 4% of countries reduced their fiscal budgets in preschool education. By country income groups, the differences between low-income, upper-middle income, and high-income countries are obvious. Taking the changes in fiscal expenditure on education from primary and secondary to high schools as an example, as shown in Figure 2.20, over 90% of high-income countries and over 80% of upper-middle income countries have increased their budgets for primary to high school education. However, less than 50% of low-income countries have achieved an increase in fiscal investment in education. These indicate that, the income level of a country will significantly affect its ability to recover and further improve its education through financial investment after the pandemic.

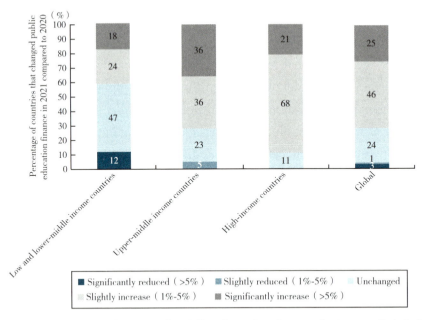

Figure 2.19   **The Change of public education finance in terms of global preschool education in 2021 compared to 2020**

Source: Survey on National Education Responses to COVID-19 School Closures.

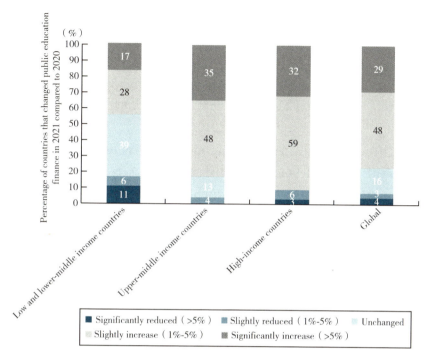

Figure 2.20   Changes of public education finance in terms of global primary-high school in 2021 compared to 2020

Source: Survey on National Education Responses to COVID-19 School Closures.

2.3 Nutrition and health

2.3.1 Progress has been made in maternal and child health, but significant regional differences need to be addressed

Nutritional and health issues continue to improve globally, including the increasing coverage and level of healthcare services for children's nutritional status. According to *Sustainable Development Report 2023*, the incidence of malnutrition has decreased from 16.87% in 2000 to 12.49% in 2017, 9.98% in 2019 and 9.79% in 2020. The prevalence of stunting in children under five years old has decreased from 26.07% in 2000 to 18.05% in 2019 and 17.67% in 2020, and further decreased to 17.32% in 2021 and 17.01% in 2022. The neonatal mortality rate decreased from 23.01‰ in 2000 to 12.7‰ in 2019, and further decreased to 12.42‰ in 2020 and 12.14‰ in 2021. The mortality rate of children under five years old has decreased from 69.54‰ in 2000 to 27.9‰ in 2019, 27‰ in 2020, and 26.22‰ in 2021. The Universal Health Service Coverage Index (UHC) and the proportion of infants delivered by skilled health personnel increased from 41.18% and 71.33% in 2000 to 60.83% and 83.73% in 2017, and to 64.37% and 93.06%, respectively, in 2019.

The differences in nutritional and health issues across countries with different income levels are still significant. According to *Sustainable Development Report 2023*, the prevalence of undernourishment and the prevalence of stunting in children under 5 years old in low-income countries in 2021 is 12 and 7 times higher than that of high-income countries. The neonatal mortality rate in low-income countries is 8 times higher than that of high-income countries; and the mortality rate of children under 5 years old in low-income countries is 12 times higher than that of high-income countries. In 2019, the National Health Service Coverage Index (UHC) and the proportion of infants delivered by skilled health personnel in high-income countries were 37.66 and 15 percentage points higher than those in low-income countries, respectively.

In high-income countries, the prevalence of undernourishment has remained at around 4% since 2000 and reached be 2.91% by 2020; the prevalence of stunting in children under 5 years old decreased from 6.77% in 2000 to 5.03% in 2019, and then increased to 5.28% and 5.22% in 2021 and 2022, respectively; the neonatal mortality rate and the mortality rate of children under 5 years old decreased from 5.89‰ and 10.92‰ in 2000 to 3.56‰ and 6.15‰ in 2019, respectively, and then to 3.33‰ and 5.72‰ in 2021, respectively. The UHC of high-income countries increased steadily from 62.98 to 78.88, and increased to 79.96 by 2019; the proportion of births attended by skilled health personnel has remained steady at over 98%.

In upper-middle income countries, the prevalence of undernourishment decreased by 3 percentage points from 9.68% to 6.46% in 2001-2018, and then increased to 6.97% in 2020; from 2000 to 2019, the prevalence of stunting in children under 5 years old decreased by 5 percentage points, from 19.31% to 14.11%, and then decreased to 11.36% and 11.19% in 2021 and 2022; the neonatal mortality rate dropped by 6 thousand points, from 16.40 per thousand to 9.99 per thousand, to 9.24 per thousand in 2021; the mortality rate of children under 5 years of age decreased by 17 per thousand points, from 36.25 per thousand to 18.84 per thousand, and to 17.01 per thousand by 2021. During the same period, the UHC of middle- and high-income countries increased from 46.79 to 68.83 in 2017, and then decreased to 68.68 in 2019; the proportion of births attended by skilled health personnel increased steadily from 91.8% to 98.37% in 2018 and then to 99.04% in 2020, approaching the level of high-income countries.

In lower-middle income countries, the prevalence of undernourishment decreased by 6 percentage points from 19.05% to 12.96% in 2001-2018 and then to 11.7% in 2020; from 2000 to 2019, the prevalence of stunting in children under 5 years old decreased by 8 percentage points, from 34.97% to 27.12%, and then decreased to 21.47% and 21.02% in 2021; the neonatal mortality rate dropped by 10 thousand points, from 28.93‰ to 18.61‰, and then to 17.06 ‰ in 2021; the mortality rate of children under 5 years of age decreased by about half, from 82‰ to 40.26‰, and then to 35.55 ‰ in 2021. During the same period, the UHC of low- and middle-income countries increased from 33.72 to 55.61 in 2017, and then increased to 56.59 in 2019; the proportion of births attended by skilled health personnel increased slowly, steadily from 63.49% to 85.95% in 2015, then decreased to only 65.52% in 2018, and then increased to 87.88% in 2020.

In low-income countries, the prevalence of undernourishment decreased by 9.57 percentage points to 25.02% from 34.59% in 2000 to 31.42% in 2020, and then gradually increased to 26.58% in 2018. The prevalence of stunting in children under 5 years old was 43.22% in 2000, still as high as 37.14% in 2019, and decreased to 31.82% and 31.3% in 2021 and 2022 respectively. The neonatal mortality rate and the mortality rate of children under 5 years of age decreased from 40.82‰ and 148.97‰ in 2000 to 26.78‰ and 69.96‰ in 2019, respectively, and then decreased to 26.44‰ and 68.97‰ in 2021, but they are still at a high level. The UHC rose from 21.22 in 2000 to 40 in 2017, and to 42.30 in 2019. The proportion of births attended by skilled health personnel increased from 31.23% in 2000 to 55.3% in 2018, and then to 84.12% in 2020.

2.3.2 The COVID-19 and increasingly severe food insecurity have exacerbated the nutritional and health crisis of the impoverished population

Although nutritional and health issues continue to improve globally, the nutritional and health crisis of impoverished populations in poor countries remains severe. The pandemic and increasingly severe food insecurity may further hinder the already slow progress in improving child malnutrition[1]. The pandemic has exacerbated the already serious nutritional challenges in poor countries, especially affecting vulnerable populations such as the poor and children. The pandemic has led to unemployment and reduced income, especially in the informal sector, making it difficult for many families to afford nutritious food. The economic impact of the pandemic has made many families in Tanzania unable to afford food. The price of corn, beans, and other staple foods has increased by 30% in some regions[2]. Moreover, disruptions in the food supply chain and restrictions on movement and trade may also lead to food shortages and higher food prices, especially in rural areas. This may be particularly problematic for vulnerable groups who rely heavily on the market for food purchases. The school closure measures taken to control the spread of COVID-19 also have a negative impact on nutrition and health, especially for school-age children who rely on school meals for most of their daily nutrition intake. The suspension of school meal delivery programs may lead to a reduction in the consumption of nutritious foods, especially for children from poor families who lack access to alternative food sources.

The Global Report on Food Crises 2023, released by the Global Network Against Food Crises (GNAFC) on May 3, 2023, shows that the number of people facing severe food insecurity increased for the fourth consecutive year in 2022.[3] More than 250 million people are facing severe hunger, and people in seven

---

1 See: *Sustainable Development Report 2022.*

2 UNICEF Tanzania. COVID-19response:nutrition.2020, https://www.unicef.org/tanzania/covid-19-response-nutrition.

3 *The Global Report on Food Crises 2023* classifies food insecurity into five levels according to the severity, and IPC Phase 1-5 respectively corresponds to the levels of None/Minimal, Stressed, Crisis, Emergency and Catastrophe/Famine the level above the crisis is severe food insecurity.

countries are on the verge of starvation. The report analyzed 42 major food crisis areas, of which 30 areas have more than 35 million children under the age of five suffering from wasting or severe malnutrition, among which 9.2 million children suffer from severe wasting. This form of malnutrition is the most dangerous and is the main reason for the increase in child mortality. The report points out that, the economic impact caused by the COVID-19 is also the main cause of food insecurity. Low-income countries, which rely heavily on imports of food and agricultural inputs, bear the brunt, as the COVID-19 has severely damaged their economic resilience and made them more vulnerable to global food prices.

According to the report *The State of Food Security and Nutrition in the World*, jointly released by five United Nations specialized agencies[1] in July 2023, In 2022, 691-783 million people worldwide were facing hunger.[2] Compared with 2019 before the outbreak of COVID-19, the number of hungry people in the world increased by 122 million. The report pointed out that, if this situation continues, countries in the world would not be able to achieve the Sustainable Development Goal of eliminating hunger by 2030 on schedule, and nearly 600 million people in the world were expected to face hunger by 2030. The report suggested that, in order to effectively strengthen food security and improve the nutritional status, it is necessary to promote the transformation of the agricultural food system, and to fully grasp the complex and changing relationship between urban-rural areas and the agricultural food system, thus to lay the foundation for policy intervention, action and investment.

Case: Social Protection Programs for the COVID-19 in Tanzania

Tanzania has launched multiple social protection plans to provide basic resources such as food and healthcare for vulnerable groups to improve their well-being and to ensure that these plans are effectively implemented to benefit the most in need. The specific plans include the followings.

1. Cash transfer programs: Regular cash transfer is provided to eligible

---

1   The five United Nations specialized agencies are the Food and Agriculture Organization of the United Nations (FAO), the International Fund for Agricultural Development (IFAD), the United Nations Children's Fund (UNICEF), the World Health Organization (WHO) and the World Food Programme (WFP).

2   In *The State of Food Security and Nutrition in the World*, hunger refers to an uncomfortable or painful physical feeling caused by insufficient dietary energy intake, which is measured by the incidence of food shortage.

households through the programs, including the Productive Social Safety Net (PSSN) and the Tanzania Social Action Fund (TASAF), to help them meet their basic needs, including food, health care, and education. Cash transfer programs are effective in reducing poverty and improving food security, especially among vulnerable groups such as the poor, women, and children.

2. School feeding programs: These programs provide free or subsidized meals to school-age children to help improve their nutrition and support their education. School feeding programs have been shown to be effective in improving school attendance and academic performance, as well as reducing malnutrition.

3. Health insurance programs: National Health Insurance Fund (NHIF) has been implemented to provide health insurance for regular sector employees and their families to help them access basic health-care services without facing financial difficulties. Health insurance plans have been proven effective in improving health outcomes and reducing poverty, especially among vulnerable populations.

4. Public works programs: Provide temporary employment opportunities for eligible families through public works projects, including the Tanzania Social Action Fund (TASAF) Public Works Program, to earn income while contributing to the development of public infrastructure and services.

2.4 Infrastructure

2.4.1 Continuous improvement has been made in the infrastructure globally

Globally, water resources infrastructure, energy infrastructure, internet infrastructure, and transportation infrastructure have all been improved, but the gap in infrastructure coverage and quality between countries with varying wealth levels remains large. According to *Sustainable Development Report 2023*, the proportion of the population with clean water increased from 75.5% in 2000 to 83.3% in 2017, 88.13% in 2019 and 88.32% in 2020; the proportion of the population with access to clean energy increased from 48.28% in 2000 to 57.2% in 2016, 67.04% in 2019 and 67.4% in 2020; the proportion of the population with access to electricity increased from 62.73% in 2000 to 77.05% in 2017, 84.73% in 2019 and 85.47% in 2020; the proportion of the population using the internet increased from 6.65%

in 2000 to 46.87% in 2017, 61.07% in 2019, 64.72% in 2020 and 69.44% in 2021, respectively; the Logistics Performance Index, which refers to the quality of trade and transport-related infrastructure with a value range of 1-5, has steadily increased from 2.53 in 2010 to 2.64 in 2016 and 2.71 in 2018.

Differences in infrastructure coverage and quality among countries with different income levels remain significant. According to *Sustainable Development Report 2023*, in 2020, the proportion of people with clean drinking water and the proportion of people with access to clean fuel in low-income countries were 37.52 and 87.8 percentage points lower than those in high-income countries. The proportion of people with electricity in low-income countries was 59.61% lower than that in high-income countries, and the proportion of people with internet use in low-income countries was 69.69% lower than that in high-income countries. In 2018, the Logistics Network Index for high-income countries was 3.46, compared with 2.08 for low-income countries.

In high-income countries, the proportion of the population with access to at least basic drinking water services increased from 98.61% in 2000 to 99.52% in 2019 and 99.59% in 2020; the proportion of the population with access to clean fuels and cooking technologies remained at 100% from 2000 to 2019 and 2020; the proportion of the population with access to electricity increased from 99.51% in 2000 to 99.99% in 2019 and 100% in 2020; the proportion of the population using the internet increased from 22.37% in 2000 to 87.86% in 2019 and 89.36% in 2020; the Logistics Performance Index was 3.46 in 2018.

In upper-middle income countries, the proportion of the population with access to at least basic drinking water services increased from 89.19% in 2000 to 96.05% in 2019 and 96.2% in 2020; the proportion of the population with access to clean fuels and cooking technologies increased from 66.83% in 2000 to 83.38% in 2019 and 83.74% in 2020; the proportion of the population with access to electricity increased from 89.03% in 2000 to 96.16% in 2019 and 96.5% in 2020; the proportion of the population using the internet increased from 3.21% in 2000 to 69.5% in 2019 and 73.66% in 2020; the Logistics Performance Index was 2.58 in 2018.

In lower-middle income countries, the proportion of the population with access to at least basic drinking water services increased from 70.34% in 2000 to 82.22% in 2019 and 82.58% in 2020; the proportion of the population with access to clean fuels and cooking technologies increased from 28.81% in 2000 to 44.13% in 2019 and 44.9% in 2020; the proportion of the population with access to electricity increased from 52.36% in 2000 to 79.85% in 2019 and 81.31% in 2020; the proportion of the population with access to the internet increased from 0.89% in 2000 to 44.35% in 2019 and 50.07% in 2020; the Logistics Performance Index was 2.36 in 2018.

In low-income countries, the proportion of the population with access to at least basic drinking water services increased from 47.4% in 2000 to 61.46% in 2019 and 62.07% in 2020; the proportion of the population with access to clean fuels and cooking technologies increased from 7.35% in 2000 to 11.93% in 2019 and 12.2% in 2020; the proportion of the population with access to electricity increased from 15.91% in 2000 to 38.66% in 2019 and 40.39% in 2020; the proportion of the population with access to the internet increased from 0.15% in 2000 to 16.48% in 2019 and 19.67% in 2020; the Logistics Performance Index was only 2.08 in 2018.

2.4.2 Infrastructure in poor countries is still lagging behind, hindering their economic recovery

The COVID-19 has illustrated the value of industrialization, technical advancement, and flexible infrastructure in remaking a better world and reaching sustainable development objectives. Economies with varied industrial sectors and strong infrastructure, including transportation, internet access, and utilities, suffer less and recover more quickly.

Case: Infrastructure Construction Before and After the COVID-19 in Tanzania

Infrastructure investment sectors in Tanzania have been significantly impacted by the COVID-19. The growth rate of Tanzania's construction industry decreased by more than 50% from 11.9% in the first quarter of 2020 to 5.8% in the second quarter of 2020, according to a report by the country's National Bureau of Statistics (NBS). The construction and infrastructure sectors were dealing with issues such as supply chain interruptions, labor shortages, a decline in the market for construction services, difficulties in financing, and project delays and cancellations. The Tanzanian government took a number of actions to assist the construction sector during the COVID-19 pandemic, including tax relief, the removal of import duties on necessities for the industry, the prompt issuance of construction permits, the provision of financial aid, the promotion of electronic construction, the implementation of security agreements, etc.

The Standard Gauge Railway (SGR), the Julius Nyerere Hydropower Station, and the extension of the port of Dar es Salaam are three important infrastructure projects which Tanzanian government has increased its investment. According to Tanzania's goal of becoming a middle-income nation by 2025, the government's investment in infrastructure projects is anticipated to boost the nation's economic growth and development in the following years.

One of the main challenges in ensuring the continued growth of Tanzania's infrastructure sector is the difficulty of financing, especially after the COVID-19, which has led to an increase in risk aversion among lenders and investors. Governments need to work closely with financial institutions to ensure funding for infrastructure projects, including through public-private partnerships and other innovative financing mechanisms. Another challenge is the shortage of skilled labour, and the government needs to invest in training and capacity-building projects to address this challenge.

2.5　Natural disasters

2.5.1　The geographical distribution of natural disasters is wide, with a large number of people affected and significant economic losses

Since 2000, Asia has seen the most of the world's natural catastrophes, followed by Africa, Americas, and Europe, and then Oceania, according to data from the International Disaster Database (EM-DAT). From 2000 to 2022, there were 161, 95, 88, 53 and 16 natural disasters in Asia, Africa, Americas, Europe and Oceania, respectively (see Figure 2.21). Asia has had a greater number and variety of natural catastrophes due to its size and diverse climate. Natural catastrophes in Africa are directly tied to land degradation, health care, and climatic conditions and changes. Volcanic activity, earthquakes, storms, and floods all have a significant impact on the Americas. Europe has few natural disasters because of its generally steady topography and climate. Oceania has experienced fewer natural disasters than other continents because of its small size, yet it is nevertheless impacted by tropical cyclones, floods, and sea level rise.

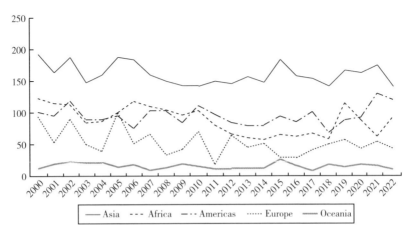

Figure 2.21　Number of natural disasters, 2000-2022

Source: EM-DAT.

From the perspective of the types of disaster, hydrological disasters, meteorological disasters and biological disasters are the three most frequent natural disasters in the world. Due to the differences in geographical environment, the types of natural disasters that occur frequently on different continents are different. Asia is prone to hydrological, meteorological and geological disasters. The geological disasters in Asia are mainly earthquakes. A total of 419 earthquakes occurred from 2000 to 2022, accounting for 66.93% of the global total. In 2022, 21 earthquakes occurred in Asia, accounting for 67.74% of the global total. The Americas are prone to hydrological and meteorological disasters and are also subject to climate shocks. From 2000 to 2022, there were 120 wildfires and 93 droughts in the Americas. In 2022, there were 7 wildfires and 3 droughts in the Americas. Due to the underdevelopment of medical care and the special natural environment, Africa is also suffering from biological disasters. From 2000 to 2022, Africa suffered from 22 insect pests and 586 infectious diseases (354 bacterial diseases, 176 viral disease, 9 parasitic diseases and 47 other types). In 2022, Africa was hit by 6 bacterial diseases and 7 viral diseases. Due to geographical location, terrain and geological conditions, climate characteristics and the impact of climate change, the number of meteorological disasters in Oceania is more than that of hydrological disasters. Tropical cyclones are the main meteorological disasters and floods are the main hydrological disasters. From 2000 to 2022, Oceania was hit by 105 tropical cyclones and 97 floods. In 2022, Oceania experienced one convective storm, one tropical cyclone and five floods. See Figure 2.22.

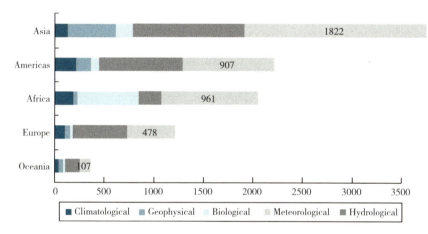

Figure 2.22   Number of natural disasters, 2000-2022

Source: EM-DAT.

Natural catastrophe victims are primarily concentrated in Asia and Africa. The types of catastrophes that have the biggest effects on the populace are hydrological and meteorological disasters. As shown in Figure 2.23, in terms of the number of people affected, Asia is the continent most affected by natural disasters. From 2000 to 2022, about 3.622 billion people were affected, accounting for 81.19% of the global affected population. Africa comes in second, with 513 million people affected, or 11.5% of the affected population worldwide. According to the data in 2022, Africa is the continent with the largest population affected by natural disasters, with about 111 million people affected, accounting for 59.49% of the total affected population. Asia followed closely, with about 64 million people affected, accounting for 34.52% of the total affected population that year. From 2000 to 2022, hydrological disasters among natural disasters affected the most population, especially in Asia. During the period, about 1,629 million people in Asia were affected by hydrological disasters, accounting for 44.97% of the affected population in the region. Climatological disasters have also affected a large number of people in Asia and Africa. In Asia, approximately 1,161 million people were affected by climatological disasters, accounting for 32.05% of the affected population in the region. From 2000 to 2022, drought, wildfires and other climate disasters affected 411 million people in Africa. In 2022, 101 million people in Africa were affected by climate disasters and 0.16 million people were affected by biological disasters. The number of people affected by geological disasters (such as earthquakes) is relatively small, but there is still a certain degree of impact in Europe and Asia.

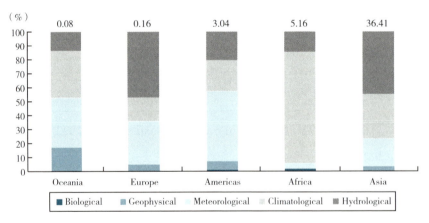

Figure 2.23   Number of people affected by various types of natural disasters, 2000-2022

Source: EM-DAT.

From 2000 to 2022, the total damages affected by natural disasters were the highest in the Americas, reaching approximately US$1,938,483 million, followed by Asia (US$1,671,533 million) and Europe (US$386,036 million). Oceania (US$110.928 million) and Africa (US$40.948 million) suffered relatively smaller damages. In 2022, the Americas was the continent with the highest total natural disaster losses, at approximately US$155,791 million, followed by Asia (US$48,746 million), Oceania (US$8,589 million), Africa (US$8,56 million), and Europe (US$2,156 million). From 2000 to 2022, meteorological disasters caused losses of US$1,494.121 million in the Americas; in 2022, it was US$125,432 million. Asia is located in the Circum-Pacific Belt. During the period of 2000-2022, geological disasters caused losses of US$638.695 million in Asia (38.21% of the damages in Asia), while hydrological disasters and climate disasters caused losses of US$554.467 million and US$415, 122 million in Asia, respectively. In 2022, many hydrological disasters occurred in Asia, causing losses of US$25.527 million, while geological disasters caused losses of US$12.194 million in Asia. See Figure 2.24.

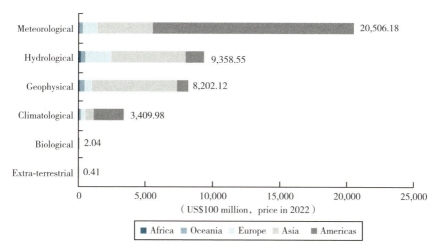

Figure 2.24   Losses due to various types of natural disasters, 2000-2022

Source: EM-DAT.

2.5.2 Natural disasters affect the process of poverty reduction. International aid is an important force in disaster response and poverty reduction

Natural disasters have a direct impact on the poor in various ways. First, disasters directly harm people's livelihoods and property. Floods, earthquakes, and storms can all ruin people's homes and farmland. Damage to infrastructure, such as water supply systems, roads, and bridges, can severely worsen the living conditions of the populace. Second, natural disasters have a huge impact on farmland and agricultural productivity. Disasters like floods, droughts, and others will damage fisheries and stock farmers by causing crop losses or even crop failure. Moreover, poverty was worsened by the disaster's casualties and unemployment. Natural disasters may cause casualties, deprive families of their main economic pillars and aggravate poverty. In the post-disaster reconstruction stage, many people face unemployment and income reduction due to the loss of job opportunities, which further deepens the poverty problem.

Natural disasters also affect poverty indirectly. First, the disaster has an impact on the economy, such as a decline in agricultural production and damage to infrastructure. This will lead to a decrease in economic activity, affecting employment and income opportunities. Second, rising prices and shortage of resources after the disaster also put pressure on low-income people. The surge in demand after the disaster has led to a rise in prices, making it hard for the poor to bear the high cost of living. At the same time, the shortage of resources, such as water and food, has also exacerbated the poverty problem. Finally, the post-disaster recovery and reconstruction phase has an important impact on the poor. The implementation of rehabilitation and reconstruction projects can provide employment opportunities and help the poor to rebuild their homes and livelihoods. However, for the poor, the opportunities for post-disaster recovery and reconstruction may be limited and the degree of demand satisfaction may be insufficient, which may lead to the continuation of poverty.

Strengthening disaster management, improving disaster response capabilities and mitigating the impact of disasters on people's livelihoods will help reduce poverty. At the same time, ensuring that the poor receive adequate support in post-disaster recovery and reconstruction is an important part of promoting poverty reduction, including state aid, social organization aid and international aid.

International aid is an important force in dealing with natural disasters and reducing poverty. As shown in Figure 2.25, Asia, which suffered the most from disasters, received the largest amount of aid, amounting to US$12,128 million, followed by the Americas (US$5,479 million) and Africa (US$1,268 million). Oceania (US$126 million) and Europe (US$70 million) received relatively low amounts of aid due to fewer natural disasters and more developed economies. In terms of the types of natural disasters, aid flows mostly to geological disasters (US$7,944 million) and hydrological disasters (US$6,290 million). The frequency of geological disasters is relatively low, but they often cause greater losses. The loss caused by hydrological disasters is relatively low, but the frequency of occurrence is relatively high. In the Americas, due to geological disasters, such as earthquakes, it received a relatively high amount of aid (US$4,939 million), which may be related to the higher earthquake risk in the region. The investment of these aid funds will help the affected countries and regions to cope with the impact of natural disasters and provide emergency relief and rehabilitation support. The government and international organizations also help the affected population by providing relief and shelter. These relief and shelters can provide basic needs such as food, water, medical care and safety, and help the victims rebuild their lives. These aid measures can help alleviate the plight of the poor, improve their ability to resist natural disasters and provide support for their sustainable development.

The process of post-disaster reconstruction and economic recovery may have a positive impact on the poor. By restoring infrastructure, providing employment opportunities and rebuilding communities, the livelihood recovery and economic growth of the poor can be promoted. The policies and measures provided by the national government to cope with and reduce poverty after the disaster are crucial to the recovery of the affected areas. This may include measures such as establishing early warning systems, strengthening disaster risk management and providing financial assistance. International organizations and external aid agencies play an important role in post-disaster reconstruction and poverty reduction. Through the provision of funds, technical assistance and expertise, international organizations and external assistance can help disaster-stricken countries to implement post-disaster reconstruction and poverty reduction plans.

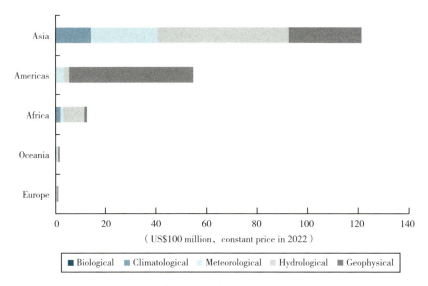

Figure 2.25   Amount of international aid received due to natural disasters, 2000-2015

Note: Due to the limitation of data integrity, the data from 2000 to 2015 are selected.
Source: EM-DAT.

In the process of post-disaster reconstruction and poverty reduction, the importance of sustainable development goals should be considered. This includes promoting social, economic and environmental sustainability to ensure disaster-affected areas are able to cope with disasters and poverty in the long term. In order to promote post-disaster poverty reduction and sustainable development, a series of strategies and suggestions can be put forward. These include strengthening disaster risk management, improving social security systems, providing vocational training and education opportunities, and promoting sustainable agriculture and renewable energy.

Case: Cyclone Yaas

Cyclone Yaas was a strong cyclone in the Indian Ocean hurricane season in 2021 and landed on the east coast of India in May 2021. The hurricane has sustained winds of 70-80 km/h and gusts of up to 90 km/h. It attacked the states of Orissa and West Bengal in eastern India, and also affected southern Bangladesh. According to EM-DAT data, cyclone Yaas affected 1.625 million people in India and 1.3 million people in Bangladesh, causing losses of approximately US$3.24 billion to India. Some rural areas in Bangladesh cannot even access to clean drinking water due to cyclone Yaas.

Cyclone Yaas has severely impacted the local economy and raised the unemployment rate. The destruction of infrastructure resulted in production disruptions and transportation difficulties, which in turn affected the operations of local enterprises and the supply chain. Key local industries such as agriculture, fishing and tourism have been adversely affected, resulting in a decline in GDP and job losses. Cyclone Yaas caused house damage. Most people used loans to repair the damaged houses. The poor people fell into a debt trap. The loss of farmland caused by cyclone Yaas has deprived the victims of their sources of income, the saline-flooded soil will not be suitable for cultivation for at least the next two or three crop cycles, and all the freshwater ponds will also become saline water, resulting in the death of farmed fish.

2.6 Regional conflicts

2.6.1 The concentration of occurrence of regional conflicts and their casualties

According to the data from the Armed Conflict Location and Event Data Project(ACLED), in 2022, there were more than 6,355 regional conflicts around the world, more than 2,796 violent conflicts in Asia and 1,226 in Europe, followed by Africa (1,211), the Americas (1,115) and Oceania (7). Regional conflicts in Asia in 2022 included 890 protests, 503 explosions/remote violence, 424 battles and 272 violence against civilians. There were more than 1226 regional conflicts in Europe, including 755 explosions/remote violence and 216 battles. Countries with more regional conflicts in 2022 include Ukraine (1,015), Syria (446), Myanmar (435), Brazil (316), Mexico (299), India (282), Iraq (249), Pakistan (237) and Yemen (231). See Figure 2.26.

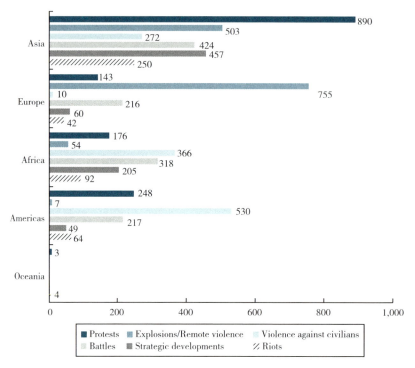

Figure 2.26   Various types of violent conflicts in five continents, 2022

Source: ACLED.

In 2022, Europe, Africa and Asia were the continents with the highest number of deaths due to political unrest, reaching 2,724, 1,904 and 1,434 , respectively, as shown in Figure 2.27. Among the subregions, West Africa and East Africa were the areas most affected by the political turmoil, with 866 and 748 people killed, respectively. The Middle East and Europe also have relatively high death toll, 702 and 2,724, respectively. This is closely related to the number and types of political unrest in the above areas. In 2022, more than 7,264 people were killed in violent conflicts around the world. Battles, explosions/remote violence and violence against civilians resulted in a large number of deaths. The three types of attacks resulted in 2,838, 2,590 and 1,218 deaths, respectively.

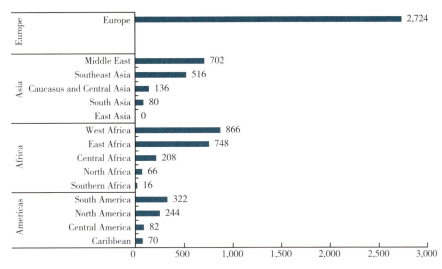

Figure 2.27   Deaths in violent conflicts in five continents and subregions, 2022

Source: ACLED.

2.6.2 Regional conflicts affect the process of poverty reduction. Achieving regional peace and stability is the key to promoting poverty reduction

Regional conflicts have caused direct damage to people's lives and property, making people facing threats to their lives. Regional conflicts have damaged infrastructure such as roads, bridges, power supply and communication networks, limiting people's transportation and logistics. Regional conflicts have destroyed farmland and agricultural facilities, causing farmers to be unable to grow and breed normally, leading to poverty. In addition, regional conflicts have also led to casualties, forced displacement and increased unemployment. At the same time, regional conflicts have also forced a large number of people to leave their homes, become refugees or internally displaced persons (IDPs), and lose their security and sources of livelihood. The conflict also severely affected industrial and commercial activities, resulting in large numbers of people losing their jobs and increasing the risk of unemployment and poverty.

Regional conflicts indirectly affect the process of poverty reduction. First, the conflict has had an impact on the economy, such as disruptions in production activities and reduced investment. At the same time, due to the uncertainties and risks caused by the conflict, investors' willingness to invest in the region has decreased, limiting economic growth and employment opportunities. Second, the conflict has led to a shortage of resources and a shrinking market, making it more difficult for the poor to access basic living resources, limiting the income sources and economic activities of the poor and exacerbating the poverty problem. Finally, the conflict also disrupted basic public services such as education, medical care and social services. War and conflict have caused the closure of schools, destroyed medical institutions and weakened the ability to provide social services. This has deprived the poor of access to good education and health care, limiting their chances of escaping poverty.

Resolving regional conflicts and achieving regional peace and stability are the keys to promoting the cause of poverty reduction. In addition, providing support and assistance to conflict-affected areas to help them rebuild and recover is the top priority in alleviating the impact of the conflict on poverty.

Chapter 3   Policy Provision and Implementation Effectiveness of Major Regions and Typical Countries of the World in Promoting Poverty Reduction

Overview

As we all know, ending global extreme poverty is the top priority of the United Nations Millennium Development Goals (MDGs) and Sustainable Development Goals (SDGs). However, complete eradication or reducing global extreme poverty to 3 percent of the world's population by 2030 remains the biggest challenge. To this end, many developing countries and emerging economies have formulated and implemented a series of poverty reduction strategies, policies and measures, while the United Nations, the World Bank, the International Monetary Fund (IMF) and many developed countries have provided various forms of assistance and support to them. A detailed review and real-time tracking of the poverty reduction policies of the world's major countries and regions will help to provide reference for the governments of many developing countries in constructing and improving poverty reduction policy systems that suit their own realities, and will in turn provide a policy model for the early fulfillment of the United Nations 2030 Agenda for Sustainable Development, in particular the goal of poverty reduction.

3.1   Types of policy provision to promote poverty reduction in major regions and typical countries of the world

3.1.1   Changes in the macro-context of global governance for poverty reduction

Despite the effective containment of the COVID-19 epidemic, countries are generally faced with economic difficulties such as sluggish growth, weak spending, monetary tightening and inflation, as well as social crises such as distributional imbalances, disparities between the rich and the poor, food insecurity and insecurity, and externally, with uncertainties such as disruptions in major supply chains, unsustainable debt and limitations on the scale of external assistance, and non-traditional security challenges such as regional conflicts, ecological degradation, environmental pollution and the spread of diseases. The new situation is not only a direct result of the food and fuel crises, but also of the social crises, such as the lack of food security. The new situation has not only led directly to soaring prices of food, fuel and fertilizer, but has also continued to impact on the world's fragile states and vulnerable populations, with the risk of plummeting deposits and foreign direct investment in Western countries, a worsening of the humanitarian crisis in Europe, the risk of collapsing food reserves and health systems in Africa, a general increase in competition for resources and extreme violence in Latin America, and a worsening of unemployment and livelihood difficulties in Asia. Unemployment and livelihood difficulties have worsened in Asia. Progress in eradicating extreme poverty globally has been slow, and the target of virtually eradicating extreme poverty globally by 2030 may be difficult to achieve.

3.1.2   Levels and implications of policies of governance for poverty reduction in different countries

As we all know, poverty is the result of a series of complex factors such as structural economic and cultural behaviour, so that poverty reduction policies should also be targeted at the different causes of poverty and different groups for integrated management. This report argues that, a country's main policy in the field of poverty reduction includes the following types. First, macro strate-gy-oriented policy, mainly referring to the state-led construction of the poverty reduction strategy framework, action programmes, target planning, legal system and regulations, special institutions, etc. Second, meso-level demand-oriented policy, mainly referring to agriculture and rural areas, human resources, social security, regional development, health care, education, science and technology, labour and employment, and other related policies. It also refers to the special poverty reduction policies and measures formulated and implemented by the relevant departments of agriculture and rural areas, human resources, social se-curity, regional development, health care, education, science and technology, and labour and employment, as well as the establishment of special poverty reduction institutions by the central and local governments. Third, the micro tool-oriented policy, which refers mainly to the combination of fiscal transfers, tax cuts, fee reductions, development and financing, and relief and assistance policies applied to push forward poverty reduction by participating entities such as the central and local governments, businesses, and the community, etc.

3.2   Policy provision practices to promote poverty reduction in major regions and typical countries of the world

This section focuses on the socio-economic conditions, evolution of the poverty situation and policy provision for poverty reduction in each region and typical country, with reference to the classification of the geographic regions by the Department of Economic and Social Affairs of the United Nations Secretariat, which divides the globe into six regions[1], namely, Africa, Asia, Latin America and the Caribbean, North America, Oceania, and Europe, with a view to provid-ing information to support the understanding of the current state of poverty and progress in poverty reduction globally.

---

1   The United Nations Department of Economic and Social Affairs divides the globe into six regions, including Asia, Africa, Latin America and the Caribbean, North America and Oceania, based on continental categories (see: http://unstats.un.org/unsd/methodology/m49/).

3.2.1 Asia

According to the United Nations , there are 48 countries in Asia. They are Afghanistan, United Arab Emirates, Oman, Azerbaijan, Pakistan, State of Palestine, Bahrain, Bhutan, Democratic People's Republic of Korea, Timor-Leste, Philippines, Georgia, Kazakhstan, Republic of Korea, Kyrgyzstan, Cambodia, Qatar, Kuwait, Lao People's Democratic Republic, Lebanon, Maldives, Malaysia, Mongolia, Bangladesh, Myanmar, Nepal, Japan, Cyprus, Saudi Arabia, Sri Lanka, Tajikistan, Thailand, Türkiye, Turkmenistan, Brunei Darussalam, Uzbekistan, Singapore, Syrian Arab Republic, Armenia, Yemen, Iraq, Iran, Israel, India, Indonesia, Jordan, Viet Nam, and China.

3.2.1.1   Characteristics and evolutionary trends of poverty in Asia

(1) Main characteristics of poverty in Asia

First, the level of public services in Asia is relatively backward, with some countries having a weak economic base, insufficient foreign exchange and dependence on imports.

For example, since 2022, Sri Lanka has experienced shortages of food, fuel and medicines due to a lack of foreign exchange. The shortage of food quickly led to a surge in food and food prices; the shortage of fuel not only led to difficulties in fuelling up motorbikes, cars and other means of transport of the general public, but also led to serious power cuts nationwide, affecting industrial production and the lives of residents; the shortage of medicines and medical equipment seriously affected the general public's access to health care, and some critically ill patients even faced life-threatening situations. Although the government has taken measures such as reshuffling the government, seeking assistance from the International Monetary Fund, and finding support through bilateral channels, it has not been able to reverse the momentum of the worsening economic crisis, and the Prime Minister of Sri Lanka, Wickremesinghe, has also said in his speech that, the state was bankrupt, and the economic crisis with shortages of food, energy, and medicines would continue until the end of 2023.[1] Bhutan has been in a state of

---

1   See: http:m.gmw.cn/baijia/2022-07//4//303044117.html.

serious imbalance for a long time due to its economy's heavy reliance on imports. In 2020, under the impact of the pandemic, Bhutan's domestic foreign exchange reserves have shrunk dramatically, from US$1.46 billion in April 2021 to US$845 million in August 2022.

Second, Asian countries have high population growth rates, large social gaps between rich and poor, and severe problems of extreme poverty.

At present, the poor in Asia is still concentrated in the South Asia. The data from Statista, a globally renowned data and statistics library, shows that, in 2022, about 38 million men and 45 million women, totalling about 83 million, Lived below the extreme poverty line in India. In 2022, the World Bank updated the international poverty line. Based on 2017 purchasing power parity (PPP), the new extreme poverty line was adjusted upward from US$1.90 per person per day to US$2.15 per person per day. Based on the original measure, the extreme poverty rate in India was 10.4%, whereas based on the new measure, it is 13.6%, the number of people living in extreme poverty has increased rather than decreased. India's population is expected to reach 1.5 billion in 2026, but the economy is not growing fast enough to meet the employment needs of at least 20 million jobs per year for this additional population. From an economic perspective, India's gross domestic product (GDP) consists of about 16% of agricultural output but employs 65 to 70% of the country's population. The lack of large-scale industrialisation and the concentration of services in high-end sectors such as finance, pharmaceuticals and IT have resulted in the inability of India's population to switch between the three sectors, especially the large rural population, resulting in large numbers of rural and urban migrants and poor people.

(2) Trends in the evolution of poverty in Asia

Good socio-economic conditions can contribute to the successful implementation of poverty reduction, while the improvement of the living standards of the population and the reduction of poverty have an impact on socio-economic conditions. This section analyses the current trend of poverty evolution in Asia, mainly from the data of the *United Nations World Economic Situation and Prospects 2023*, the Human Development Index, and the World Bank.

According to the *United Nations World Economic Situation and Prospects 2023*, Asia is facing pressures such as tightening financial conditions due to the impact of the COVID-19 pandemic. Among them, the GDP growth rate of East Asian countries is expected to be 4.4% in 2023, but the economic recovery is still fragile; the average GDP growth rate of South Asian countries will slow down from 5.6% in 2022 to 4.8% in 2023; the West Asian countries have gradually escaped from the economic downturn, but the recovery of the non-oil-producing countries is still weak, and it is expected that the average GDP growth rate will drop from 6.4% in 2022 to 3.5% in 2023. See Figure 3.1 and Figure 3.2.

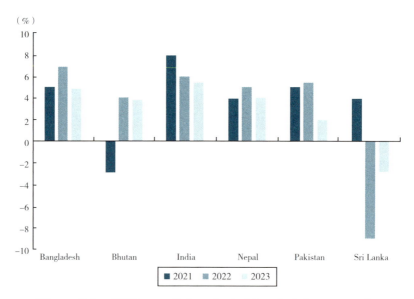

Figure 3.1　GDP growth in selected South Asian countries

Source: United Nations Department of Economic and Social Affairs; assessments based on World Economic Projection Modelling (WEPM) .

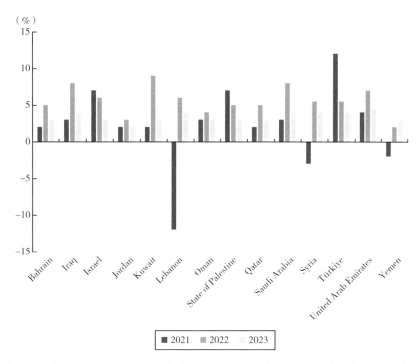

Figure 3.2   Economic growth forecasts for selected West Asian countries

Source: United Nations Department of Economic and Social Affairs; assessments based on
the World Economic Projection Model (WEPM).

3.2.1.2   Key policy provisions for advancing poverty reduction in Asian countries

**(1) Active optimisation of poverty identification and provision of
specialised poverty reduction support**

According to the 2022 *Global Multidimensional Poverty Index*, poverty
in Asia is characterized by poor infrastructure and difficulties in industrial
restructuring. To address this, Asian countries can carry out more targeted poverty
identification and assessment, so as to effectively strengthen the construction
of infrastructure and promote industrial transformation and upgrading, thereby
gradually better addressing the regional poverty problem in Asia.

With regard to upgrading poverty identification and promoting industrial
transformation, Asian countries should focus on analysing the factors that have

led to poverty in recent years, accurately identifying the target regions and populations, and making sustained investments to implement region-specific basic poverty reduction. For example, in upgrading the identification of poverty, reference can be made to the Benazir Income Support Programme (BISP) in Pakistan, which targets the poor and disadvantaged, eliminates poverty, and upgrades the social status of the marginalized and disadvantaged classes, and draws on its method of identifying the poor by adopting the Poverty Scorecard tool designed by the World Bank to conduct a survey on the economic situation of households in the country, and using the Proxy Mean Test (PMT) to rate households on a scale from 0 to 100. The PMT is used to assess the poverty level of a household on a scale of 0 to 100, and BISP is provided to poor households with a score of 16.7 or less. In terms of industrial transformation, reference can be made to the Doi Tung Development Project in Thailand, which eradicates extreme poverty and promotes the development of the local economy through a combination of measures such as the improvement of infrastructure and the development of the tourism industry, etc. The programme can be regarded as an exemplary experience in poverty reduction in mountainous areas for countries in Asia that have similar cases, so as to enable Asian countries to adapt to local conditions and to develop their own economic strategies. The programme can be considered a model experience in mountain poverty reduction for countries in Asia with similar cases, enabling Asian countries to implement pro-poor development projects at different regional scales in accordance with local conditions, thus achieving the effect of economic recovery and poverty reduction in the aftermath of the pandemic.

(2) Implementation of public service projects and upgrading of infrastructure

Public services and programmes have always been a key driver of poverty reduction. Poor public service is one of the key characteristics of poverty in Asia, which will be highlighted in 2022 in areas such as public health and safety. In this regard, with reference to the 2022 *Global Multidimensional Poverty Index*, the targeting of public programmes for poverty reduction in Asia can be further extended and refined to include public health in the areas of drinking water, sanitation and basic education, so as to improve the status quo of poverty in Asia in terms of basic public services.

For example, in the area of drinking water for public health, Nepal's experience with the Clean Water Programme in 2022 has been effective in reducing poverty. Under this locally adapted poverty reduction project, Nepal has improved access to drinking water through increased investment in sanitation, improved child nutrition, and reduced child mortality by reducing diarrhoea. Among the changes in Bajhang district is a vivid testimony to the effectiveness of the government of Nepal's poverty reduction efforts. The *2022 Global Multidimensional Poverty Index* released by the United Nations Development Programme in October 2022 shows that, during 2011-2019, Nepal's Multidimensional Poverty Index (MPI) has declined significantly from 0.185 to 0.075, and the poverty rate has fallen from 39.1% to 17.7%. According to the United Nations Development Programme (UNDP), Nepal has seen significant improvement in public health facilities and positive progress in health. The government of Nepal has formulated a multi-phase nutrition programme, which is being implemented in collaboration with various agencies in the country in the fields of health, education, sanitation, agriculture, etc, with the aim of further improving food security, sanitation and hygiene facilities. For example, in order to improve public sanitation in Nepal, the government has spent nearly 10 years to provide every household with a new type of hygienic toilet. The government has also implemented a clean water programme to ensure safe water for the population, which has significantly reduced child mortality. Nepal has increased its cooperation with international organisations to introduce successful experiences and advanced technologies. The government, together with the United Nations Development Programme (UNDP), has launched a pilot project for the development of small and micro enterprises to increase employment opportunities, improve people's livelihoods and reduce poverty. On this basis, the government has launched the " Development of Micro and Small Enterprises for Poverty Reduction" programme, which now covers all parts of the country. The International Bamboo and Rattan Organization(INBAR) has implemented a bamboo forest restoration and management project in Nepal, promoting practical experience and modern technology to help local farmers increase bamboo shoot production and expand sales markets, and some 3 million households in Nepal are now involved in activities related to the bamboo industry.

In education, Malaysia allocated RM52.6 billion to the Ministry of Education (MOE) in 2022 for the implementation of the Higher Education Fund Loan Scheme (Public Education), which accounted for 16% of the total Federal Development Expenditure (FDE), making it the sector with the largest allocation. Specifically, RM746 million was allocated to repair schools in East Malaysia (112 of which were in Sabah and 165 in Sarawak); to provide special incentives for teaching materials for the first time by offering a one-off incentive of RM100 to more than 400,000 staff members under the Ministry of Education, in recognition of the dedication of teachers to teaching at home; and to increase the Start-up Assistance Grant (SAG), from RM100 in 2021 to RM150 in 2022, totalling RM450 million, is expected to benefit 3 million students.

(3) Attempts to tighten monetary policy in an effort to accelerate economic recovery

Factors such as rising global commodity prices, slowing global demand growth, and global investors turning to safe-haven markets have led to risk premiums in developing economies. For example, in the face of accelerating consumer inflation caused by rising global prices of fuel and food, the Reserve Bank of India and the Central Bank of Bangladesh tightened monetary policy as early as the second quarter of 2019, and Pakistan and Sri Lanka started a policy cycle of monetary tightening at the end of 2022.

(4) Optimizing self-employment systems and implementing cash transfers

The establishment of a self-employment system and conditional cash transfers, which are part of social welfare, are key to a country's long-term development. In recent years, many Asian countries have adopted similar policy measures in their poverty reduction initiatives to achieve national well-being and poverty reduction goals.

The social safety net programme in Bangladesh exemplifies this aspect of poverty reduction. In its poverty reduction efforts, the Government of Bangladesh has been consistently promoting social safety net programmes in the hope of alleviating poverty by improving the socio-economic conditions of the extreme poor. Using the social safety net life-cycle approach, the government has been making budgetary planning to help the poorest of the poor at the policy level. The revised government budget for 2020-2021 allocates a total of BDT 956.83 billion, which is about one-fifth (17.75%) of the total budget, for poverty. This allocation is 3.1% of the GDP for the fiscal year, which shows the Government's commitment to pro-poor interventions. The social safety net project consists of multiple interventions that fall under different sub-programmes and sub-projects, such as one-family-one-farm, shelter, housing, and reintegration. These policy interventions focus on bringing about positive changes in the lives of the poor and building a better and more liveable society. Sociologists have pointed out that social safety net programmes can effectively contribute to sustainable development, and that these programmes are well-targeted and designed to benefit specific segments of the society, such as the widowed population, poor women abandoned by their husbands, the elderly, persons with disabilities, freedom fighters, and so on. Projects that help the poor in cash or in kind should be channelled through formal channels in order to benefit the target population. Mechanisms include government banks, rural savings banks, mobile banking services run by various operators and the active participation of local administrations.

(5) Focusing on the extreme poor and improving social security systems

Paying attention to the living situation of the extreme poor, implementing special loan programs, and improving the social security system is an important starting point for the implementation of poverty reduction plans. Asian countries actively implement special loan programmes, improve the social security system, help economic recovery, enhance the effectiveness of poverty reduction.

For example, in 2022, extreme weather conditions and natural disasters have led to a rise in inflation in South Asian countries, and a growing number of the poor. In Pakistan, the government has introduced targeted subsidies in response to high food prices, and efforts to increase social protection; in Bangladesh, the government has lowered tariffs on rice imports, and increased fertiliser subsidies and budgetary allocations for the agricultural sector. Nepal, on the other hand, announced a monetary policy, with its central bank governor, Adhikari, announcing relief measures at the time of announcing the monetary policy for the fiscal year 2021-2022 (from mid-July 2021) on 13 July, including extension of loan repayment period, reduction in the amount of instalments, restructuring and rescheduling of loan repayment plans, and provision of credit at more favourable interest rates. Among them, restaurants, public transport, educational institutions and entertainment can extend loan repayment for one year and repay it in at least four instalments, and tourism and cinema can restructure and reschedule loan repayment. In Bangladesh, the government has taken measures to help the extremely poor but labour-ready rural population to get employment by increasing the allocation to BDT16.5 billion in 2020-2021. In Japan, the government has, since March 2020, urgently implemented a " special case loan" for families living in difficulty, which is an interest-free loan that can be applied for without a guarantor. See Table 3.1.

Table 3.1 Poverty reduction policy provision in typical asian countries in recent years

Country	Poverty reduction strategy	Focus area	Poverty reduction target	Year
India	Economic relief package- Expansion of PMGKY, Direct Benefit Transfer, DeenDayal National Livelihood Project, Ujjawala Scheme; Employees' Provident Fund, " Rural Youth Employment Scheme", "Prime Minister/National Skill Development Scheme", "Prime Minister/National Poverty Benefit Scheme", "National Health Guarantee Scheme", "Prime Minister/National Poverty Benefit Scheme", "National Health Security Scheme"	Food resupply, health care, cash relief, women's rights, infrastructure	economic assistance, mainly for farmers, is expected to benefit 86.9 million farmers and 70 million women in four months	2020

Continued

Country	Poverty reduction strategy	Focus area	Poverty reduction target	Year
Pakistan	Zakat system,Pakistan Foundation Board (PBM),Benazir Income Support Programme (BISP)	Financial relief, food support, child support, vocational training, medical centre support, women's rights	Zakat is collected only for Muslims and the tax is then transferred to the poor Muslim, especially widows, orphans and the handicapped; PBM provides assistance mainly to the poor such as widows, orphans, the handicapped, the infirm and the sick; and BISP targets the poor and the vulnerable, eradicates poverty, and uplifts the status of the marginalized and disadvantaged sections of the society (especially women)	2024
Bangladesh	" Elderly Persons' Allowance Project", "Disabled Persons' Allowance", "Private Orphanage Allowance (per person)", "Freedom Fighters' Honour Allowance Project", "Honour Allowance and Medical Allowance for the Families of Wounded Freedom Fighters and Martyrs", "Mothers' Allowance", "Allowance for Breastfeeding Mothers", "Financial Aid for Extremely Poor Females", "Special Project for the Gypsies", "Project on the Third Sex" , etc.	Financial relief, allocation of funds for social empowerment, women's rights, post-disaster reconstruction, employment support	The Social Safety Net Project includes a series of sub-projects aimed at improving the livelihoods of the poor and thus upgrading their economic and social status; specialised poverty alleviation measures targeting the most vulnerable and poorest people	2025
Sri Lanka	Tax reform,Facilitating the implementation of the IMF's US$2.9 billion bailout programme	Financial relief	Responding to economic hardship as well as food insecurity	2023

Continued

Country	Poverty reduction strategy	Focus area	Poverty reduction target	Year
Nepal	Clean water measures, Multiple nutrition programmes, " Development of Micro and Small Enterprises for Poverty Reduction Project ", International Organisation for Bamboo and Rattan (INBAR) project for rehabilitation and management of bamboo forests in Nepal, Monetary policy relief measures for FY2021-2022 (from mid-July 2021)	Sanitation infrastructure, clean water, food safety, employment support, increased agricultural production, monetary policy	Improved child nutrition, reducing child mortality by reducing diarrhoea; pilot projects for small and micro-enterprises, increasing employment opportunities, improving livelihoods and reducing poverty; for local farmers, increasing bamboo shoot production and expanding the sales market; and for restaurants, public transport, educational institutions and the entertainment industry, arranging for a one-year extension of the loan and repayment of the loan in at least four instalments, and restructuring and rescheduling of repayments for the tourism and film industries	2022
Bhutan	Asia-Pacific Disaster Relief Fund (APDRF), Asia-Pacific Vaccine Assistance Programme (ACVAX), Japan's Asia-Pacific Fund for Prosperity and Vitality (APFPV), India supports Bhutan's Twelfth Five-Year Plan (2019-2023), Bhutan's suspension of motor vehicle imports to reduce foreign exchange losses, lifting of the ban on cigarette imports	Vaccine assistance, medical relief, financial relief, food relief, food aid, import and export trade reform, vocational education aid, trade support	Upgrading the professional skills of Bhutanese medical personnel and the level of emergency medical care in the country; India has provided development assistance to a number of projects in Bhutan through the Trade Support Facility (TSF) and Project Aid (PA) modalities to enhance bilateral trade facilitation through the Cross Border Trade Support Facility (CBTSF); Bhutan has suspended the import of motor vehicles to reduce the loss of foreign exchange; and lifting the smoking ban to ease the worsening financial situation caused by the pandemic	2023,2024
Maldives	China-Maldives Friendship Bridge	Tourism, transport		until now

Source: Synthesis of poverty reduction policy provisions in recent years of selected typical Asian countries.

3.2.2 Africa

According to the United Nations, there are 54 countries in Africa: Algeria, Egypt, Ethiopia, Angola, Benin, Botswana, Burkina Faso, Burundi, Equatorial Guinea, Togo, Eritrea, Cabo Verde, Gambia, Congo, Democratic Republic of Congo, Djibouti, Guinea, Guinea-Bissau, Ghana, Gabon, Zimbabwe, Cameroon, Comoros, Côte d'Ivoire, Kenya, Lesotho, Liberia, Libya, Rwanda, Madagascar, Malawi, Mali, Mauritius, Mauritania, Morocco, Mozambique, Namibia, South Africa, South Sudan, Niger, Nigeria, Sierra Leone, Senegal, Seychelles, Sao Tome and Principe, Eswatini, Sudan, Somalia, Tanzania, Tunisia, Uganda, Zambia, Chad, and Central African Republic.

3.2.2.1 Characteristics and evolutionary trends of poverty in the Africa

Generally speaking, as the continent with the highest concentration of developing countries (especially the least developed countries), Africa has a large number of poor people, a weak capacity to reduce poverty, and insufficient international assistance, resulting in widespread poverty, deep poverty, a high poverty rate, and a high rate of absolute poverty. In terms of the types of challenges to poverty reduction, poverty in African countries is mainly manifested in the absence of social security systems, low levels of basic education, climate change and ecological degradation, the difficulty of maintaining basic food security, the increasingly prominent issue of poverty in rural areas, and the lack of employment opportunities for the urban population. According to the World Bank's projections, by 2030, the number of people living in extreme poverty in Africa will account for 86 percent of the world's total extreme poor, and Africa will continue to have the highest concentration of people living in extreme poverty and the highest poverty rate in the world.

In the past two years, African countries have not achieved significant poverty reduction targets, and the progress of poverty reduction has been slow in most African countries. The extreme poverty rate has risen significantly in some countries, and the process of poverty reduction is clearly lagging behind the rest parts of the world. For example, based on the data from PovcalNet in June 2022, in South Sudan,76.4% of people living in absolute poverty (i. e., per capita household living costs below US$1.9 per day), with a CPIA[1] score of 1.6; in Malawi,73.5% of people living in absolute poverty, with a CPIA score of 3.1; in Burundi,72.8% of people living in absolute poverty, with a CPIA score of 2.9; in the Democratic Republic of Congo, 77.2% of people living in absolute poverty, with a CPIA score of 3; in Central African Republic, 65.9% of people living in absolute poverty, with a CPIA score of 2.6; in Somalia, 68.6% of people living in absolute poverty, with a CPIA score of 2.1;in Mozambique, 63.7% of people living in absolute poverty, with a CPIA score of 3.1; in Zambia, 58.8% of people living in absolute poverty, with a CPIA score of 3.1; in Liberia, 44.4% of people living in absolute poverty, with a CPIA score of 3; and in Chad, 38.1% of people living in absolute poverty, with a CPIA score of 2.8. See Figure 3.3.

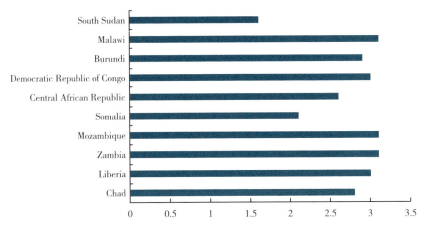

Figure 3.3   CPIA scores of selected poor African countries, 2022

Source: CPIA database, 2022.

---

1   The Country Policy and Institutional Assessment(CPIA) is specifically composed of four parts: economic management indicators, structural policy indicators, social inclusion and equity policy indicators, and public sector management and institutions indicators.

3.2.2.2   Key policy provisions for advancing poverty reduction in African countries

(1) Positioning poverty reduction governance prominently in national development strategies

Since 1999, the World Bank, the International Monetary Fund (IMF) and governments of African countries have been working together to develop *Poverty Reduction Strategy Reports* (PRSRs), which have been used by most African countries as their national poverty reduction plans and programmes of action. For example, in Rwanda, the government has successively launched a series of medium-term transformation strategies, including the Poverty Reduction Strategic Plan (PRSP1) for 2002-2005, the Economic Development and Poverty Reduction Strategy I (EDPRS I) for 2008-2012, and the Economic Development and Poverty Reduction Strategy Ⅱ (EDPRS Ⅱ) for 2013/14-2017/18, and the National Transformation Strategy (NST-1) for 2018/19-2023/24. Over the past two decades, Rwanda's poverty reduction policies have been effective, with the domestic poverty rate falling from 78% in 1994 to 38% in 2017. In 2020, in the concluding year of Rwanda's "Vision 2020", the Rwandan government promulgated " Vision 2050", which sets the country's development goal to become an upper-middle income country by 2035, and a high-income country dominated by a knowledge-based economy by 2050, with a fundamental focus on improving people's livelihoods as the foundation of its strategic vision and policy framework. The Government of Burundi has also formulated the National Development Plan (2018-2027), which also specifies the development goals of " feeding everyone and saving for every family" and " building Burundi into an emerging country by 2040". The year of 2022 has been designated as the "Year of Agriculture in Burundi", with a view to combining agricultural and rural development with the eradication of absolute poverty. The Government of Somalia has also formulated its ninth national development plan, the National Development Plan 2020-2024. In Côted'Ivoire, the national statistics department has launched a special survey on poverty in the country for 2011-2021, with a view to focusing on the poor and vulnerable through detailed and continuous data tracking and data comparisons in order to provide a policy basis for the formulation and implementation of poverty reduction programmes. In addition, in order to better respond to the country's economic and social development, the Government of Mauritania has developed a new Strategy for the Development of Statistics (2020-2030) and a Priority Action Plan (2021-2025), which has led to the implementation of major reforms in the national statistical agency[1]. The Statistical Institute of Jamaica, in collaboration with the Ministry of Health and other experts, led a committee to match data needs with existing data required to guide policy during the crisis. To help fill the data gap on the sustainable development goals, the National Bureau of Statistics in Kenya initiated a partnership with civil society organisations and incorporated a set of quality standards for citizen-generated data into its newly released Kenyan Statistical Quality Assurance Framework.[2]

(2) Promoting the upgrading of infrastructure and public services in poor areas

For example, in South Africa, the government plans to allocate 100 billion rand over 10 years (2021-2030) to an infrastructure fund, with priority given to support in the areas of energy, roads, water, electricity, communications, public health, welfare housing and other areas of livelihood protection. Specifically, South Africa has proposed that it would expand its rural bridge construction programme, gradually increasing the number of bridges delivered from 14 to 95 per year by 2021, and will also upgrade and build 685 kilometres of rural roads by 2023.

In response to the unfavourable situation of the country's infrastructure growth rate in recent years, which has significantly lagged behind the population growth rate, the Federal Government of Nigeria in July 2022 allocated 50 billion naira for the country's traditional industrial infrastructure and technological upgrading, such as the Ministry of Agriculture will be earmarked for the construction of rural roads and the development and utilisation of renewable energy sources, such as solar energy. Under the "Decent Life" policy initiative

---

1 World Bank, Office of the Chief Economist for the Africa Region. *Assessing Africa's Policies And Institutions.* OCT. 2022, P.48.

2 UN, *The Sustainable Development Goals Report 2022.*

proposed by President Sisi in 2019, the government of Egypt plans to allocate nearly one trillion Egyptian pounds to implement more than 1,000 projects targeting nearly 5,000 villages in 20 impoverished governorates and 52% of the country's population, in three phases, to progressively improve the infrastructure in the areas of healthcare, education, housing, roads, electricity, water supply, and so on. Specifically, in the construction of natural gas pipelines, as of August 2022, Egypt has completed the construction of natural gas pipelines in 120 villages, allowing more than 410,000 poor families to use natural gas. In Algeria, the Ministry of Energy and Mines, together with the Ministry of the Interior, the Ministry of Land and Local Authorities, conducted a survey to identify more than 8,000 so-called "grey zones" (named after the grey colour of these zones on the national governance map) with shortcomings in infrastructure such as electricity and natural gas and launched a special programme to help more than 140,000 poor families to access to electricity and 70,000 poor families to access to natural gas in the 2020-2024 period. In September 2022, the Société Générale de Petrol et de Gaz de l'Algérie (SGPGA) also launched a new social investment programme providing 37 development projects in the "grey zones" of the country's 21 wilayas, and the communications companies have given priority to the "grey zones". The communications companies have given priority to the installation of Internet and mobile networks in the "grey zones"; and health-care institutions have organised key visits to the "grey zones" and set up mobile clinics.

(3) Efforts to improve the efficiency of fiscal spending on poverty reduction

Governments of some African countries have endeavoured to improve the efficiency of fiscal spending, especially for poverty reduction. For example, in South Africa, the government has decided to flexibly expand financing channels and extend the social assistance scheme for poor households until March 2023. In July 2022, the Federal Government of Nigeria approved 400 billion naira for specific welfare programmes, including government enterprise and empowerment programmes, conditional cash transfers, farmers' funds, and market-based financial support in the light of the National Poverty Reduction and Growth

Strategy (NPRGS). In January 2022, Ministry of Finance of Ghana announced a 20% cut in fiscal spending for the current year in response to the fiscal crisis brought about by the heavy financial burden, for which it adopted fiscal spending restrictions such as limiting the hiring of retired person and suspending the implementation of the Poverty Reduction Framework Programme (IPEP) projects.

(4) Promoting social cohesion and inclusion through youth employment and entrepreneurship

In view of the persistently high unemployment rate among youth groups in the country, the Presidential Employment Stimulus Programme was launched in South Africa in 2020 is progressing steadily, with more than 500,000 education and teaching staff to be employed in schools of all types nationwide, and the Department of Home Affairs gradually recruiting about 10,000 unemployed youths to be responsible for paperless office work and digital processing of documents in government agencies, as well as the social and economic development of the country. In Egypt, the government launched "Decent Life" initiative which includes policies designed to provide training and employment for people in disadvantaged areas. In its poverty reduction plan for FY2021-2022, the government continues to launch projects to support small-scale entrepreneurship and home-based production, and to provide new employment opportunities for women and young people through the Youth Vocational Training Centres.

3.2.3 Latin America and the Caribbean

According to the United Nations, Latin America and the Caribbean comprises 33 countries: Argentina, Antigua and Barbuda, Bahamas, Belize, Bolivia, Brazil, Barbados, Chile, Colombia, Costa Rica, Cuba, Dominican Republic, Dominica, Ecuador, Grenada, Guatemala, Guyana, Honduras, Haiti, Jamaica, Saint Kitts and Nevis, Saint Lucia, Mexico, Nicaragua, Panama, Peru, Paraguay, El Salvador, Suriname, Trinidad and Tobago, Uruguay, Saint Vincent and the Grenadines, and Venezuela.

3.2.3.1   Characteristics and evolutionary trends of poverty in Latin America and the Caribbean

(1) Main characteristics of poverty in Latin America and the Caribbean

Firstly, social poverty and social division have increased, making it difficult for low-income groups to reap the benefits of economic growth.

Latin America and the Caribbean (LAC) has always been the region with the largest gap between the rich and the poor in the world, and this gap is widening due to the impact of the COVID-19 pandemic. According to the United Nations Economic Commission for Latin America and the Caribbean (ECLAC), in 2020, the region will have about additional 22 million poor people, with a poverty rate of 33.7% and an extreme poverty rate of 12.5%. The total number of the poor in the region has increased to 209 million, with 78 million living in extreme poverty, an increase of 8 million from 2019, according to the *Social Panorama of Latin America 2020* released by ECLAC. While the COVID-19 pandemic has led to a rise in the number of the poor and unemployed in LAC, it has also made the region's rich group become richer. From March to June 2020, the total wealth of at least 73 billionaires in LAC grew by US$48.2 billion. In Brazil, 49.6% of the country's resources are in the hands of the richest 1% of the population (about 2.1 million), ranking it second among the ten countries with the largest gap between the rich and the poor, according to the *Global Wealth Report 2020* released by Credit Suisse Group.

During the pandemic, the United States was experienced downward pressure due to block downs and restrictions. This paralysed a number of economic and trade activities, with sectors such as tourism, transport and trade, which happen to host a significant number of migrants from Central America. Reduced incomes and unemployment pressures have led to expatriates being unable to work with capital, resulting in a significant decrease in the total amount of remittances flowing to Central America. In El Salvador, for example, according to the country's Central Reserve Bank, remittances totalled more than US$5.6 billion for the whole of 2019, equivalent to 16% of its GDP. However, due to the impact of the pandemic, in April 2020 alone, the total amount of remittances fell by 40% compared with the same period in 2019, and the national economic situation is not optimistic.

Not only is it challenging to improve the economic and social development situation in the short term, but it is also worsening the downward mobility of LAC countries. This trend is causing the new middle class, which was expected to act as a "buffer", to move to the next social class in large numbers. The serious polarisation between the rich and the poor in the region has led to demonstrations and protests in many countries, greatly intensifying social conflicts.

Secondly, some countries have a disproportionately high share of informal employment, making this group highly vulnerable to external factors.

LAC countries, in general, have a significant proportion of informal sector employment among the urban economically active population. However, there has been no significant change in this proportion since the 21st century. Historically, informal employment ratios have risen in response to national economic transitions and external shocks to the domestic economy. Informal employment in LAC countries was affected in the immediate aftermath of the COVID-19 pandemic. According to the statistics from 15 countries such as Guatemala, Peru and on employment in 2019, 11 countries had more than 50% of their non-agricultural sector workforce engaged in informal employment (see Figure 3.4). Among these countries, Honduras topped the list with 76% of its population involved in informal employment. In countries such as Chile and Saint Lucia maintain, the informal employment share is 30% or less. Even in higher-income countries such as Argentina and Colombia, informal employment plays a significant role in the social employment.

The low barriers to informal employment facilitate the integration of job seekers of all ages, genders and skill levels into the labour market This contributes to an increase in the labour force participation rate overall, leading to the expansion of employment opportunities and higher incomes for workers. Informal employment in this sense, has a positive effect on reducing poverty. However, when workers move from formal employment to informal sector, for example, during an economic downturn, it can lead to an increase in poverty. People with informal employment is usually the most vulnerable to economic downturns and unemployment. Moreover, informal employment is often

associated with inadequate social protection systems, which can adversely affect
long-term poverty reduction efforts.

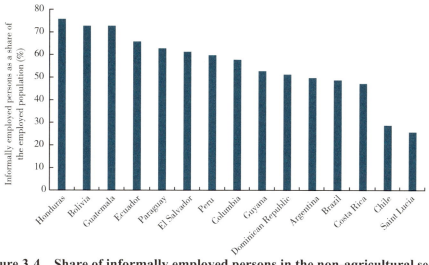

**Figure 3.4   Share of informally employed persons in the non-agricultural sector
of LAC countries, 2019**

Source: Martin Abeles et al. *The COVID-19 Crisis and the Structural Problems of Latin
America and the Caribbean: Responding to the Emergency with a long-term Perspective.* https://
www. cepal. org/en/publications.

Thirdly, in most countries, social security systems are weak, and there are
significant gaps in the construction of social security systems.

In LAC, only a few countries have unemployment insurance in their social
security systems. For example, Mexico, Argentina, Brazil, Chile, Colombia,
Ecuador and Uruguay in South America have established unemployment
insurance programmes. Two of these countries, Mexico and Ecuador, provide
pensions only for elderly individuals who are no longer working; Brazil's
programme to assist the unemployed is not part of unemployment social insurance
system. In LAC, unemployment is not only persistent, long-term and structural,
but also characterized by high levels of underemployment and informality. The
coverage of unemployment insurance programs in LAC countries is limited,
and workers in some sectors are excluded. For example, in Uruguay, workers in
agriculture, domestic services and banking are not covered. The vast majority of

LAC countries do not seem to be in a position to invest much in unemployment protection. As a result, the unemployed are often denied adequate benefits and subsidies, or even lose their livelihoods altogether. As a result, the shocks and pressures on the lives of the unemployed in LAC countries are much stronger and heavier than those on the unemployed in developed countries.

Fourthly, extreme poverty coexists with multidimensional poverty, and the phenomenon of "growth poverty" occurs occasionally.

While the poverty rate declines steadily only when economic growth reaches a certain level, in LAC, poverty is very sensitive to economic downturns or fluctuations. The poverty rate rebounds as soon as economic growth declines or fluctuates. Both growth and distributional factors have a large impact on the poverty rate, but growth factors are relatively more important. Economic growth reduces unemployment and increases household income, which in turn reduces the poverty rate. It is only when the economy growth reaches a certain level that the unemployment rate can be reduced and the goal of poverty reduction can be truly achieved.

ECLAC has measured and observed multidimensional poverty in 17 LAC countries around 2005 and 2012. It was found that: a) the countries with the most serious multidimensional poverty among these 17 countries are basically in Central America. In 2012, in Nicaragua, Honduras, and Guatemala, more than 70% of their inhabitants living in multidimensional poverty. b) the LAC countries with the lowest multidimensional poverty rate are almost exclusively those with higher levels of economic development, such as Chile, Argentina, Uruguay, Brazil and Costa Rica, whose multi-dimensionally poor populations account for about 10% of their entire populations. c) countries with a higher poverty rate also have a higher intensity of multidimensional poverty, i. e., the greater the number of multi-dimensionally poor populations or households, the greater the number.

(2) Trends in the evolution of poverty in Latin America and the Caribbean

Steady economic growth in Latin America and the Caribbean has contributed positively to global poverty reduction. In 2021, it continued the positive development trends of the first two decades of the 21st century, with a general increase in income levels of countries in LAC according to the World Bank's income classification criteria. There was a jump from lower-middle income countries to upper-middle income clusters. Over the two decades, the number of high-income countries increased from 1 to 6 in 2020 and 10 in 2021, and the number of upper-middle income countries increased from 13 to 17 in 2020 and 18 in 2021. By 2021, the only remaining low- and middle-income countries are Haiti, Honduras, El Salvador, Nicaragua, and Bolivia. In addition, LAC have a wide disparity in per capita national income, with the highest per capita national income (Bahamas, US$27,780 per person) being 22 times higher than the lowest per capita national income (Haiti, US$1,250 per person). See Figure 3.5.

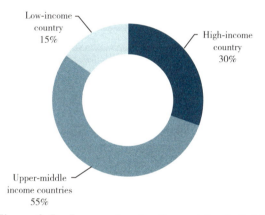

Low-income country 15%

High-income country 30%

Upper-middle income countries 55%

Figure 3.5   Income levels of countries in LAC

Source: Compiled from World Bank global development data.

Since the beginning of the century, when the poverty rate was high in many low- and middle-income countries, LAC has made significant progress over the two decades to reduce the poverty rate in most low- and middle-income countries. However, in the *Sustainable Development Report* (SDR)estimates, the WSDG index has continued to decline from 0.5 points and then stagnate since the outbreak of the COVID-19 and other overlapping crises. Since 2020, the COVID-19 pandemic has slowed down the process of poverty reduction in low- and middle-income countries. COVID-19 adjusted Human Development Index (HDI) show a broad but uneven decline. Among hem, LAC, with a decrease of 30.4% in the COVID-19-adjusted HDI, far exceeding the world average of

21.7%, was the region most affected by the COVID-19 pandemic. See Figure 3.6.

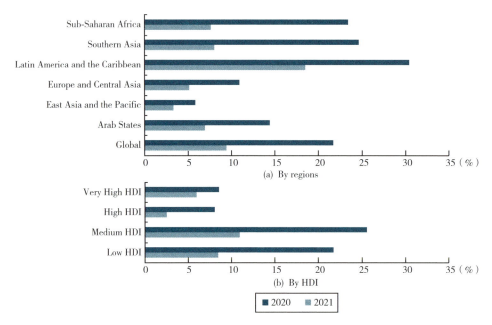

Figure 3.6   Losses in COVID-19-adjusted HDI, 2020 and 2021
Source: *Human Development Report* Office.

The Sustainable Development Goals (SDGs), proposed by the United Nations Development Programme (UNDP), set 17 global development goals, which combine three dimensions of development – social, economic and environmental – to provide a comprehensive measure of the level of development of countries and regions.

Among the 33 LAC countries counted in *Sustainable Development Report 2023*, the scores of 8 countries, including Cuba, Brazil, and Argentina, exceed the average score of the region (70.2), 15 countries, including Bolivia and Paraguay, exceed the world's average score (66.7), and 8 countries, including Nicaragua, Belize, and Honduras, are at or below the world's average, ranking among the bottom 50% of the 194 countries and territories. Meanwhile, Haiti is in the bottom of the region with a score of 52.6. See Table 3.2.

Table 3.2   **SDG scorecard in LAC, 2023**

Country	2023 SDG score	2023 Ranking
Uruguay	77.7	32
Cuba	74.1	46
Brazil	73.7	50
Argentina	73.7	51
Dominican Republic	72.1	62
Peru	71.7	65
El Salvador	70.7	73
Ecuador	70.4	74
Jamaica	69.6	82
Barbados	69.4	84
Bolivia	68.9	87
Paraguay	68.8	88
Suriname	68.2	92
Guyana	67.4	96
Panama	67.3	97
Nicaragua	64.8	104
Belize	64.6	107
Trinidad and Tobago	63.0	114
Honduras	62.9	116
Venezuela	62.9	117
Bahamas	60.9	124
Guatemala	59.4	127
Haiti	52.6	152

Source: *Sustainability Development Report 2023.*

Note: The United Nations Sustainable Development Goals Index, which requires 80% (at least 75%) of countries to meet the index indicator, lists 27 countries that do not meet the index indicator requirement, with five countries in Latin America and the Caribbean. Data of Antigua and Barbuda, Dominica, Grenada, Saint Kitts and Nevis, Saint Lucia are missing.

3.2.3.2 Key policy provisions for advancing poverty reduction in Latin American and the Caribbean

(1) Relying on financing to promote economic recovery

The Inter-American Development Bank (IDB) plays a significant role in providing economic support for LAC in terms of financing and specialised poverty alleviation programs. It is the most important source of funding for socio-economic development in the region. The IDB suggested that, the sluggish growth, rising interest rates, tightening of monetary policy, gradual fiscal consolidation, and the existing high level of debt are the main reasons for the lack of growth of the economy in the region. As a result, IDB has urged LAC countries to tackle the growing social demands and limited fiscal resources to confront the challenges of decreasing inflation and reducing public debt burdens, and has recommended that countries utilize the long-term financing options offered by multilateral development banks to improve the composition of their debt. Since 2023, the institution has provided a number of credits for poverty alleviation to 16 countries in the LAC.

(2) Exploring the development of family farming and eco-agriculture

Countries in LAC have conducted many explorations in the development of family farming and ecological agriculture. For example, the federal government of Brazil has introduced the Low-Carbon Agriculture Programme. It provides long-term, low-interest credits to encourage agriculture, forestry and animal husbandry production. At the same time, the government is improving access to food and supporting family farming in rural areas through the implementation of the programme.

(3) Sustained financial support for vulnerable groups

LAC countries have actively implemented targeted financial support programmes. For example, Brazil relaunched the Bolsa Família (Family Grant) programme in 2023, targeting poor families and vulnerable groups with low resilience to risks. The programme is financed through the Citizen's Income Benefit, the Supplementary Benefit, the Early Childhood Benefit, and the Family Variable Benefit, with a focus on young children, youths, and pregnant women.

The Early Childhood Benefit began to be distributed in March 2023. Other benefits of the project would be disbursed from June 2023 onwards. Until then, the Brazilian aid programme's basket of benefits would continue to be paid, including the early childhood benefit from the project. In the past, the Bolsa Família programme has provided significant financial assistance to destitute and poor families in the areas of education, health and food. By the end of 2022, the Bolsa Familia programme had increased the number of beneficiaries from 14 million to 17 million, with the average value rising from R$189 to R$400.

For example, Costa Rica launched the Avancemos programme, which aims to encourage poor out-of-school young people aged 12 to 25 to either remain in school or reintegrate into the secondary education system. The Avancemos programme is implemented by the Joint Institute for Social Welfare (IMAS). In 2014, the programme's budget was close to 49 billion colones (US$90 million), equivalent to 0.2% of the country's GDP for the year. In August 2015, the programme helped 157,000 students from 124,000 families nationwide, representing about 40% of Costa Rica's high school students. The Beyond Yourself programme the Targeted Demographic Information System (SIPO) and the Social Information Worksheet (FIS) to identify the target persons from poor, extremely poor or vulnerable households. SIPO is a targeting mechanism used to categorize households based on their socio-economic, demographic, and housing conditions. FIS is administered by collecting data through direct interviews with households and, in some cases, by conducting a census of the poor in neighborhoods with a high concentration of poor residents. Under the same concept, Costa Rica implemented a strategy called Puente al Desarrollo (Bridge to Development), which focuses on the 75 poorest regions of Costa Rica. The strategy aims to identify the poor through social workers called co-managers, who provide direct, personalized support to families.

(4) Active exploitation of the potential of special employment programmes

Employment is crucial for reducing poverty and inequality. LAC countries have launched a number of initiatives to boost employment and the economy, including the introduction of social welfare programmes for individuals, the strengthening of distance training, the expansion of infrastructure in disaster-affected sectors, the expansion of loan disbursements and support for the development of small and medium-sized enterprises. For example, concerning unemployed young people, Mexico has implemented the Youth for the Future programme, which aims to provide skills training for unemployed young people in order to increase employment opportunities. Additionally, it covers expenses such as health insurance during the training period. For business, tourism, transport and construction, the government of Chile introduced a US$2 billion employment subsidy programme in 2020 to subsidize wages in sectors severely affected by the pandemic. Chile has also invested US$34 billion in new roads, ports, airports, cultural and sports centers, among other projects, in an effort to create jobs by improving urban infrastructure.

3.2.4 Oceania

According to the United Nations, there are 16 countries in Oceania: Australia, Papua New Guinea, Fiji, Kiribati, Cook Islands, Marshall Islands, Micronesia (Federated States of), Nauru, Niue, Palau, Samoa, Solomon Islands, Tonga, Tuvalu, Vanuatu, and New Zealand.

According to the World Bank's income classification criteria, of the 14 countries in Oceania in 2023 (data for Cook Islands and Niue are not available at this time), there are four high-income countries (Australia, New Zealand, Nauru, Palau), four upper-middle income countries (Fiji, Marshall Islands, Tonga, Tuvalu), and six lower-middle income countries (Papua New Guinea, Solomon Islands, Vanuatu, Federated States of Micronesia, Kiribati, Samoa).

3.2.4.1 Characteristics and evolutionary trends of poverty in Oceania

Based on the World Bank's US$2.15 poverty line, three of the eight Oceania countries with poverty rate above 10% in 2023 are Vanuatu, Papua New Guinea, and Solomon Islands, while in Tonga, Fiji, and Samoa, the poverty rate is between 1% and 2%, and in Australia, it is below 1%. This suggests that poverty in Oceanian continues to be bifurcated, with lower poverty rate in high-income and upper-middle income countries such as Australia, New Zealand, and Tonga, and higher poverty rate in lower-middle income countries such as Vanuatu, Papua

New Guinea and Solomon Islands. The future of poverty reduction in Oceania continues to depend on these three low- and middle-income countries.

Compared to the situation before the outbreak of COVID-19, poverty rate in Australia and New Zealand remains low in 2023. In other Pacific island countries, the economy is still recovering, with a slight decline in poverty rate compared to 2022 and 2021. However, the current economic recovery and poverty reduction dynamics in the Oceania region remain very fragile overall. See Table 3.3.

Table 3.3   Poverty rate of Oceanian countries

Country	Codes	Poverty rate(%)				
		2019	2020	2021	2022	2023
Australia	AUS	0.34	0.34	0.34	0.34	0.34
New Zealand	NZL	0.01	0.01	0.01	0.01	–
Tonga	TON	1.19	1.29	1.07	1.09	1.06
Fiji	FJI	1.65	2.92	3.47	2.44	2.00
Samoa	WSM	1.70	1.51	1.20	1.36	1.23
Vanuatu	VUT	12.39	15.53	16.10	16.09	15.44
Papua New Guinea	PNG	27.76	29.61	29.79	29.04	27.89
Solomon Islands	SLB	25.04	33.53	34.83	38.98	38.53

Source: https://dashboards. sdgindex. org/profiles; *Sustainable Development Report 2023.* Data for New Zealand refer to 2022.

3.2.4.2   Main policy provisions to promote poverty reduction in Oceania

(1) Implementing economic recovery programmes to support the development of small and medium-sized enterprises(SMEs)

To support the recovery of SMEs, the Government of Australia introduced the SME Recovery Loan Scheme. The scheme which was launched in March 2021 and ended on June 30, 2022, is mainly for SMEs that are most seriously affected by the pandemic. Eligible enterprises can apply for an interest-free loan of up to two years, with a maximum loan amount of up to AUD$5 million, and the government will provide 80% guarantee for the loan[1]. The Government of New Zealand also introduced the Small Business Cashflow Scheme and the Government Business Finance Guarantee Scheme in May 2020.The Small Business CashFlow Scheme provides support of up to NZ$10,000 for companies employing 50 or fewer full-time employees, with an additional loan of NZ$1,800 per full-time employee. In February 2022, the government announced that the program's base loan would increase from NZ$10,000 to NZ$20,000. The loan repayment period is five years (60 months). The loan is interest-free if repaid within one year. The project was originally scheduled to expire at the end of December 2020, but was later extended to December 31, 2023, in light of the pandemic.[2]

The Government Business Finance Guarantee Scheme provides New Zealand SMEs with annual revenues between NZ$250,000 and NZ$80 million with the ability to apply for a loan of up to NZ$500,000 from an accredited bank in partnership with the Government of New Zealand for a period of three years, which is expected to provide New Zealand businesses with a total of NZ$6.25 billion, and which ends on June 30, 2021.[3]

(2) Launching a digital economy strategy that builds on transformation for poverty reduction

Oceania island countries have been significantly expanding their digital infrastructure over the past few years. Following the outbreak of the COVID-19, Oceanian countries have increased their focus on digital economy development. In October 2021, the Pacific Islands Forum Trade Ministers endorsed *Pacific Regional E-Commerce Strategy and Roadmap* of US$55 million.

In 2021, UNCTAD and the United Nations Development Programme (UNDP) collaborated on the launch of the Pacific Digital Economy Programme (PDEP), which is designed to support the development of an inclusive digital

---

1 The Treasury, Australian Government.SME Recovery Loan Scheme, https://treasury.gov.au/coronavirus/sme-recovery-loan-scheme.

2 Revenue. COVID-19 Small Business Cashflow Scheme (SBCS), https://www.ird.govt.nz/covid-19/business-and-organisations/small-business-cash-flow-loan.

3 The Treasury, New Zealand Government.Business Finance Guarantee Scheme, https://www.treasury.govt.nz/information-and-services/new-zealand-economy/covid-19-economic-response/measures/bfg.

Pacific economy, starting with Fiji, the Solomon Islands and other countries. The first phase was launched over a two-year period and ended in December 2022. After two years of hard work, the program me is already bearing fruit. Solomon Islands officially approved the country's National E-Commerce Strategy (NECS) in September 2022, partnering with Island Tech's KlikPei platform to launch its own e-commerce aggregation platform, KlikPe. Vanuatu launched its own e-commerce platform, Maua, in September 2022 to help MSMEs access markets more easily, cost-effectively and fairly. Tonga also launched its own e-commerce platform, Digicel, in November 2022. Fiji drafted a Financial and Digital Literacy Strategy in 2022. In the future, the initiative will also be extended to Papua New Guinea, Kiribati, the Federated States of Micronesia, and Marshall Islands.

Enhanced market participation through the development of an inclusive digital economy for rural communities, women, labor-mobile workers, and micro, small and medium-sized enterprises could promote economic growth, improve livelihoods, reduce poverty and contribute to the achievement of the sustainable development goals.[1]

(3) Re-launching the tourism industry and developing the blue economy

Tourism is the mainstay of many South Pacific island countries. Many countries re-opened their borders to international tourists when the pandemic eased. Fiji opened its international borders in December 2021, phasing out all entry restriction requirements for global tourists. Its tourism industry recovered rapidly, with tourist arrivals in 2022 reaching 71% of 2019 levels and a projected GDP growth rate in 2022 of 16%[2]. Papua New Guinea also decided in May 2021 to develop gaming tourism to attract tourists and increase government revenue.[3]

For Small Island Developing States (SIDs), the blue economy is another

---

1   UNCDF. Pacific Digital Economy Programme Annual Report 2022, March 13, 2023, https://unctad. org/system/files/information-document/PDEP_Annual_Report_2022_13Mar2023_Final.pdf

2   IMF. Fiji's Economy Rebounds Strongly on Tourism Recovery, June 29, 2023, http://dmc-global.com/ news/guonei/6339.html.

3   National Gaming Control Council Looks at Gaming Tourism,10 May 2021, http://www.png-china. com/forum.php?mod=viewthread&tid=13444&highlight=%B2%A9%B2%CA.

opportunity, which would be a unique development strategy of these countries. Many SIDs are exploring mariculture, the mining of rare earth minerals from the seabed and bioprospecting for resources such as medicines and cosmetics. The exclusive economic zone of the Cook Islands is estimated to contain 12 billion tonnes of cobalt-rich nodules. The Cook Islands may become the first country to allow deep-sea mining when the country issued deep-sea exploration licences to three companies in 2022, allowing them to survey within its territorial waters and determine the feasibility of sustained mining over the next five years.[1]

3.2.5 North America

North America, located in the northern part of the Western Hemisphere, is the second most economically developed region in the world, with two countries (the United States and Canada) and three regions (Bermuda, Greenland, and Saint-Pierre and Miquelon) according to the United Nations.

3.2.5.1 Characteristics and evolutionary trends of poverty in North America

Two countries in North America – Canada and the United States – are developed countries. The poverty rate (US$2.15) in Canada in 2023 is 0.2%, which has remained essentially stable since 2016. [2] The poverty rate in the US in 2023 is 0.55%, largely stable since 2015, 0.64% in 2016 (lowest) and 0.71% in 2020 (highest).[3] As a whole, in the US and Canada, the absolute poverty rate is low and the number of poor people is small. The current poverty in the two countries is mainly characterised by relative poverty.

According to data released by the Government of Canada in May 2023, the poverty rate in Canada was 7.4% in 2021, up from 6.4% in 2020 and down slightly from 10.3% in 2019. This includes a poverty rate of 6.4% for people under the age of 18, 8.2% for people aged 18-64, and 5.6% for people aged 65

---

1 Pacific Island Countries Divided on Deep Sea Mining,29 August 2022, http://ggmd.cgs.gov.cn/DepositsNewsCen.aspx?id=4703.

2 Sustainable Development Report 2023 ,Canada,https://dashboards.sdgindex.org/profiles/canada.

3 Sustainable Development Report 2023 , United States, https://dashboards.sdgindex.org/profiles/united-states.

and over.[1] See Table 3.4.

Table 3.4　　Changes in poverty rate in Canada (in % of low-income population)

Groups	2015	2016	2017	2018	2019	2020	2021
All	14.5	12.9	11.9	11.2	10.3	6.4	7.4
Under 18 years old	16.3	13.9	11.7	10.6	9.4	4.7	6.4
18-64 years old	15.7	14.0	13.4	12.8	11.8	7.8	8.2
65 years old and above	7.1	7.1	6.1	6.0	5.7	3.1	5.6

Source: Statistics Canada.

According to data released by the US Census Bureau in September 2022, based on the official poverty measure, the total US population in 2021 was 328.2 million, with 37.9 million people living in poverty, and an overall poverty rate of 11.6%, up 0.2 percentage points from 2020 (11.4% in 2020). This compares with six consecutive years of annual declines in the poverty rate from 14.8% in 2014 until 2020. By age, the poverty rate of seniors over 65 years is lower than the overall level (10.3%), and the poverty rate of children under 18 years is 15.3%. By race, there are racial disparities in the poverty rate, for Blacks, poverty rate (19.5%) is the highest, for non-Hispanic whites, poverty rate (8.1%)is the lowest. By marital status, for married couples, poverty rate (4.8%)is the lowest, and for single mothers, poverty rate (23%) is the highest. By educational attainment, an individual's level of education had a significant impact on poverty, for adults without a high school diploma, the poverty rate is 27.2%, compared to adults with a college degree of only 4.1%.[2]

According to World Bank, Canada and the US have seen little change in poverty since 2020, and while both countries have seen a slight increase in their poverty rates in 2021 compared to 2020 according to data released by the

---

1　Statistics Canada, Low income statistics by age, sex and economic family type, May 23,2023, https://www150.statcan.gc.ca/t1/tbl1/en/tv.action?pid=1110013501.

2　John Creamer, Emily A. Shrider, Kalee Burns, and Frances Chen. Poverty in the United States: 2021 Current Population Reports, September 13, 2022, https://www.census.gov/library/publications/2022/demo/p60-277.html.

Canadian and US governments. Indications show that, Canada's poverty rate continued to rise in 2022, reaching 9.8%, and could climb back to 2019 levels[1]; the US's poverty rate in 2022 also likely to continue to rise[2]. An article by the Center on Poverty and Social Policy of Columbia University noted that, the child poverty rate in the US rose from 12.1% in December 2021 to 16.6% in May 2022, an increase of 3.3 million children living in poverty, due to the expiration of the Child Tax Credit in the Relief Act during the COVID-19 pandemic.[3] These data show that, the poverty rates in both countries have worsened after 2020. It is mainly because the relief programmes and economic stimulus packages launched by the governments during the pandemic have expired. In addition, there has been no fundamental improvement in the persistent problems of poverty reduction in the two countries-regional inequality in poverty in the countries, and structural inequality in the poor population.

3.2.5.2 Main policy provisions for promoting poverty reduction in North America

(1) Actively develop climate and energy transition strategies to create entirely new jobs

The US Government attaches great importance to energy and climate issues. The Biden Administration has proposed an overall goal of achieving a 100% clean energy economy and net-zero emissions by 2050, envisaging an energy transition and upgrade in the United States through the creation of new jobs and the rebuilding of infrastructure.

On 16 August 2022, US President Joe Biden signed the Inflation Reduction Act of 2022 (hereinafter referred to as the "Inflation Reduction Act") into law. The Act is the most important economic reform plan in recent years for the US

---

1 Burton Gustajtis ,Andrew Heisz,Market Basket Measure poverty thresholds and provisional poverty trends for 2021 and 2022,January 17, 2023,https://www150.statcan.gc.ca/n1/pub/75f0002m/75f0002m2022008-eng.htm.

2 Santul Nerkar,Michael Tabb,The U.S. Poverty Rate Hit A Record Low-But Don't Expect It To Stay That Way,Dec. 16, 2022, https://fivethirtyeight.com/videos/the-u-s-poverty-rate-hit-a-record-low-but-dont-expect-it-to-stay-that-way/.

3 Li zhiwei, U.S. needs to face up to the stark reality of child poverty, 9 August 2022, People's Daily Online. http://world.people.com.cn/n1/2022/0809/c1002-32497677.html.

to promote green transformation, reduce the healthcare burden of the vulnerable, optimise the tax system to promote fairness, and tackle the fiscal deficit, and is expected to generate US$433 billion in fiscal spending and US$740 billion in new revenue. Although named "Inflation Reduction", the Inflation Reduction Act is actually the most aggressive action taken in US history to address the climate crisis, and will create more good-paying, secure jobs across the US and provide more manufacturing jobs; reduce the burden of health care on the public and fulfil Biden's campaign promise of affordable prescription drugs; narrow the gap between rich and poor, improve the fairness of the income tax system, raise revenue and fund much-needed US government investment projects through tax reform.[1]

The federal Government of Canada has also placed great importance on climate goals and has made achieving large-scale emissions reductions an important part of the transition to a green, low-carbon economy. Canada will further encourage the innovation and growth of low-carbon cutting-edge technologies and support the continuous improvement and expansion of the structure and scale of new low-carbon industries, so as to create a new low-carbon economic pattern, which is conducive to enhancing Canada's emissions reduction efficiency and promoting the achievement of climate goals, and creating a new growth point in the green economy, so as to give impetus to Canada's economic recovery in the wake of the end of the epidemic.

On 2 June 2021, the Government of Canada launched the Smart Renewables and Electrification Pathways Program. Administered by Natural Resources Canada, the programme provides up to C$964 million over four years for smart renewables and grid modernisation projects. It supports building Canada's low-emission energy future and renewable electrification economy by focusing on clean energy technologies and modernising power system operations. The program will support projects in three areas: existing renewable energy, emerging technologies and grid modernisation. The goal is to increase the renewable energy capacity of Canada's electricity grid and improve its reliability and resilience to

1 Zhou Jinghong, Hu Yijian. The Policy Background, Formation Process and Response Ideas of the U.S. Inflation Reduction Act, International Taxation, No. 3, 2023, pp. 39-40.

provide Canadians with a cleaner, more reliable supply of electricity. The plan aims to achieve net-zero emissions by 2050. As of 1 May 2023, 88 projects have been signed under the program with funding of C\$967 million. Funding has been approved for 73 projects that, when completed, will add approximately 2,800 megawatts of renewable energy capacity, equivalent to an annual reduction of 3.3 million tonnes of carbon dioxide emissions. 38 projects are aboriginal-owned, amounting to more than C\$700 million, and are projected to generate 14,000 jobs annually.[1]

(2) Addressing the challenges of inequality, such as ethnic poverty, and introducing differentiated policies for poverty reduction

The wide disparity in poverty rates across different ethnic groups in the US and Canada is a structural problem that has long plagued the cause of poverty reduction in both countries. Data released by the US Census Bureau in September 2022 show that, the US economy is showing signs of recovering from the COVID-19 pandemic, but poverty disparities across gender, race, and ethnicity persist, with poverty rates for blacks and Hispanics in the US nearing their lowest levels in decades, but disparities between whites and blacks and Hispanics remaining large (see Figure 3.7).[2]

---

1 Government of Canada, "Smart Renewables and Electrification Pathways Program", May 23, 2023, https://natural-resources.canada.ca/climate-change/green-infrastructure-programs/sreps/23566.

2 John Creamer, Emily A. Shrider, Kalee Burns, Frances Chen, Poverty in the United States: 2021 Current Population Reports, September 13, 2022, https://www.census.gov/library/publications/2022/demo/p60-277.html; American Progress, The Latest Poverty, Income, and Food Insecurity Data Reveal Continuing Racial Disparities, December 21, 2022, https://www.americanprogress.org/article/the-latest-poverty-income-and-food-insecurity-data-reveal-continuing-racial-disparities/.

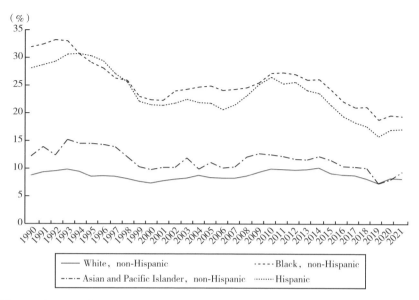

**Figure 3.7   Official poverty rates of ethnic groups in the United States,
1990-2021**

Sources: American Progress, The Latest Poverty, Income, and Food Insecurity Data Reveal
Continuing Racial Disparities, December 21, 2022, https://www. americanprogress. org/article/the-
latest-poverty-income-and-food-insecurity-data-reveal-continuing-racial-disparities/.

In Canada, poverty rates are significantly higher than the national poverty
rate for all minority groups except Filipino Canadians (8.1%), more than twice
the national average for Korean Canadians (19.0%), and not much lower for
Chinese Canadians and African Americans (15.3% and 12.4%, respectively).[1] For
this reason, the governments have also introduced fair but differentiated policies
in an attempt to reduce or alleviate inequalities between ethnic groups. In the US,
the Biden administration has provided economic opportunities for black families
and communities by signing the American Rescue Plan Act, the Bipartisan
Infrastructure Investment and Jobs Act and the Inflation Reduction Act, which
have helped to create new economic opportunities for African Americans and
strengthened investment in black businesses and the black community. In its

---

1   Statistics Canada, Disaggregated trends in poverty from the 2021 Census of Population, November 9,
2022, https://www12.statcan.gc.ca/census-recensement/2021/as-sa/98-200-x/2021009/98-200-x2021009-eng.
pdf.

2022 budget, the Government of Canada proposes to invest an additional C$11 billion over the next six years to continue to support aboriginal children and their families and to help aboriginal communities to continue to develop and shape their futures. These measures include, inter alia, supporting aboriginal children through the Jordan's Principle, implementing aboriginal child welfare legislation, addressing the legacy of the infamous residential schools, improving health in aboriginal communities, providing mental health and health care services, increasing investment in housing in aboriginal communities, and supporting aboriginal businesses and community economic development. These measures by the US government and Canadian government may go some way toward improving the poverty differentials of ethnic groups, but the problem of racial inequality is a systemic one, and short-term measures pale in the face of a long history of racial inequality.[1]

(3) Continued expansionary fiscal policy and the introduction of inclusive social welfare programmes

In the US and Canada, the governments initiated relief programmes during the COVID-19 pandemic. In March 2021, the US Congress passed the US$1.9 trillion American Rescue Plan Act which provided additional assistance to state and local governments for additional welfare benefits and mass vaccinations. The Government of Canada has also introduced programmes such as Canada Emergency Response Benefit, Canada Recovery Benefit, Canada Recovery Caregiving Benefit and Canada Recovery Sickness Benefit. In order to further address the outstanding problems of economic and social development, the government of these two countries have adjusted their anti-pandemic relief measures and introduced new support measures for enterprises and employees. For example, the Canadian government extended the Caregiving Benefit and Canada Recovery Sickness until 7 May 2022, providing a weekly subsidy of C$300 for people who were unable to work due to local shutdown. In March 2023, the Canadian government also announced targeted inflation relief for 11

---

1 Chunman Zhang, Can Political Veterans Solve Old Problems? A Brief Review of the Biden Administration's Measures to Promote Racial Equality, 14 January 2022, Fudan Institute of Development Studies, https://fddi.fudan.edu.cn/_t2515/93/05/c21253a430853/page.htm.

million Canadians and families most in need. The US, in response to rising child poverty rates, plans to expand the Child Tax Credit, raising it from US$2,000 to US$3,600 for each child under age 6, and US$3,000 for those over age 6.

3.2.6 Europe

According to the United Nations, there are 44 European countries or regions: Albania, Ireland, Estonia, Andorra, Austria, Belarus, Bulgaria, Belgium, Iceland, Bosnia and Herzegovina, Poland, North Macedonia, Denmark, Germany, Russian Federation, France, Holy See, Finland, Netherlands, Montenegro, Czech Republic, Croatia, Latvia, Lithuania, Liechtenstein, Luxembourg, Romania, Malta, Republic of Moldova, Monaco, Norway, Portugal, Sweden, Switzerland, Serbia, San Marino, Slovakia, Slovenia, Ukraine, Spain, Greece, Hungary, Italy, and United Kingdom.

3.2.6.1 Characteristics and evolutionary trends of poverty in Europe

With better overall economic and social development conditions, relatively well-developed infrastructure and generally higher household incomes, countries in Europe have become one of the most developed ones in the world. The governance process of poverty reduction in Europe is mainly directed at the sphere of relative poverty, where countries face a series of challenges such as the structuring of poverty groups, the persistence of the risk of social exclusion, and the uneven development of poor regions, and where poverty reduction strategies combining general welfare and employment promotion are commonly applied. As the birthplace of the global welfare state, European countries have generally enacted laws and regulations specialising in social welfare. A comprehensive social welfare system has been established to provide universal insurance and relief protection for all nationals, which has become the first line of defence for the protection of poor social groups. At the same time, European "welfare states" have generally implemented a poverty reduction strategy that combines universal welfare with employment promotion, with the competent authorities actively assuming responsibility for poverty reduction and implementing policy interventions in terms of financial expenditure and resource allocation, in an effort to overcome the policy tension between competitive and secure employment.

For example, the Government of Bulgaria has specifically developed and implemented an Action Plan for 2021-2022, and a National Strategy for Poverty Reduction and Promotion of Social Inclusion for 2030. The Government of Bulgaria plans to reduce the absolute share of the poor to 31% of the total population by 2022, and a further 25% by 2030, while reducing the relative share of the poor from 23.8% in 2020 to 22.5% in 2022 and 18% in 2030.

At the same time, the Government of Romania officially approved the National Strategy for Social Inclusion and Poverty Reduction 2022-2027, and the Action Plan, deciding to allocate 161 million lei, including for the creation of 100 social service centres for the elderly, with the objective of reducing by 2027 the number of people at risk of poverty or social exclusion by at least 7%. In addition, thanks to a combination of sustained economic growth and government policy support, the domestic poverty rate in Croatia has been reduced to 1.6% in 2022, and is expected to be further reduced to 1.5% by 2024.[1]

3.2.6.2 Main policy provisions for promoting poverty reduction in European countries

(1) Continued implementation of innovative growth and balanced development relief measures

The further relaxation of COVID-19 restrictions and the further release of pent-up demand provide a solid foundation for the continued implementation of relief strategies and policies by governments of European countries. For example, in April 2022, the UK government decided that a range of green technologies used to decarbonise buildings will be exempt from business rates, among other things, which will reduce costs for businesses by more than £200 million over the next five years. The Managed and Digital Growth Enablement Programme will provide thousands of pounds' worth of support to relevant SMEs, including annual investment allowances worth £1 million. In Portugal, the Ministry of Territorial Integration has decided to extend the Inland Employment Promotion Project to the end of 2023, with a view to reducing the number of SMEs in

---

1 World Bank/International Bank for Reconstruction and Development. *Macro Poverty Outlook*, Washington DC, Oct., 2022,p.55.

the country. The Inland Employment Promotion Project, which aims to create conditions to attract more people, especially young people, back to rural areas, has been extended until the end of 2023, with people who have moved to the countryside for more than a year being eligible for up to €4,827 in settling-in allowances. 27 villages and towns in seven autonomous communities in Spain launched the National Teleworker Friendly Villages programme in 2021, which is open to all villages with a permanent population of less than 5,000 and wishing to attract more inhabitants, with 50-100 villages expected to join in the future.

(2) Actively promote universal social security coverage

In view of the fact that vulnerable populations, such as children, women, the elderly, ethnic minorities and disabilities, account for a rising proportion of the world's poor, the European Union(EU)and European countries have actively implement policies and resources to try to achieve synergistic poverty reduction by improving the development space of the region as a whole and the livelihood space of the poor. For example, the government in Germany decided to replace the Hartz IV subsidy policy, which had been in place since 2002, with the Bürgergeld, which offers higher subsidies and tax exemptions than the Bürgergeld, while requiring less housing space and household assets. In July 2022, the German federal government launched a subsidy programme specifically for children from poor families, which was granted at a rate of 20 euros per person per month until the introduction of basic child security. In September 2022, the ruling coalition agreed on a third bailout package (totalling €65 billion) to subsidise the losses suffered by people and businesses as a result of the sharp rise in energy prices and high inflation, with recipients of housing benefit receiving a one-off additional heating subsidy from September to December. At the same time, the basic social security benefit for recipients of social security benefits raised from €449 to €500 per month from 1 January 2023, pensioners received a one-off energy subsidy of €300 from 1 December, students and apprentices received a one-off energy subsidy of €200, and the monthly child benefit for families with children increased by €18 per child. For families with children, the monthly child benefit per child increased by €18.

In Spain, the government's third round of relief measures, with an investment of more than €10 billion, is aimed at mitigating the impact of rising energy and food prices on people's lives in 2022. Specifically, the government provides a one-off grant of €200 by the end of 2022 to low-income earners, freelancers and the unemployed with annual incomes of less than €14,000; increases non-contributory pensions by 15%; provides fuel subsidies for people working in agriculture, fishing, shipping and road transport, and subsidizes fuel by 20 euro cents per litre, and sets a cap on the price of natural gas for power generation in order to level out the price of electricity; provides discounts and concessions on public transport to the general public by reducing the price of monthly passes for state-owned public transport by 50% from 1 September 2022 and by 30% everywhere; and abolishes in the first half of 2023 the value-added tax (VAT) that applies to foodstuffs such as bread, milk, eggs and vegetables.

(3) Efforts are being made to improve diversified employment training and support policies

In the aftermath of the pandemic, European countries' poverty reduction policies have focused more on employment and the labour market, highlighting the concept of comprehensive, multidimensional and wide-ranging integration of poverty reduction in the context of regional social support policies. For example, with the support of the €100 billion local recovery programme and the €45 billion Next Generation EU Funds, the French government is determined to combat poverty by promoting employment through policy frameworks such as the Inclusion in the Economy (IAE), to benefit young people, immigrants and the unemployed. By the end of 2022, the government has committed to spending €150 million in an effort to create 270,000 jobs, while €120 million have been earmarked for employment upgrading in urban priority zones, and the share of policies including State subsidies has been increased from 50% to 80%.

At the same time, policy provision in the EU and its member states has paid more attention to factors such as mental health behind poverty rather than purely material, capability and absolute poverty agendas, which highlights the concept of a holistic, multidimensional and broadly integrated approach to poverty reduction in the context of a regional social support policy perspective. For example, in view of the increase in the underage poverty rate to nearly 4% in the country, the

Government of the Russian Federation has launched 42 social support policies, including retraining for 2 million people and recruitment for 200,000 people.

3.3 Effectiveness of policy implementation in promoting poverty reduction in major regions and typical countries of the world

Sound macroeconomic policies, good governance structures and the active participation of society are essential for the effective formulation and implementation of poverty reduction strategies and policies. The basic path out of poverty for a country is to rely on the government to overcome market failures during the take-off phase of the economy, to develop modern and large-scale industries through the mobilization and allocation of resources, to pay active attention to the pro-poor aspects of economic growth. At the same time, the poverty-reducing impact of a country's economic growth is directly affected by the level of social inequality. It is only through a model of inclusive growth and a focus on the distribution of income in favour of the poor that a country's poor can truly benefit from the process of economic and social development.

3.3.1 Cash transfers help to protect vulnerable groups, but government deficits and public debt tend to rise

Governments around the world have made efforts to increase policy inputs in the fields of education, health care, social security and human capital, while many international organisations and NGOs have actively participated in the governance of poverty reduction in developing countries through the provision of financial assistance, technical support and the exchange of experience, etc. This mode of policy provision in the form of "giving things" has helped to reduce the burden on the daily lives of individuals, improve the living standards and the quality of life of the poor, and to a certain extent, improve their living environment and health. However, the rapid increase of interest rate has triggered capital outflows and currency depreciation in developing countries, and the balance-of-payments pressures and debt vulnerability of many countries have been worsening; the pandemic may lead to rising inflation, and expansionary fiscal spending may lead to a doubling of fiscal deficits and further aggravation of sovereign debt crises, thus further aggravating the problem of the "welfare trap". The problem of the "welfare trap" has to a certain extent weakened the effectiveness of policy provision. For example, against the backdrop of slowing economic growth superimposed on inflationary shocks, in Netherlands, the government deficit will continue to rise in the next few years, public finance will be deteriorating. The government is phasing out temporary support measures. It is expected that more residents will be at risk of falling below the poverty line next year. The latest economic analysis report released by the Netherlands Bureau for Economic Policy Analysis (CPB) predicts that, the proportion of the poor in the total population of the Netherlands will rise from 4.7% in 2023 to 5.8% in 2024, totalling about 995,000 people, and that there is already limited room for expanding the provision of inclusive social policies, and the actual effectiveness of such policies has failed to meet the public's expectations. The UN's *Sustainable Development Goals Report 2022* notes that, while almost all countries have introduced new social protection measures in response to the crisis, many are short-term in nature.[1] In addition, in some countries, special poverty reduction projects consist of many sub-projects and independent programmes. The specific policy formulation and implementation involve a wide range of actors, such as central and local governments, enterprises and NGOs, which undoubtedly increases the difficulty of coordination and cooperation among different projects, and the efficiency of policy operation, operational costs and even the risk of wasting resources.

3.3.2 Tax leverage helps to reduce income disparities, but financing innovations and financial regulation need to be strengthened

The price rises, inflation triggered by the COVID-19 pandemic have forced the monetary authorities of more than 85% of countries around the globe to raise

---

1 UN, *Sustainable Development Goals Report 2022*.

interest rates and introduce emergency relief measures such as tax exemptions, economic subsidies and employment protection in the production, consumption and distribution in a bid to alleviate to a certain extent the pressure on the production and living conditions of market players such as labourers, operators, consumers and small and micro-enterprises. It is well known that, the absolute poverty rate and the number of the poor of a country tends to decline or even disappear altogether with the process of economic and social development, but even when a country reaches a high level of economic development, low-income groups of society will always remain and groups of people living in relative poverty will not disappear altogether. In particular, the proportion of people living below half of the national median income level is an important indicator of social exclusion, income distribution and relative poverty of a country, and large income distribution gaps will affect the extent to which economic development benefits the poor. In this regard, tax policy levers to flexibly regulate income distribution gaps, social polarisation and the relative poverty rate can help to alleviate the resulting social tensions in a country. For example, the Conditional Cash Transfers program (CCTs) in LAC and other regions have had a positive impact on poverty reduction, but there are still some shortcomings in the process of policy formulation and implementation, such as insufficient coverage and a need to improve the precision of the relevant mechanisms. In addition, the New Partnership for Africa's Development (NEPAD) has attempted to encourage private sector investment and economic growth through the promotion of microfinance institutions and projects, and the improvement of marketing systems to reduce poverty and promote sustainable development, but most of these programmes have been implemented in the form of cash assistance, which is also prone to inflation, rising commodity prices and the suppression of private cash, among other negative effects. Rising food and energy prices are affecting the most vulnerable groups in the region, and public debt and inflation are at their highest levels in decades, starting in 2022, with about half of the countries experiencing double-digit inflation.[1]

---

1   IMF, Regional Economic Outlook for Africa 2023, https://www.imf.org/en/publications/reo?sortby=Date&series=Sub-Saharan%20Africa.

3.3.3 Human capital investment helps mitigate economic contraction, but education and training and community empowerment need to be expanded urgently

Although the above relevant policy programmes and projects are essential for hunger reduction and poverty alleviation, they do not really address the problem of balancing between providing employment opportunities for the disadvantaged and enhancing the competitiveness of enterprises. In other words, improving human capital is a fundamental strategy for poverty eradication, and the policy provisions simply provide help to the poor in some countries has not produced effectiveness of policy provisions that enable the poor to help themselves. Developed countries such as European countries and the US have accumulated experiences in the design and implementation of policies such as "Welfare-to-Work" type of policy provisions for the poor in some countries. One of the main challenges for the future of poverty reduction in European countries is to prevent the poverty trap caused by welfare dependency. According to data from the Government of Portugal, in the first year of implementation of the Inland Employment Promotion Programme 2020, the Ministry of Territorial Integration received 560 applications, benefiting more than 980 people. More than 50% of the applicants were under 34 years of age, and 63% of them had received higher education. However, in Portugal, people are currently concentrated along the Atlantic coast, while inland rural areas often lack the necessary public infrastructure and services to attract large numbers of people, especially young people. In South Africa, the government, with the support of the Food and Agriculture Organisation (FAO), has developed a Youth Empowerment Strategy for the Agricultural and Rural Development Sector to address the country's high youth unemployment rate. The strategy, which aims to ensure the effective and equitable integration of youth into rural agriculture, has held a launch meeting and a series of project steering committee meetings in 2022, followed by a number of stakeholder consultation workshops to solicit inputs from key stakeholders. Prolonged economic weakness and slow income growth tend to limit the capacity of countries to invest in health, education, physical and digital infrastructure, and energy transformation, thus undermining the effectiveness of policy provision for poverty reduction governance, while the sustainability of participatory poverty reduction in terms of behavioural modification and community empowerment of the poor remains to be seen.

Chapter 4　China Consolidates and Expands the Achievements of Poverty Alleviation and Effectively Connects Policies and Practices with Rural Revitalization

Overview

　　The achievements in poverty alleviation are fundamental for fully advancing rural revitalization, and China's efforts to consolidate and expand these achievements in conjunction with rural revitalization are of great significance. Consolidating and expanding the outcomes of poverty alleviation initiatives form the foundation for achieving rural revitalization. Establishing and improving mechanisms to prevent people that have been lifted out of poverty from falling back into it again, and implementing effective assistance measures, are crucial for stabilizing and increasing income. High-quality development of rural industries, expanding employment opportunities, developing and enlarging new types of rural collective economies, and enhancing poverty alleviation capabilities through skill training, are all important measures to strengthen the capacity of impoverished residents for sustaining self-development. To continue advancing rural revitalization, it is necessary to learn from and implement typical practices, which include but are not limited to promoting high-quality development of rural industries, vigorously advancing the construction of livable and business-friendly beautiful villages, and improving the rural governance system led by the CPC.

　　After China's complete victory in the fight against poverty, the primary issue it faces is to prevent a return to poverty. In response, China has implemented measures such as establishing a five-year transition period for counties that have been lifted out of poverty and establishing key counties for rural revitalization in the western regions. During the transition period, the assistance policies in the poverty alleviation stage will be optimized and adjusted by category, and the gradual transition from concentrating resources to support poverty alleviation to comprehensively promoting rural revitalization will not only achieve all-round consolidation and expansion of the outcomes of poverty alleviation, but also help areas that have been lifted out of poverty clarify the development ideas for rural revitalization, formulate rural revitalization development paths according to local conditions, and achieve an effective connection between poverty alleviation and rural revitalization.

4.1 Consolidate and expand the results of poverty alleviation

Consolidating and expanding the outcomes of poverty alleviation is the bottom-line task of comprehensively promoting rural revitalization. The 14th Five-Year Plan for Promoting Agricultural and Rural Modernization emphasized that the policy system and working mechanism for poverty alleviation are effectively connected with rural revitalization, the outcomes of "Two Assurances and Three Guarantees"[1] for the people who have been lifted out of poverty are effectively consolidated, and dynamic monitoring and assistance are required to prevent people from returning to poverty. The poverty alleviation mechanism must be sound and functioning effectively to ensure that no large-scale return to poverty occurs. The No. 1 Central Document released in 2022 focuses on comprehensively promoting rural revitalization and clarifies two bottom-line tasks: ensuring national food security and preventing large-scale return to poverty. Monitoring and providing assistance to prevent people from returning to poverty is a key measure to consolidate and expand the results of poverty alleviation. China has entered a new development stage of comprehensively implementing the rural revitalization strategy. More than 30 transitional policies have been introduced and implemented, and a dynamic monitoring and

---

1 It refers to assurances of adequate food and clothing, and guarantees of access to compulsory education,basic medical services, and safe housing for impoverished rural residents.

assistance mechanism to prevent people from returning to poverty has been fully established. Through joint efforts from all parties, the results of poverty alleviation have been further consolidated and expanded, and the bottom line of preventing large-scale return to poverty has been maintained.

4.1.1 Establish and improve a monitoring mechanism to prevent people from returning to poverty

The scope of dynamic monitoring to prevent people from returning to poverty is fully covered. Adhere to the principle of "full coverage, dynamic monitoring, and no one left out", carry out dynamic monitoring, and take multiple measures such as centralized inspections, key screenings, and daily inspections to ensure that everything is covered; rely on industry departments to give full play to the role of monitoring multiple departments, carry out regular surveys and surveys, organically combine business work with dynamic monitoring and assistance work to prevent people from returning to poverty, and intervene in advance to prevent problems; broaden channels and guide the whole society to participate in monitoring. Give full play to the role of early warning and response, effectively achieve early detection, early intervention, and early assistance, control the risk of returning to poverty from the beginning, and implement timely discovery, rapid response, precise assistance, dynamic management, and dynamic clearing.

Comprehensively improve the quality of dynamic monitoring data for preventing people from returning to poverty. Improving the quality of dynamic monitoring data for preventing people from returning to poverty is an indispensable task to consolidate and expand the outcomes of poverty alleviation and effectively connect them with rural revitalization. High-quality monitoring data is the cornerstone for consolidating and expanding the effective connection between poverty alleviation and rural revitalization. It is the basic prerequisite for precise management and an inevitable requirement for promoting rural revitalization. The first is to assign a designated person to take charge and consolidate work responsibilities. The second is to strengthen data cleaning and improve data quality. The third is to adhere to a problem-oriented approach and seize the opportunity to rectify problems. Carefully sort out the doubtful data fed back by provinces, cities, and counties, carefully summarize and analyze it, sort it out one by one, find out the crux of the problem, and ensure that all the doubtful data fed back are rectified as soon as possible.

Improve the mechanism and system to build a strong monitoring defense line. It should improve the work leadership mechanism and set up a special task force to monitor and provide assistance to prevent people from returning to poverty; improve the investigation mechanism for all employees. Each district, county, and town has clearly defined the contact person and person in charge of the investigation work. Each village has divided all farmers into zones, and each farmer household has clearly defined the person responsible for investigation visits, and ensures that the person is present at each household. It should improve the screening and consultation mechanism, strengthen consultation and discussion with industry departments, connect with dedicated personnel from departments, conduct timely consultation and judgment on important and difficult monitoring issues and policy blockages, and collectively study and solve them. It should improve the entry and review mechanism, and the person in charge of the inspection visit, the information entry clerk, and the first person in charge of the information review are fully responsible for the accuracy of the information data within their scope of responsibility. It should improve the training and supervision mechanism to ensure that the investigation work is consistent in pace, content, and standards. It should improve the responsibility review mechanism and incorporate the centralized inspection of monitoring and assistance to prevent return to poverty into the annual assessment of consolidating and expanding the results of poverty alleviation and rural revitalization. For example, in Bijiang District, Tongren City, Guizhou Province, it has established the "553311" mechanism in the process of continuous exploration and innovation and improvement of the dynamic monitoring and assistance mechanism to prevent people from returning to poverty, and continues to make efforts in terms of responsibility, monitoring, early warning, assistance, and consolidation, and tighten Build a strong defense line against falling back into poverty.

4.1.2 Implement support measures to stabilize the fundamentals of increasing income

Optimize assistance measures. The first is to provide assistance in advance. For farmers who are at serious risk in the "Three Guarantees" due to disasters, accidents and other emergencies, it should first provide assistance and then implement relevant procedures to enhance the effectiveness of assistance. The second is development assistance. For rural households with ordinary or skilled labor but with sudden, hidden, transitional and other temporary difficulties, it should focus on implementing policies such as industrial assistance and employment assistance to improve their capacities of sustaining self-development and achieve stable development. The third is comprehensive assistance. For rural households that have no labor force, resulting in low income and difficult living conditions, policies will be implemented on a household-by-household basis, focusing on implementing basic security measures such as subsistence allowances, "Five Guarantees", and subsidies for the disabled. For farmers with overlapping risks and households without labor due to obstacles, comprehensive safeguard measures that combine public welfare posts, supporting industry promotion and bottom-up protection will be implemented nearby.

Refine assistance management. Combined with the consolidation and expansion of poverty alleviation achievements and rural construction information collection results, departmental data comparisons and regular visits to towns and villages (communities), farmers are accurately classified based on household income and comprehensive consideration of "Two Assurances and Three Guarantees" and other factors. Based on the classification situation, the person responsible for assistance shall be adjusted in a timely manner, and one-on-one assistance shall be provided to key households lifted out of poverty and monitoring households, and targeted assistance measures shall be formulated to achieve precise assistance. Taking the strengthening of village-based assistance management as an important starting point, it should strengthen organizational leadership, consolidate assistance responsibilities, strengthen selection and dispatch management, optimize assistance forces, strictly rotate management, and strengthen supervision and guidance.

Strengthen assistance. The first is to deepen the cooperation between the east regions and the west regions, ensure that financial aid funds, cadres and talents are in place as soon as possible, and speed up the implementation of cooperation projects and the progress of capital expenditures. For example, Beijing and Inner Mongolia join hands to promote the construction of "two bases" and write a new chapter in Beijing-Inner Mongolia cooperation;

Guangdong-Guangxi and Guangdong-Guizhou implement "four projects"[1] to help people who have been lifted out of poverty stabilize their employment; Shandong actively implements the project of "moving production from East to west" to help the industrial development of Chongqing and Gansu turning "capital transfusion" into "industrial hematopoietic". The second is to strengthen the connection with the central government's designated assistance units and actively seek guidance and support for the designated assistance counties. In the practice of targeted assistance to Huangping County, Guizhou Province, the Agricultural Bank of China has innovatively established "three funds" (anti-poverty fund, rural revitalization industry development fund, and education and training fund) to build short, medium and long term security net for preventing people from returning to poverty, and sustainable interest linkage mechanism. The third is to increase social support. Give full play to the "leading goose" role of the first secretary in the village, and closely integrate the promotion of targeted poverty alleviation with strengthening position construction, increasing basic security, and expanding opportunities to get rich, so as to provide a strong guarantee for advancing targeted poverty alleviation and targeted poverty alleviation work in the region. The fourth is to strengthen assistance to enterprises and social organizations. For example, based on the advantages of the new media industry, Beijing ByteDance Technology Co., Ltd. relies on digital platforms such as Tiktok and Head lines Today to implement "mountain products in the headlines" and new farmer training projects, and carry out activities such as consumer assistance, rural tourism development, talent training, and public welfare assistance, bring distinctive and high-quality "mountain products" out of the countryside, bring rural customs, rural features out of mountainous areas, and train farmers into new media powerhouses.

4.2 Enhance the capacity of areas and people who have been lifted out of poverty for sustaining self-development

There will be no national rejuvenation without a thriving countryside. The

---

1   "Four projects", namely, "building achievements" project, "quality construction" project, "harmonious creation" project, "people's livelihood assistance" project.

report to the 20th National Congress of the Communist Party of China stated that, "we will consolidate and expand our achievements in poverty alleviation and help areas and people that have just shaken off poverty build their own momentum for growth". The No. 1 Central Document of 2023 made a comprehensive deployment of the key tasks of comprehensive rural revitalization in 2023, especially specific arrangements on how to enhance the momentum for growth of poverty-stricken areas and people who have been lifted out of poverty. Cadres and people in poverty-stricken areas must adhere to the systemic concept and take multiple measures to enhance the momentum for growth of poverty-stricken areas and people who have been lifted out of poverty, promote the accelerated development of poverty-stricken counties, increase the income of people who have been lifted out of poverty, comprehensively promote rural revitalization, and accelerate the construction of agricultural and rural modernization.

4.2.1 High-quality development of rural industries

The development of rural industries is a growth engine that enhances the momentum for growth of areas and people who have been lifted out of poverty. **First, promote the development of agricultural specialty industries**. Further explore the potentials of local characteristic resources, ecological environment, land, labor force, capital and other factors, and implement policies according to local conditions and villages to cultivate and develop industries. Implement the spirit of the No. 1 Central Document and seize the opportunities of "National Rural Revitalization Key Assistance County to implement a number of key projects to address shortcomings and promote revitalization" to drive people out of poverty to increase their income. **Second, promote industrial scale operation**. Taking scale operation as the leading factor, through the development of new rural collective economy, integrating agricultural factors to form a certain scale and producing economies of scale effects. Give full play to the leading role of leading enterprises to promote the comprehensive and rapid development of large planting and breeding households, farmers' professional cooperatives, etc. At the same time, it should improve the interest linkage mechanism to drive farmers to increase their income. **Third, promote the extension of**

the industrial chain and industrial upgrading. Focus on making up for the shortcomings in technology, facilities, marketing, talents, and so on, that support development momentum, give better play to the role of village cadres and science and technology commissioners in industrial assistance, accelerate digital and intelligent transformation, create science and technology industries, smart industries, etc, and improve agriculture level of informatization and modernization.

4.2.2 Actively expand employment

Strengthening employment assistance for people who have been lifted out of poverty is an effective way to increase their income, a basic measure to consolidate the results of poverty alleviation, and an important guarantee for guarding the bottom line of preventing large-scale return to poverty. **The first is to highlight the employment priority policy.** Enterprises that employ people who have been lifted out of poverty will be provided with entrepreneurial guaranteed loans, employment subsidies and social insurance subsidies. Employment service subsidies will be provided to intermediaries that provide labor transfer services. For individuals who have been lifted out of poverty, those employed in public welfare positions will be given job subsidies, and those who participate in training will be given vocational training subsidies, subsidies for food, accommodation and transportation during the training period. **The second is to increase support for entrepreneurship and encourage people to return to their hometowns to start businesses**. Make full use of existing park and other resources to build a number of entrepreneurial parks for returning to hometowns; provide "one-stop" entrepreneurial services such as training, loans, and business start-up guidance for entrepreneurs who have been lifted out of poverty, and implement tax exemptions and entrepreneurial guaranteed loans in accordance with regulations and other policy support; carry out in-depth construction of entrepreneurial guaranteed loan credit villages in poverty-stricken villages, exempt counter-guarantee procedures, and support poverty-stricken labor force to start their own businesses. **The third is to cultivate and strengthen distinctive labor service brands to stimulate new impetus for employment.** In the process of building and cultivating labor service brands, people who have been lifted out of poverty and rural laborers have a lot of opportunities to master the skills of working as a labor force through participating in skills training and achieve high-quality and stable employment. **The fourth is to continue to deepen labor cooperation and stabilize labor employment**. Establish a normalized cross-regional job information sharing and release mechanism. Give full play to the role of the counterpart assistance mechanism, strive to improve the degree of organization and employment quality of labor cooperation, actively expand counterpart collaboration between inter-provincial and intra-provincial labor import and export regions, and improve the cross-regional and normalized labor cooperation mechanism. Establish a platform for information exchange, cross-regional recruitment, tracking services and so on to achieve effective connection of information.

4.2.3 Develop and expand the new rural collective economy

Developing and strengthening the new rural collective economy is an important part of improving the basic rural management system and an important measure to consolidate the outcomes of poverty alleviation and promote the rural revitalization strategy. **The first is to adapt measures to local conditions.** China has a vast territory, and there are great differences in rural resource endowments and market conditions among the east, middle and west regions. The development of rural collective economy can not rely on model. It must strive to build an operating mechanism with clear property rights, scientific governance structure, stable management methods, and reasonable income distribution, and strengthen the rural collective economy. In economically developed regions, the development of urban agriculture and leisure agriculture has broad market prospects; in villages with industrial foundations but lack of skilled people, it can be driven by various new business entities to closely connect the interests of farmers and jointly expand the industry; and for some areas with weak industrial foundations, it can develop through joint villages and group development to give full play to their scale advantages. **The second is to actively revitalize collective asset resources.** Give full play to the important role of rural collective economic organizations as the main body for exercising the ownership of collective asset, actively revitalize collective asset and resources, and lead collective members to achieve common development, and flexibly use various methods, including resource contracting, property leasing, intermediary services, asset participation and so on, which are relatively stable business activities, direct operation, shareholding operation, cooperative operation, entrusted operation and other flexible and diverse operation methods, agricultural production, property services, leisure tourism, B&B and health care and other industries. **The third is to effectively ensure that farmers benefit**. On the one hand, it is necessary to mobilize farmers' enthusiasm for participation through a close interest linkage mechanism, encourage everyone to work together, promote internal and external linkage of talents, technology and other elements, and tap the potential between mountains, rivers and fields. On the other hand, it is necessary to improve the rural collective asset supervision system and properly manage the responsibility fields of capital, asset and resource of agriculture and rural areas ("Three Capitals").

4.2.4   Vigorously promote skills training and improve skills for poverty alleviation

To consolidate and expand the outcomes of poverty alleviation and help rural revitalization, it is necessary to highlight the accuracy and effectiveness of skills improvement so that the people who have been lifted out of poverty with skills could find good employment, and can become rich. Skills training is an important measure for the poor labor force to increase their employment income and achieve poverty alleviation.

The first is precise training to promote improvement. Combined with the characteristics of the poor labor force's employment, different groups are provided with classified training. Comprehensively understand the training intentions of the poor labor force in detail, and provide targeted training types according to the training intentions. Poverty-stricken households can sign up for skills training based on their quality level, ability level, willingness to find employment and start a business, and carry out short-term skills training based on their own needs. **The second is to take multiple measures to increase effectiveness.** Vigorously develop practical technical training in rural areas, and carry out practical vocational skills training such as planting, breeding, processing and connecting production and market, rural e-commerce live streaming and e-commerce teachers around the characteristic and advantageous industries; "mobile classrooms" enter the countryside, inviting teachers to the countryside, and equipment is moved into the village, classes are opened at home, so that students can learn and work at the same time; carry out work-for-training to promote job stabilization, support rural cooperatives, poverty alleviation workshops and so on in absorbing the employment of poor laborers, and carry out pre-job training and work-for-training in an orderly manner and skills improvement training, make good use of policy stacking, and implement the role of training subsidy funds in stabilizing and maintaining employment.

4.3 Typical practices for continuing to promote rural revitalization

4.3.1 Promote high-quality development of rural industries

The first is to focus on developing characteristic industries. Accelerate the development of modern rural service industries and cultivate new rural industries and new business formats. **The second is to strengthen support for agricultural science and technology.** Accelerate the improvement of the national agricultural science and technology innovation system; continue to strengthen basic agricultural research; significantly enhance the status of enterprises in agricultural science and technology innovation; stimulate the innovation vitality of agricultural science and technology innovation talents. **The third is to make the agricultural products processing and distribution industry bigger and stronger.** Implement actions to improve the agricultural product processing industry, support family farms, farmer cooperatives, the SMEs in developing primary processing of agricultural products in origin of there products, and guide large agricultural enterprises to develop intensive processing of agricultural products. **The fourth is to cultivate and expand industries that enrich the people in the county.** Improve the spatial layout of rural industries in the county, enhance the industry carrying and supporting service functions of the county, and enhance the agglomeration function of key towns. Implement the "one county, one industry" project to strengthen the county and enrich its people. Support national high-tech zones, economic development zones, and agricultural high-tech zones to jointly host county industrial parks.

4.3.2   Solidly promote the construction of livable, industrial and beautiful countryside

The first is to strengthen village planning. Adhere to county-wide coordination, support villages with conditions and needs to prepare village plans by division, and reasonably determine village layout and construction boundaries. Incorporate village planning into the list of village-level discussions and consultations. Standardize and optimize the administrative divisions in rural areas, and strictly prohibit the annexation of villages and the establishment of large communities against the wishes of farmers. **The second is to solidly promote the improvement of rural living environment.** We will increase efforts to renovate public spaces in villages and continue to carry out village cleaning operations. Consolidate the outcomes of the investigation and rectification of rural household toilet problems, solidly promote the renovation of household toilets, and effectively improve the quality and effectiveness of rural toilet renovations. Strengthen the construction and maintenance of sanitary public toilets in rural areas. Promote rural domestic sewage treatment by zoning and classification, and strengthen the treatment of black and odorous water bodies in rural areas. Improve the rural domestic waste collection, transportation and disposal system, and promote source classification and reduction where conditions permit. **The third is to continue to strengthen rural infrastructure construction.** It should deepen the demonstration and creation of "Four Good Rural Roads", strengthen the construction of hardened roads for natural villages (groups) with large populations and qualified rural households, and promote rural road construction projects to be more oriented towards villages and households. Promote the construction of large-scale rural water supply projects and the standardized transformation of small-scale water supply projects, accelerate the resolution of seasonal water shortages in rural areas and temporary drinking water difficulties due to drought, and continue to consolidate the results of drinking water safety. It should continue to consolidate and improve the level of rural electricity security, carry out the construction of rural energy revolution pilot counties, accelerate the clean and low-carbon energy transformation in rural areas, promote the in-depth integration of digital technology with rural production and life, and continue to carry out digital rural pilots. **The fourth is to improve basic public service capabilities.** Promote the sinking of basic public service resources and focus on strengthening weak links. Promote the high-quality and balanced development of compulsory education within the county and improve the level of rural schools. Implement the living subsidy policy for rural teachers. Promote county-level coordination of medical and health resources, and strengthen the construction of rural-level medical and health and medical security service capabilities. It should coordinate and resolve the issues of salary distribution and benefits security for rural doctors, and promote the professionalization and standardization of the rural doctor team.

4.3.3 Improve the rural governance system led by CPC

The first is to focus on the construction of grassroots democracy and strengthen the political and organizational functions of rural grassroots Party organizations. In the process of rural governance, it is necessary to give full play to the role of villagers' committees, strengthen villagers' autonomy, allow villagers to participate in decision-making and management, and improve villagers' participation and satisfaction. At the same time, it is necessary to strengthen the construction of villagers' congresses and villagers' councils, so that villagers have more voice and decision-making power, and promote the democratization and legalization of rural governance. **The second is to focus on cultural inheritance and innovation and strengthen the construction of rural spiritual civilization.** In the process of rural governance, it must pay attention to inheriting and promoting local culture, exploring and exploring rural cultural resources, promoting the development of cultural and creative industries, and increasing the influence and attraction of rural culture. At the same time, it must focus on innovation, promote the modernization and technologicalization of rural governance, introduce new technologies and new models, and improve the efficiency and quality of rural governance. **The third is to focus on ecological protection and green development to improve the quality and sustainability of the rural ecological environment.** Promote the exploration and implementation of modern agricultural and rural ecological environment governance models. Strengthen the construction of modern ecological environment management capabilities in agriculture and rural areas. Promote the implementation of ecological environment system governance in agriculture and rural areas. Strengthen scientific and technological innovation and application in agricultural and rural ecological environment management.

Chapter 5   Global Outlook for Poverty Alleviation

Overview

Global poverty reduction is currently facing multiple challenges: economic development is uncertain, regional conflicts affect political stability, food insecurity is increasingly severe, and the nutrition and health crisis is worsening. Multiple measures should be taken to promote the development of global poverty reduction, maintain regional peace and stability, increase investment in education, prioritize healthcare development, strengthen infrastructure construction, and jointly address climate change. With common development and cooperation as the core, it should actively promote the process of globalization, enhance international aid and cooperation, help reduce poverty and inequality in developing countries, deepen multilateral cooperation, and actively contribute China's strength to global poverty reduction.

5.1   Multiple challenges to global poverty alleviation

Global efforts to recover from the pandemic and alleviate poverty are confronted by a multitude of challenges and economic uncertainties. After the pandemic, worldwide economic development is characterized by significant instability due to the convergence of various crises, including regional conflicts. While some nations and regions have achieved a relatively swift economic rebound through effective management and proactive economic stimulus initiatives, others continue to grapple with multiple challenges and a sluggish pace of economic recovery. As of 2022, the global unemployment rate stood at 5.77%. The closure of numerous businesses and workforce reductions have resulted in substantial job losses, even though the labor market is gradually improving as the economy stabilizes. Nonetheless, a substantial portion of the global population still confronts formidable employment challenges, including reduced income, creating considerable pressure and obstacles for global poverty alleviation efforts. These challenges make it imperative for countries and international organizations to redouble their commitment to poverty reduction and address the underlying economic and social factors that hinder progress.

Regional conflicts present significant hurdles to poverty alleviation. In 2022, there were more than 6,355 incidents of regional conflicts worldwide. These conflicts have dual impacts on the poverty alleviation process. Firstly, regional conflicts disrupt political stability, impeding governments from effectively formulating and implementing poverty alleviation policies. A substantial portion of government resources is diverted toward military operations, security maintenance, and post-conflict reconstruction. This diverts attention and funding away from poverty alleviation and social welfare initiatives, thereby seriously undermining the poverty reduction efforts. Secondly, regional conflicts have a profound negative impact on economic development and job creation, consequently reducing the efficacy of poverty alleviation endeavors. The destruction of infrastructure, lowered productivity, and restraints on investment and economic activities during conflicts result in increased unemployment and a rise in poverty levels. Furthermore, regional conflicts exacerbate the global challenge of poverty alleviation by triggering population displacement and migration. A significant number of individuals are forcibly uprooted from their homes, endangering their lives and livelihoods. This, in turn, places immense strain on host areas and gives rise to social and economic instability, adding an extra layer of complexity to the pursuit of global poverty alleviation objectives.

Food insecurity is growing and the nutritional health crisis has intensified. Restrictive measures in the context of the pandemic have led to shortages of agricultural labor, affecting agricultural production and food availability. In addition, rising food prices, due to trade restrictions, regional conflicts and transportation, have put poor people at greater risk of food insecurity and inadequate nutritional intake among the poor. At the same time, the economic downturn caused by the pandemic has deprived many people of their sources of income, and many families have had to cut back on their food expenditures, opting for cheaper and less nutritious foods, such as processed foods high in sugar, salt and fat. This unbalanced diet has led to an increase in chronic diseases, such as obesity, diabetes and cardiovascular disease, further exacerbating the nutritional health crisis among the poor.

5.2 Multiple measures of global poverty alleviation

Maintaining peace and stability and addressing the food crisis. Reducing regional conflicts and coping with the food crisis are the top priorities in addressing global poverty. Firstly, governments should strengthen conflict prevention and resolution mechanisms and promote peaceful inter-regional dialogues through diplomatic means to avoid conflicts. Secondly, countries should increase their assistance to conflict areas to help them rebuild their infrastructure and improve the living standards of their people. To address the food crisis, it is necessary to further strengthen agricultural production capacity and encourage agricultural production by, inter alia, raising farmers' incomes. The government should formulate and implement a food security strategy, effectively increase the area under food cultivation, and provide farmers with technical guidance and financial support. Thirdly, it should promote scientific and technological innovation in agriculture and introduce new crop varieties that are drought-resistant and resistant to pests and diseases, so as to increase crop yields and safeguard food supply. Finally, in respect of nutrition and health, it should strengthen nutrition and health services for poor areas. The government should formulate and implement an inclusive health policy, provide free or low-priced nutritional supplements and conduct nutritional dietary guidance to provide comprehensive nutritional support. At the same time, it should promote a healthy food culture based on local agricultural products and advocate balanced diets in an effort to address malnutrition in impoverished areas.

Increase investment in education. The abilities and qualities of individuals can be enhanced through education. It should strengthen their ability to adapt to social development, thereby increasing employment opportunities and sources of income. In order to promote global poverty alleviation, countries should increase their investment in basic education, and in particular should pay more attention to the allocation of educational resources to poor areas and disadvantaged groups, provide good educational conditions and opportunities, and break the intergenerational transmission of poverty. Governments should raise education budgets and increase financial expenditure on education to ensure that more resources are allocated to the field of education. Establishing and expanding a universal compulsory education system to ensure that all children receive quality basic education. Education grants or scholarships should be provided to poor families to pay for their children's tuition, textbooks and other related expenses, so as to alleviate the financial burden on poor families and promote children's access to education. In addition, efforts should be stepped up to train teachers and improve their professionalism and teaching ability. At the same time, the remuneration and benefits of teachers should be improved to attract more outstanding talents to work in education. It should improve educational resources and facilities in impoverished areas, including the construction of schools, libraries and the upgrading of teaching equipment, so as to ensure that children in impoverished areas can also enjoy good educational conditions. It should increase international assistance to provide education infrastructure and related technical and training support to poor areas to help them improve their education level and quality.

Emphasize medical and health development. Poverty and health are closely related, and the lack of basic medical protection will make it easier for people to fall into the vicious circle of disease and poverty. In order to promote global poverty alleviation, countries should increase their investment in medical and health care, provide universal medical services and basic medical protection, especially in poor and remote areas, so that everyone can enjoy basic medical services and reduce poverty caused by illness and return to poverty due to illness. First of all, it should actively carry out the universalization of medical services and community health facilities to ensure that the poor have access to basic health care services, including health examinations, vaccinations and basic medicines. The construction of hospitals, clinics, laboratories and other medical infrastructure is being actively pursued to improve the accessibility and quality of medical services. Especially in impoverished areas, the quantity and quality of medical facilities need to be upgraded. Second, a comprehensive medical insurance and social security system should be established to ensure that the poor and disadvantaged have access to reasonable medical services and to provide subsidies and protection for medical expenses. The quantity and quality of medical personnel should be improved, the skill level of medical personnel should be raised, medical education and training should be strengthened, and more medical talents should be attracted to provide services in impoverished areas. Third, disease prevention, control and monitoring should be strengthened, including the provision of adequate vaccinations, the improvement of sanitary conditions, and the enhancement of disease surveillance and prevention and control measures, so as to effectively reduce the spread of diseases and improve overall health. Finally, the international community should strengthen cooperation and provide assistance and financial support, especially to help impoverished countries establish and develop healthcare systems, provide technical support and training, and work together to promote the development of healthcare, so as to effectively contribute to the process of global poverty alleviation.

Strengthening infrastructure development. Good infrastructure can help create employment opportunities and promote economic growth, increase the productivity and competitiveness of poor areas, thus drive poor people out of poverty. Countries should invest more resources in improving transportation, communication, water supply and electricity conditions, upgrading infrastructure in poor areas and providing better development opportunities for the poor. Firstly, infrastructure investment and construction should be strengthened by increasing government budgets, attracting foreign direct investment and using international bank loans. Secondly, governments and international organizations should strengthen cooperation in infrastructure construction to achieve resource sharing, technology transfer and experience sharing, so as to improve the efficiency and quality of infrastructure construction. Thirdly, infrastructure construction should focus on equity to ensure that poor regions and vulnerable groups can share the fruits of development. Finally, it should focus on sustainability and adopt environmentally friendly and resource-saving construction methods to avoid damage to the environment and ensure long-term sustainable development. The efficiency and quality of infrastructure should be improved through the introduction of new technologies and innovative models. For example, smart technologies should be used to optimize transportation systems, renewable energy should be used to build clean energy infrastructure.

Jointly addressing climate change. Climate change is affecting global poverty patterns, particularly the rural poor and groups whose livelihoods depend on natural resources. In order to promote global poverty alleviation, countries should strengthen international cooperation to jointly address climate change, reduce greenhouse gas emissions, promote sustainable development, adapt to the impacts of climate change, increase development resilience, and reduce the risk of damage to the livelihoods of the poor. Firstly, the use of fossil fuels should be reduced and the proportion of renewable energy sources should be increased, such as clean energy sources including solar and wind power. Secondly, protect and restore ecosystems, especially forests, wetlands and oceans, to help absorb carbon dioxide and other greenhouse gases. Thirdly, adopt agricultural technologies with low carbon emissions to reduce the use of pesticides and fertilizers, to increase crop yields and farmers' incomes, and to improve energy efficiency and reduce energy waste. Fourthly, improve urban planning and management to encourage sustainable transportation, energy efficiency and waste management, among other things. Finally, the international community should strengthen cooperation and ensure the sharing of resources and technology, especially by providing financial and technical assistance to developing countries in their joint efforts to combat climate change.

5.3   Promoting the Global Development Initiative and joining hands to build a community of human destiny

To actively promote the process of globalization with common development and cooperation at its core. At the seventy-sixth session of the United Nations General Assembly, Chinese President Xi Jinping put forward the

Global Development Initiative (GDI), which, with the goal of building a global development community and upholding the concepts of prioritizing development and putting people first, focuses on promoting cooperation in the areas of poverty alleviation, food security, anti-COVID-19 and vaccine protection, climate change and green development. The Global Development Initiative is closely related to poverty alleviation and the enhancement of people's well-being, helping to realize the United Nations 2030 Agenda for Sustainable Development, and providing ideas and inspiration for countries to formulate sustainable development policies. As the world is currently facing a serious situation in the field of economic and social development, the international community's full cooperation and active implementation of global development initiatives will be the only way to promote post-pandemic economic recovery and make continuous progress in poverty alleviation. The Global Development Initiative has hit the nail on the head with regard to the major changes in the world and the pandemic, focusing on people's aspirations for peaceful development, fairness and justice, and win-win cooperation, and is highly suited to the needs of all parties. China will join hands with other countries to combat the pandemic, continue to deepen international cooperation on poverty alleviation, and actively build a Global Alliance for Poverty Alleviation Cooperation to provide a platform for international cooperation on poverty alleviation. It should give full play to the role of the China-United Nations Fund for Peace and Development, accelerate the recovery from the pandemic, and vigorously promote the global poverty alleviation. It should also actively address the challenges of climate change and play a greater role in global poverty alleviation in areas such as health, digitalization, and the green economy.

Strengthen international assistance and cooperation to help reduce poverty and inequality in developing countries. Strengthening international assistance and cooperation is one of the effective ways to help developing countries out of poverty. By providing economic assistance, technical support and human resources training and other assistances to impoverished areas, local socio-economic development can be effectively promoted. This not only creates local employment opportunities and increases people's income, but also improves local infrastructure and social welfare, thus effectively reducing poverty. At the same time, international assistance and cooperation can also help reduce inequality among developing countries. In the context of globalization, the economic gap between developing countries is widening, which also leads to inequality in other aspects, such as social welfare and education level. By strengthening international cooperation mechanisms, such as international financial organizations and multilateral development banks, it is possible to provide developing countries with equal and fair development opportunities and to promote more balanced economic development and resource allocation among countries. In addition, strengthening international assistance and cooperation is crucial to addressing global challenges. Problems such as climate change, outbreaks of infectious diseases and trade protectionism are no longer confined to a particular country or region, but require global cooperation to address. Through enhanced international cooperation, global responses can be jointly formulated, technologies and experiences can be shared, and these challenges can be jointly addressed to radically reduce the poverty and inequality faced by developing countries.

Deepening multilateral cooperation and actively contributing China's strength to the global poverty alleviation. China's achievements in poverty alleviation have provided a Chinese model and a Chinese solution for promoting global poverty alleviation. President Xi Jinping's Global Development Initiatives also place poverty alleviation as a key area of cooperation. To this end, China will continue to promote international exchanges and cooperation, form international poverty alleviation synergies, and strive to establish a new type of international poverty alleviation governance system centered on win-win cooperation. At the same time, in the light of its own development realities, it will pay attention to the urgent challenges faced by countries around the world, especially developing countries, and actively respond to the needs of other countries in specific priority areas. Under the current circumstances, it is particularly important to improve solidarity and cooperation among countries of the Global South, continue to support and help developing countries in general, and the least developed countries (LDCs) in particular, to eradicate poverty, strengthen cooperation with Southeast Asian countries in the areas of digital villages, cross-border e-commerce, ecotourism and other areas, and to push forward the quality and upgrading of cooperation in poverty alleviation, as well as to improve cooperation in poverty alleviation with the Pacific island states and assist them in completing the transformation of their digital economies.

In conclusion, the advancement of global poverty alleviation is a collective endeavor that requires solidarity and cooperation among nations. Achieving the goals of global prosperity and sustainable development is possible only through the joint efforts of all countries, leading to a harmonious, stable, and sustainable world. As a member of the international community, each country should adhere to a long-term vision and strategic perspective, integrate the concept of the global sustainable development goals into the economic and social development framework, strengthen exchanges, sharing and cooperation on issues such as poverty alleviation and rural development, food security, education development and others through various multilateral and bilateral exchange mechanisms and platforms. We shall work together to implement the 2030 Agenda for Sustainable Development, build an equal and balanced global partnership for development, join hands to promote the global poverty alleviation process, and build a poverty-free community of shared future for mankind.

References

［1］Asian Development Bank. Asian Development Outlook 2023［R］. 2023.

［2］Burton Gustajtis, Andrew Heisz. Market Basket Measure Poverty Thresholds and Provisional Poverty Trends for 2021 and 2022［EB/OL］. https: //www150.statcan. gc.ca/n1/pub/75f0002m/75f0002m2022008-eng.htm.

［3］C.W. Lee. U.S. Needs to Face Up to the Stark Reality of Child Poverty［EB/OL］. http: //world.people.com.cn/n1/2022/0809/c1002-32497677.html.

［4］Chen Xi. Innovation of Monitoring and Early Warning Mechanism for Preventing Large-scale Poverty Return. A Case Study Based on Longhui County, Hunan Province［J］. Rural Economy and Technology, 2023, 34（2）: 167-172.

［5］IMF: Fiji's Economy Rebounds Strongly On Tourism Recovery［EB/OL］. http: //dmc-global.com/news/guonei/6339.html.

［6］Deininger Klaus, Ali Daniel Ayalew, Fang Ming. Impact of the Russian Invasion on Ukrainian Farmers' Productivity, Rural Welfare, and Food Security ［EB/OL］. Policy Research Working Papers, 2023, 10464. http: //hdl.handle. net/10986/39911 License: CC BY 3.0 IGO.

［7］Developing Industry, Promoting Employment, and Aiding Revitalization: A Typical Case of Ruicheng County Finance Bureau's Assistance in Villages［J］. Shanxi Finance and Taxation, 2022（4）: 18-19.

［8］Dong Zhanfeng. Building A Beautiful China Promoting Modern Ecological and Environmental Governance in Agriculture and Rural Areas［EB/OL］. http: // f.china.com.cn/2022-02/28/content_78076006.htm.

［9］Global Assessment Report on Disaster Risk Reduction 2022: Our World at Risk: Transforming Governance for a Resilient Future［R］. United Nations Office for

Disaster Risk Reduction (UNDRR) .

[10] Global Humanitarian Assistance Report 2022 [R]. 2022.

[11] Government of Canada: Smart Renewable and Electrification Pathways Program [EB/OL]. https: //natural-resources.canada.ca/climate-change/green-infrastructure-programs/sreps/23566.

[12] Hart Tom, Lauren Blaxter.Ceasefire Divisions: Violations of the Truce with Gaza Lead to Rising Political Pressures in Israel [EB/OL]. Armed Conflict Location & Event Data Project (ACLED) . https: //www.acleddata.com/2018/11/23/ceasefire-divisions-violations-of-the-truce-with-gaza-lead-to-rising-political-pressures-in-israel/.

[13] He Shuo. Preventing the Return of Poverty to Fight A Good "Protracted Battle" More to Fight A Good "Active Battle": Xinyu City, to Prevent the Return of Poverty Monitoring and Help the Work of the Main Practices [J]. Old District Construction, 2020 (23) : 23-24.

[14] Hunan Huaihua: Improve Skills to Fight Poverty to Help Fight Poverty Perfect "Finish" [EB/OL]. https: //www.toutiao.com/article/6913845753635013128/?&source=m_redirect.

[15] John Creamer, Emily A. Shrider, Kalee Burns, Frances Chen. Poverty in the United States: 2021 Current Population Reports [R]. https: //www.census.gov/library/publications/2022/demo/p60-277.html.

[16] Liu Meijun. National Rural Revitalization Bureau Issued A Document 24 Measures to Consolidate and Expand the Results of Poverty Alleviation [EB/OL] . https: //finance.qianlong.com/2022/0602/7260687.shtml.

[17] Liu Ruiping. Shanxi Xiankang: Four Mechanisms to Prevent Poverty [J] . China Rural Revitalization, 2021 (12) : 2.

[18] Nugroho Dita, Pasquini Chiara, Reuge Nicolas, Amaro Diogo. COVID-19: How are Countries Preparing to Mitigate The Learning Loss as Schools Reopen? Trends and Emerging Good Practices to Support the Most Vulnerable Children [R] . Innocenti Research Briefs, No. 2020-20.

[19] Pacific Island Nations Divided Over Deep-sea Mining [EB/OL] .http: //ggmd.cgs.gov.cn/DepositsNewsCen.aspx?id=4703.

[20] Qiao Jinliang. New Situation of New Rural Collective Economy [EB/OL]. https: //m.gmw.cn/baijia/2022-12/06/36210827.html.

［21］Statistics Canada: Disaggregated Trends in Poverty From the 2021 Census of Population［EB/OL］. https: //www12.statcan.gc.ca/census-recensement/2021/as-sa/98-200-x/2021009/98-200-x2021009-eng.pdf.

［22］Statistics Canada: Low Income Statistics by Age, Sex and Economic Family Type［EB/OL］. https: //www150.statcan.gc.ca/t1/tbl1/en/tv.action?pid=1110013501.

［23］Tan Zi. Province Introduces New Policy to Assist Enterprises to Stabilize and Expand Employment［J］. Workers, 2020.

［24］The United Nations Development Programme Human Development Report Office. Global Multidimensional Poverty Index 2019［R］. 2019.

［25］The United Nations Development Programme Human Development Report Office. Global Multidimensional Poverty Index 2023［R］. 2023.

［26］The United Nations Development Programme Human Development Report Office. Global Multidimensional Poverty Index 2022［R］. 2022.

［27］The White House: FACT SHEET: CHIPS and Science Act Will Lower Costs, Create Jobs, Strengthen Supply Chains, and Counter China［EB/OL］. https: //www.whitehouse.gov/briefing-room/statements-releases/2022/08/09/fact-sheet-chips-and-science-act-will-lower-costs-create-jobs-strengthen-supply-chains-and-counter-china/.

［28］World Bank, OECD, UNICEF, UNESCO Institute For Statistics. Learning Recovery to Education Transformation Insights and Reflections From the 4th Survey on National Education Responses to COVID-19 School Closures［R］.2022.

［29］World Bank, UNESCO. Education Finance Watch［R］. 2022.

［30］UNESCAP. Asia-Pacific Disaster Report 2021［R］. 2023.

［31］UNICEF, Tanzania. COVID-19 Response: Nutrition［R］. 2020.

［32］United Nations. 2030 Agenda For Sustainable Development［R］. 2016.

［33］United Nations. World Economic Situation and Prospects 2023［R］. 2023.

［34］Wang Shiman. Multi-pronged Approach to Make the Results of Poverty Alleviation More Consolidated and Better Rural Development［EB/OL］. https: //sichuan.scol.com.cn/ggxw/202212/58775924.html.

［35］Wei Jian. New Collective Economy to Promote Common Prosperity in Rural Areas［EB/OL］. https: //theory.gmw.cn/2022-09/23/content_36044211.htm.

[36] Wei Min. Consolidating the Results of Poverty Alleviation Hebei's Multi-measures to Help The Poverty-stricken Population Stable Employment [EB/OL]. http://district.ce.cn/newarea/roll/202301/06/t20230106_38329902.shtml.

[37] Why Does the Central Government Repeatedly Emphasize "the Establishment of A Five-year Transition Period in Poverty-eradication Areas" ? [EB/OL]. https://www.toutiao.com/article/6945449823893979662/? &source=m_redirect.

[38] World Bank, Office of the Chief Economist for the Africa Region. Assessing Africa's Policies And Institutions [R]. 2022.

[39] World Bank. East Asia and the Pacific Economic Update [R]. 2023.

[40] World Bank. Global Economic Prospects 2023 [R]. 2023.

[41] World Bank. Macro Poverty Outlook 2023 [R]. 2023.

[42] World Bank. Poverty and Shared Prosperity 2022 [R]. 2022.

[43] World Bank. The Destiny of Turbulence: The Long Term Impact of Rising Prices and Food Security on the Middle East and North Africa [R]. 2023.

[44] Xing Mo, He Ye. Analysis of Long-term Mechanism for Preventing Poverty Return in the Context of Rural Revitalization [J]. Shanxi Agricultural Economics, 2022 (15) : 28-30.

[45] Yang Guang. Heilongjiang A-Cheng District First Secretary in the Village to Help Precise Poverty Alleviation [EB/OL]. https://www.nrra.gov.cn/art/2016/6/20/art_5_50681.html.

[46] Yang Shiyun. Developing and Enlarging New Collective Economy to Promote Common Prosperity of Farmers and Rural Areas [J]. Masses, 2022 (10) : 3.

[47] Zhao Shaofeng, Wang Zuocheng. Blue Book on the Development of Pacific Island Countries 2022 [M]. Beijing: Social Science Literature Publishing House, 2022.

[48] Zhou Jiansheng. Attacking the Difficulties to Make up for the Short Boards and Revitalizing the Living Environment [J]. Jiangsu Rural Economy, 2021 (6) : 3.

[49] Zhou Jinghong, Hu Yijian. Policy Background, Formation Process and Response Ideas of the U.S. Inflation Reduction Act [J]. International Taxation, 2023 (3) : 39-40.